The Aesthetic Border

Bucknell Studies in Latin American Literature and Theory

Series editor: *Aníbal González, Yale University*

Dealing with far-reaching questions of history and modernity, language and self-hood, and power and ethics, Latin American literature sheds light on the many-faceted nature of Latin American life, as well as on the human condition as a whole. This highly successful series has published some of the best recent criticism on Latin American literature. Acknowledging the historical links and cultural affinities between Latin American and Iberian literatures, the series productively combines scholarship with theory and welcomes consideration of Spanish and Portuguese texts and topics, while also providing a space of convergence for scholars working in Romance studies, comparative literature, cultural studies, and literary theory.

Recent Titles in the Series

Brantley Nicholson, *The Aesthetic Border: Colombian Literature in the Face of Globalization*
Ronald J. Friis, *White Light: The Poetry of Alberto Blanco*
Cecily Raynor, *Latin American Literature at the Millennium: Local Lives, Global Spaces*
Alberto Villate-Isaza, *Exemplary Violence: Rewriting History in Colonial Colombia*
Marília Librandi, Jamille Pinheiro Dias, and Tom Winterbottom, eds., *Transpoetic Exchange: Haroldo de Campos, Octavio Paz, and Other Multiversal Dialogues*
Naida García-Crespo, *Early Puerto Rican Cinema and Nation Building: National Sentiments, Transnational Realities, 1897–1940*
Earl E. Fitz, *Machado de Assis and Narrative Theory: Language, Imitation, Art, and Verisimilitude in the Last Six Novels*
Tara Daly, *Beyond Human: Vital Materialisms in the Andean Avant-Gardes*

For more information about the series, please visit www.bucknelluniversitypress.org.

The Aesthetic Border

Colombian Literature in the Face of Globalization

BRANTLEY NICHOLSON

Lewisburg, Pennsylvania

Library of Congress Cataloging-in-Publication Data
Names: Nicholson, Brantley, author.
Title: The aesthetic border : Colombian literature in the face of globalization /
   Brantley Nicholson.
Description: Lewisburg, Pennsylvania : Bucknell University Press, [2022] | Series:
   Bucknell studies in Latin American literature and theory | Includes bibliographical
   references and index.
Identifiers: LCCN 2021032905 | ISBN 9781684483655 (paperback ; alk. paper) |
   ISBN 9781684483662 (cloth ; alk. paper) | ISBN 9781684483679 (epub) |
   ISBN 9781684483686 (mobi) | ISBN 9781684483693 (pdf)
Subjects: LCSH: Colombian fiction—20th century—History and criticism. |
   Colombian fiction—21st century—History and criticism. | Literature and
   globalization—Colombia. | LCGFT: Literary criticism.
Classification: LCC PQ8172 .N53 2022 | DDC 863/.64099861—dc23/eng/20211102
LC record available at https://lccn.loc.gov/2021032905

A British Cataloging-in-Publication record for this book is available from the British Library.

References to internet websites (URLs) were accurate at the time of writing. Neither the
author nor Bucknell University Press is responsible for URLs that may have expired or
changed since the manuscript was prepared.

♾ The paper used in this publication meets the requirements of the American National
Standard for Information Sciences—Permanence of Paper for Printed Library Materials,
ANSI Z39.48-1992.

www.bucknelluniversitypress.org
Distributed worldwide by Rutgers University Press

Manufactured in the United States of America

For Helen, Ruth, and Clara

Contents

Contents

Preface and Acknowledgments

Casting back to the idea stage and coming up to the date of publication, the completion of this book has been a long and meandering affair. As such, it is difficult to give just due or to thank all of the people involved. I have long had an interest in the overlap between economics, literature, and politics and am indebted to all of the interlocutors I have been lucky enough to have over decades. Time spent in the graduate program at Duke University, where I completed my doctorate, was a natural incubator for this approach. It was a place where this seemingly odd nexus of ideas came across as natural, and I am grateful for time spent with some of the profession's leading thought-makers. More recently, I have had the benefit of working through my ideas with a wide cast of talented students at Georgia College. Fresh perspectives from a variety of generations and viewpoints have kept me on my toes and easy conclusions at bay. That is a privilege.

I owe the genesis of this specific project to a chance conversation with José María Rodríguez García, while at Duke. He had the early vision to show me that the best place to tie together the threads of my interests was Colombia. This drew me out of my comfort zone of Chile and set me on a decade-long exploration of a country that I have come to think of as not just intellectually fascinating but metonymic for the Americas. Likewise, it is difficult to think of how my understanding of the way we apply narrative to geography would exist without the instruction of Walter Mignolo. He took my fascination with psychogeography and blew it up to the world scale and changed the time signature from half a century to a millennium.

I have enjoyed the luxury of intellectual dialogue with an incredible group of peers, and a list of their names could fill pages. For this project, I will be specific to the scholars who have either read early versions, offered insightful feedback, or pointed me in fruitful directions, while I worked on this book. Be it in working groups in the United States, over coffee in Bogotá and Medellín, or at conferences throughout the world, Jean Franco, Fernando Vallejo, Rory O'Bryen, Juanita Aristizábal, Jeffrey Cedeño, and Camilo Hernández Castellanos gave helpful direction on the topic of Colombia over the past decade. Clearing the final hurdles of publication during the COVID-19 pandemic has presented extraordinary challenges. I am grateful for the hard work and diligence of the editorial team at Bucknell University Press, ranging from Aníbal González, who edits one of the most exciting lines in Latin American Studies, through to the director, Suzanne Guiod, and the managing editor, Pam Dailey. I have long been a reader of the high-quality material that comes out of Bucknell University Press and am happy to be able to add my own voice to the conversation. Emma Clements offered a very helpful and professional fresh set of eyes in the eleventh hour, and I am grateful for it. Susan Hurst, my department's administrator at Georgia College, is forever dutiful in keeping the trains running on time, while we faculty amble around the world thinking big ideas. The same goes for my department's recent chair, Peggy Elliott. I have also had two trustworthy intellectual sparring partners in Aaron Castroverde and Justin Izzo, with whom I have been able to develop ideas from inkling to public consumption in a safe space for almost fifteen years.

A book project requires the patience of many people. Both my parents, Bart and Pam Nicholson, and my parents-in-law, Derek and Elspeth Anthony, have at times offered enormous help with child care, while I both toiled in the archives and made trips to South America. The same goes for my wife, Helen Nicholson. On a more topical level, while working on this project, I have spent countless hours reading and writing in libraries, studies, and coffee shops. The British Library, the Reform Club in London, La Universidad de los Andes in Bogotá, and practically every independent coffee shop (with the occasional Juan Valdez) in Medellín and Bogotá have offered invaluable respite and motivation.

Lastly, I should acknowledge the privilege it is to write a book about a country to which I am a foreigner. To be able to unpack my own fascination and intellectual interest through the history and culture of Colombia has been both a large undertaking and a pleasure. I do not take it for granted that the multifaced, ever-complicated, and splendorous country that is Colombia is a place where real people go about their daily lives. I simply and humbly offer my perspective to be taken for what it is worth.

The Aesthetic Border

The Aesthetic Border

Introduction

In Fernando Vallejo's (1942–) biography of José Asunción Silva, *Chapolas negras* (1995), he structures the thread of Silva's life around a circuitous return to the shipwreck that on January 28, 1895, just under a year before Silva's eventual suicide, would lose him the only existing copies of his entire life's work. In the Bocas de Ceniza, not far from Colombia's coast, Silva's boat capsized while he was returning to Bogotá from Paris, where he had fulfilled the aesthetic promise of his generation in a trip to the City of Lights. Colombia was in the midst of the third of four consecutive civil wars and a series of presidencies occupied by high literary idealists with a belief that grammatical precision and aesthetic modernism could serve as sufficient philosophical and political models for young American nation-states. When Silva's boat upended, he, like his country, was suspended between the nation and the world.

This is a book about Colombia and its relationship to the wider world. It is a study of the Colombian literary canon and the impression that globalization has left on it. Colombia has been the site of one of the Americas' most tumultuous entrances into globalization. By turns embracing the discourse and economics of elsewhere and radically turning inward, Colombia has produced iconic literature that oftentimes encapsulates the struggle of young nations to define themselves. This book analyzes how Colombian literature has acted as a hologram to the lived experience of an existentially charged half century, from the publication of Gabriel García Márquez's *One Hundred Years of Solitude* to Juan Gabriel Vásquez's status as new "global" Colombian writer. While these literary icons, one canonical, the other emergent, bookend Colombia's fall and rise on the world stage, the period between the two is inordinately violent, spanning the Colombian urban novel's evolution into narco-literature. This study marks Colombia's relationship to the world and its literary manifestations as threefold: García Márquez's poetics of early globalization, in a retreat to romanticism that paradoxically made him a world literary icon; the country's violent end of the twentieth century, in which the populace attempted to come to terms with a fractured nation whose largest economic export was narcotics; and the contemporary period in which a new major author has emerged to create what I refer to as a *literature of national reconstitution* that grapples with the literary clichés built up over the previous half century.

As I describe in the chapters that follow, Colombia is a nation built on paradoxes. It is geographically central to the Americas, has maritime access to both the Atlantic and Pacific, and has the *terroir* and natural resources that make it ripe for an export economy. Yet the two periods during which Colombia engaged wholesale with the global economy, the first in the turn-of-the-century coffee craze and the second during the narcotics trade, marked the most salient moments in the fracturing of the national economic model (more on this in chapter 1). It is a nation that took the aesthetic citizen and lettering-of-the-nation sociopolitical models at their word, only to end in urban disorder through the mid-twentieth-century Violence period and the 1990s, when urban centers were ungovernable, which I detail in chapters 2 and 3. It is also a country on the verge of reemergence, as it tries to learn from previous mistakes, both economic and sociopolitical, in order to create a Colombia that is both true to its past and at ease in the twenty-first century, as I describe in chapter 4.

As nations and institutions throughout the world reexamine their cultural hallmarks and the iconography of nationhood after a seventy-year period of unflinching globalization, there are lessons to be learned from Colombia. While many of the experiential changes intrinsic to moments of national expanse and economic liberalization happen over decades in a geographical spread that is not easy to map, in Colombia the hyperbolic nature of swings in the economy and the cultural artifacts that accompany them make for a telling subject in the relation between nations and global socioeconomic systems. The spaces at which cultures reify, hybridize, reject, and transmute in the face of the outside and new is something I define as the *aesthetic border*, the place where multiple forms of systematic and institutionally buttressed perception converge. What unites García Márquez, the urban novelists of the mid-twentieth century, and the literature of national reconstitution in the twenty-first century is the shared project of capturing the fission and fusion intrinsic to global and local convergence in form. Authors are naturally drawn to these moments and spaces. Inherent to the buoyant and deflating energies in both the coffee boom and its subsequent crash, the expansion of the cocaine industry and the havoc it unleashed, and the attempt to reconstitute local symbolisms is the notion that there is a novel subjective and aesthetic dynamism that points toward deeper truths of the Colombian, if not pan-American, experience.

The notion that there is an aesthetic energy that reveals itself naturally at borders is one with a long history. It makes for an especially revelatory study of Colombia, which, as I describe in chapter 3, is a country that used high institutional aesthetics as a model to evoke citizenship at the turn of the twentieth century. This is a theoretical approach that goes beyond Colombia, however. Any expansion of cultural, economic, and aesthetic systems has presented a parallel overwriting, hybridization, or resistance. The stakes of the overwriting of multiple systems of perception with a singular aesthetic epistemology have always been vast. Walter Mignolo points to the high Enlightenment as the moment in which such perception becomes set on the global scale. Mignolo refers to the semantic shift from aesthesis to aesthetics.[1] He defines aesthetic globalization as the simultaneous totalization of an aesthetic epistemology and the reduction of an idea of an "evolution of perception" to a singular telos. The formation of the modern European citizen occurs in aesthetic terms as much as sociopolitical terms: just as Montesquieu lays out the modern nation-state, Kant—and he is really a stand-in for many others who took part in the theorization of the modern aesthetic citizen, with Alexander Baumgarten as a forebear and Friedrich Schiller as a pupil—lays out an ordering of the world according to a hierarchy of perceptive capability.[2]

Engaging with aesthetics and socioeconomics in Latin American spaces that are sites of ongoing reinvention, then, always situates local writers and artists in the position of border dweller. The Latin American *ciudad letrada*, or lettered city, that for Angel Rama acted as an outpost of high perception, ordered government, and lettered citizens, does not cover over the spread of aesthetic distance. By contrast, in the *ciudad letrada*, intellectuals write from the border between the civilized elsewhere that creates knowledge, literary aesthetic framework, and ideal perception and the local space of incongruous experience. Even within the context of incipient and postglobalization Latin America, Colombian urban and narco-novels address this breach by calling into question the novel's limits.

Latin American criticism has been particularly ripe for the development of globalization theory. Nestor García-Canclini's vocabulary of hybrid modernities and Mariano Siskind's more updated consideration of the Latin American intelligentsia's traditional "desire for the world" have structural parallels to my theorization of the aesthetic border.[3] This place where multiple forms of perception converge can play out in new cultural artifacts and spatial experiences in which subjects enter and exit older constellations of embodiment. My rendering of globalization encompasses the cultural affects that follow global financial and commodity markets. To make strictly economic arguments is fodder for another book under another genre, but the ways in which macroeconomic decisions and commodity markets affect the cultural superstructure in both Colombia and Latin America cannot be overstated. The minutia of day-to-day affectual interaction in Latin America, according to Dierdra Reber, betrays the embossment of commodities.[4]

Beyond notions of hybridity and assumption, there is a subcanon of what we could call *resistance theory*. These theories envision local aesthetic and socioeconomic practices as remaining external to, or at least not wholly subsumed by, global flows. Enrique Dussel's notion of an analectic perhaps goes the farthest in structuring a theory of externality. For Dussel, the local is not so concerned by entering into a dialectal mode of resistance as it is completely ambivalent or agnostic to it. Knowingly or not, for Dussel, local modes of being refuse to reify in the face of international cultural markets, because they simply do not take them into consideration. Antonio Cornejo Polar's dialectical heterogeneity, one might wager, acts as theoretical bridge between Dussel's stubborn externality and Ignacio Sánchez Prado's strategic Occidentalism, which reluctantly acquiesces to the inrush of the world. For Cornejo Polar, there is a natural blend or hybridization in a space, such as the Americas, where so many modes of embodiment share a common geography. Orality mixed with a written tradition creates a cultural dynamism in which nodes in the culture map dialogue and blend with each other, while retaining their original form of expression. These theoretical conversations have helped me develop the nomenclature and description of possible outcomes at the aesthetic border as theorized globally.[5]

In Colombia more precisely, aesthetics and the "investigation into the nature of beauty" goes hand in hand with such a self-reflective national literary tradition—or a group of writers that meditates heavily on the limited capabilities of literary aesthetics. This questioning leads to a further dissection of aesthetic idealism, or the belief in a purity of aesthetics that can lead to a social order: a faith in beauty that when viewed through the looking glass of interpretations of the evocation of a national and urban citizen through aesthetics sits uncomfortably with both writers in exile and those who lament decaying urban infrastructure. In *El atravesado* (1971), to use one example, the urban novelist Andrés Caicedo, to whom I return in chapter 2, offers an example in which aesthetics undo rather than constitute the citizen. In an inversion of Schiller's theory that through artistic beauty the individual and collective will come together in the harmony of the state, Caicedo's characters use art as a catalyst to reproduce the boundary-subjectivity that they experience precisely at the state level. Caicedo and other urban novelists attempting to chronicle city life under the Violence comment on the limits of aesthetic idealism in and of itself, as their characters navigate the intersections and competing energies of market logic, beauty, and the struggle of the lettered city to keep pace with the constant arrival of both new ideas and migrants from the Colombian hinterland.

One may argue that Colombia stands out, even within the context of Latin American countries, in presenting an inordinately complex relationship between culture and violence. Since independence, Colombia has experienced no shortage of overlap between cultural idealism—largely through the commingling of politics and poetic and grammatical transcendentalists, whom I explore further in chapter 3—and violence. Giving representation to violence, in the sense that it would require a memorializing literary marker to begin to quantify and categorize trauma, is doubly complicated, given that the violence is ongoing. In the book *Literature, Testimony and Cinema in Contemporary Colombian Culture: Spectres of La Violencia*, Rory O'Bryen discusses the problems of remembering and situating violence through culture, when he argues, "The fact that there exists a strong discourse that posits Colombia's current situation as a continuation of the Violence should alert us to the uncomfortable sense that to talk of 'remembering' here—or, indeed, of 'memory'—may not only be inappropriate, but also flagrantly anachronistic."[6] Colombia presents a problematic situation in that its political and aesthetic discourses still find themselves muddled by the extreme contrasts in a nation-state struggling to stay afloat as a unified entity: one that, with regard to globalization, offers many intrinsic contradictions to both global developmentalist projects and the aesthetic infrastructure that accompanies them. Jean Franco, for one, claims, "The contemporary narrative of globalization as purveyed by the World Bank and by official circles in Europe and the United States is a narrative of development fantasized as a journey into prosperity. Seen from Latin America, the outcome is not so certain and the pauperization of those left behind hardly makes for a heartening 'story.' The stigmatized bodies of those marked for death in the drug wars and in urban violence reveal the other side of the globalization narrative."[7]

To the extent that shear dynamism is enough to destabilize even the most conservative of social infrastructures, the Colombian lettered city is challenged throughout the twentieth century by prolonged periods of internal migration and mass urbanization. Between the period of 1938 and 1951, Medellín alone increased in population by 77 percent.[8] While the period of 1930 to 1950 saw improvements in urban design and public transportation in Bogotá, the wave of urban migrants between 1950 and 1970, both through daily use and violent eruptions, undid any collective urban progress made over the previous fifty years. Bringing to the urban space a fresh set of visual and literary signifiers, the presence of new collective subjectivities upended the already arcane literary systems put in place by the Colombian founders. Almost instantaneously, new cultural forms began to spring up that challenged the urban cultural hegemony, and popular culture, mixed with until then unknown forms, gained increasing importance to the collective urban experience. Still, old institutions had reason to reinstate their control over novel affect. The lettered elite and their newly urban unlettered counterparts began to rub against one another, causing both symbolic and real political tension.

Functionaries of the lettered city took a notable hit during the Bogotazo of April 9, 1948, one of Colombia's most collectively traumatic moments. Just over fifty years after Caro modified the Constitución de 1886 and used his knowledge of Latin and Greek authors to project his political exceptionality, the politics and aesthetics that the state excluded came back to haunt its governing bodies. In a moment of political and affective groundswell, following the assassination of the populist leader Jorge Eliécer Gaitán, the lack of state representation of new subjectivities and urban infrastructure to account for the presence of new massive publics led to a prolonged period of violence. In just one day, a third of Bogotá was demolished by angry mobs that "left the nation's capital a smoldering ruins; churches and public buildings were transformed into heaps of rubble; trolley cars were derailed and burned; stores looted; the city's sidewalks overflowed with the debris of broken glass and ruined merchandise. Meanwhile, decomposing corpses hurriedly thrown in piles in Bogotá's central cemetery seemed to give material testimony to the existence of an anonymous, dangerous crowd that had captured the elite imagination and provoked increasing anxiety of an impending attack upon elite privilege by a ragged, bloodthirsty army of the nation's excluded."[9]

The "rural barbarian" that had propped up nineteenth-century Latin America's most influential political treatises had finally come to the Colombian city; and the group of migrants challenged the aesthetic model embedded in the "civilization and barbarism" paradigm, latently at first and manifestly through rioting later. If Caro's exceptionalism that fostered a singular aesthetic and epistemological order proved to be a failure, he had not acted in a vacuum. Conversely, he had taken the Latin American political map at its word: the city establishes a cultural elite with its aesthetic weight based in Europe, and the government applies its interpretation of the singular, universalized standard to the unlettered body. Colombia, more than most Latin American nations, had the tendency to tie aesthetic registers in with geography; it is a nation that has always contrasted a small urban stretch—Cali, Bogotá, and Medellín—with the countryside, using the literary discourses of the "barbarian" jungle to affirm the suspicions and fears of the urban elite. As María Ospina points out in her article "Las naturalezas de la guerra: Topografías violentas de selva en la narrativa contemporánea colombiana," there is a strong discourse, ranging from the early writings of Francisco José de Caldas through José Eustasio Rivera's *La vorágine* (1924) and to Ingrid Betancourt's testimonial account of the FARC-laden jungle, *No hay silencio que no termine* (2010), that openly draws on an imagistic contrast between the disorder of the rugged, chaotic countryside and the civility of the ordered city.[10]

Allusions to the lettered city as a civilizing project are clear in Colombian history, and arguably more so than in most Latin American nations, the governing bodies of Colombia tie aesthetics into legislation. Angel Rama observes a prescription to civilize Latin America that is emphatically singular: "Este es obra de la *ciudad letrada*. Sólo ella es capaz de concebir, como pura especulación, la ciudad ideal, proyectarla antes de su existencia, conservarla más allá de su eje-cución material, hacerla pervivir aun en pugna con las modificaciones sensi-bles que introduce sin cesar el hombre común." (This is the work of the lettered city. Only it is capable of conceiving, as pure speculation, the ideal city, project it before it even exists, preserve it beyond its material execution, and make it hold up in the face of the constant changes in taste of the common person.)[11] Though in line with Rama's description of the "ciudad ideal," his formula, both in material and subjective terms, never leads to a politically functioning and inclusive Colombia; and his "hombre común" never makes it off the ground. On the contrary, the map of the civilizing, lettered elite fails to account for real aesthetic subjectivities in Colombia: the outside-of-accounting indigenous com-munities, the untestimonialized African populations, the migrant lumpen, and the hybrid and syncretic subjectivities borne out of migratory flux.

When Rama describes the full authorial weight given to the written word, he identifies the singular literary aesthetics at the heart of the civilizing map. Yet a look at the persistent lapses of the Colombian state, both in aesthetic and political terms, shows another side to the story. Those subjectivities who argu-ably tended toward a culture of orality or who were kept at bay by the carefully controlled literary archive would take exception to such a limiting approach to civil modernity. Rama's aesthetic state, exemplified *avant la lettre* by Caro, would not save the nation from streaming civil war, acute moments of violence, and a continuation of disorder and displacement. In the period between 1980 and 2000, the century-long displacements continued, and four million citizens not factoring into the logic of the lettered city were forced to migrate.[12] And the problems surrounding the failure of the state to bind continue to be largely representational; Flor Edilma Osorio Perez claims, for example: "Millions of women and men have suffered the pain and terror of war, which has left them sunk in poverty and total uncertainty to face their immediate future, amidst a society that ignores them when it is not looking at them with disdain and distrust."[13]

One of the most visible failures in representation in post-Violence Colom-bia consists of urban anomie and *pandilla* (street-gang) violence. A branch of the urban novel, the *narco-novela*—a form that *La virgen de los sicarios* along-side other popular renditions such as Jorge Franco's *Rosario Tijeras* (1953) helped to consolidate—has gone to great lengths to represent the street youths who make up Colombia's *pandillas*. The importance of representation could hardly be overestimated, according to sociologists. It is visibility that *pandilleros* (gang members) seek out when they join rivaling groups, alongside a *sicariato* that forms part of an economic infrastructure based in a liberalism gone awry. Through urban anomie and the *sicariato*, we witness a paralleling economic and aesthetic underrepresentation, according to Maria Guadalupe Pacheco: "El sicariato no es sólo la condensación de las violencias sociales, económicas, políticas, históricas y estructurales de Colombia. Medellín es apenas un escenario de lo que se anuncia para muchos otros lugares del planeta en tiempos de globalización: el vaciamiento de sentidos, el cierre de horizontes, el desencanto de un mundo que predica el consumo como única forma de pertenencia ciudadana." (The *sicariato* is not only a condensation of structural social, economic, political, and historical forms of violence. Medellín is simply a snapshot of what happens throughout the world in times of globalization: the hollowing out of meaning, the closing of horizons, the disenchantment of the world that is followed by consumption as the only form of citizenship and belonging.)[14]

The lack of state and aesthetic representation that leads to anomie and social exclusion operates on three interworking levels. The first consists of the fact that the long duration of unsuccessfully testimonialized violence creates what the social historian Daniel Pécaut has referred to as the "banalization of violence" in Colombian history. As history repeats and reiterates situations of violence in Colombia, it produces a normalizing frame around the politically violent setting, which creates a need for an alternative perspective to aid collective memory. For Pécaut, an altern narrative is necessary to process cultural memory and testimonialize traumatic experiences under a logic that escapes the tremendous frame of Colombian history.[15] This approach exacerbates the problems of the appropriation of literary aesthetics by a government that, until recently, has largely been used to justify the ongoing processes of violence, rather than to work through them.

On another level, physical and institutional infrastructure built around the Colombian city have failed to evoke and govern a functioning citizenry throughout the twentieth century. Despite investment in urban design, many times employing Europe's foremost midcentury modernist designers, such as representatives of the Bauhaus and L'esprit, the urban collective has not responded as planned. Marco Palacios puts the distortion between utopian, Continental design and Colombian cityscapes succinctly when he writes, "Si desde una perspectiva latinoamericana Colombia es notable por la armonía relativa de la distribución geográfica de su población urbana, las ciudades por dentro revelan, mejor que en ningún otro plano de la realidad social, el fracaso del ideal urbano de modernización occidental. En unos 20 años, c. 1950–70, las avalanchas de inmigrantes arrasaron con la exquisita racionalidad cartesiana de los planos que entre c.1930–50, trazaron urbanistas europeos como H. Bartholomew, Carlo Brunner y Le Corbousier en Bogotá, José Luis Sert en Cali, Wierner y Sert en Medellín." (If from the Latin American perspective, Colombia is notable for relative harmony in geographic distribution of its urban populations, viewed from the inside, its cities reveal, more than in most other maps of social reality, the failure of Western modernized urban idyll. In just twenty years, c. 1950–70, avalanches of immigrants razed the exquisite carte-sian reality laid out in the urban maps that between c. 1930–50, leading Euro-pean urbanists had designed: H. Bartholomew, Carlo Brunner and Le Corbousier in Bogotá, José Luis Sert in Cali, Wierner and Sert in Medellín.)[16]

Interestingly, architectural modernists parallel Caro's aesthetic state, though from an opposing perspective. While, for Caro, aesthetic distance is used to create a chasm between the government and the Colombian body politic, for these utopian architects and engineers, modern urban design ideally would lead to embracing inclusivity. Both approaches are met with a similar destructive response, however. When the excluded, unlettered migrant comes to the Colombian city, idealistic infrastructure collapses under the weight of a sub-jectivity that is not accounted for in the aesthetic nation, which is where the third level of underrepresentation arises. The unlettered status of the majority of Colombian citizens creates a political atmosphere, in which the populace does not have the ability to leave an inscription on the literary archive that lends the lettered city its authorial weight. At no point during the foundation of the Colombian nation-state does the cultural bedrock of nationhood act as a dia-logue, or diatopical hermeneutic, with its citizens. By contrast, Colombia's aes-thetic epistemology is undergirded by a politics of exception that letters the Colombian body on the basis of an incongruous modernism that finds its ulti-mate referents in a European, and largely Kantian and Baumgartean, order. An unrepresentative literary modernism props up an exclusionist state, beginning with the transcendental political poets of the end of the nineteenth century and coming back to haunt the government through the unquiet of the mid- to late twentieth century—one could point to the absence of a stable constitution throughout the nineteenth century as leading to the tendency to use a literary archive to lend governmental credibility, a modus operandi that would have been at the forefront of Caro's mind, since he, himself, altered the constitution in 1886. When the excluded subject makes their presence felt through migra-tion to the city, they challenge the government, its self-referential aesthetic par-adigm, and the infrastructural projects that only account for small portions of the Colombian populace. The Colombian aesthetic state does not lend stabil-ity so much as it creates bare lives, and the bare lives eventually demand to be taken into account when they move to the urban context.

In Colombia, governing bodies continued to feed off the literary-political privilege well into the twentieth century. As popular cultures and new urban subjectivities arose, institutional figures moved into media that were tradition-ally associated with popular aesthetics.[17] Newspapers, radio shows, and maga-zines also felt the weight of the archive, in a globalized, post-Violence context. Yet authority and its aesthetic registers were increasingly challenged by Colom-bia's urban populations as the century progressed, and the extreme lived experiences of many urban Colombians were not displaced by the literary archive so much as they increasingly became represented, giving birth to new Colombian literary genres: the *novela de la Violence* and the *novela urbana*. The birth of these new genres reflects a rippling in the aesthetic map, the increasing mediation between an aesthetically distant state infrastructure and its citizens, and the intervention of mass publics in old symbolic systems. For Jesús Martín Barbero, we begin to see a mixture of media and subjectivity that challenges the foundational archive. Martín Barbero discusses the dynamics of the late twentieth-century urban cultural map when he writes, "It is a map with many populations halfway between peasant village and urban neighborhood, with *villages* where social relations no longer have the stability or elemental nature of the rural and with *neighborhoods* in which feudal authoritarianisms survive alongside the horizontality woven into urban illegality and informality. These are villages that remain centered on religion while at the same time experiencing changes that affect not only the world of labor and housing but also the world of subjectivity, affectivity, and sensuality."[18]

As new urban subjectivities challenged old cultural institutions in Colombia, the traditional lettered city undertook a double affront. On the one hand, the politics of the Cold War exacerbated the distance between Latin American *modernismo* and the institutionalized North American modernism.[19] At the same time, the very *modernismo* that had been celebrated by proponents of the lettered city was, itself, radicalized. Popular culture and new literary aesthetics challenged the content of *modernismo* in Latin America, which, according to Jean Franco, "succeed in breaching the walls of what Angel Rama termed 'the lettered city'; through this breach, indigenous languages and cultures [enter] into productive contact with lettered culture."[20] More specifically in Colombia, the literary archive was radically altered when the *novela de la Violencia* and the *novela urbana* took aesthetics out of the hands of governing bodies and placed them in the context of urban cityscapes.

I have therefore turned to literature to unpack the inherent contradictions, paradoxes, and dynamism at the heart of Colombia's very existence. Literature has always been a lodestar for Colombia, even if that literature has often excluded large swaths of the population. It would seem that a country that has thrown so much weight behind aesthetic idealism, that has left governance to literary acts of faith and urban infrastructure to modernism, would need to work through itself *aesthetically*. Nationhood is a collection of stories we tell ourselves; that Colombia's compendium resonates so far beyond its borders is telling at a time in which so many countries, be they young or old, turn inward for reflection.

In chapter 1, "Gabo against the World: Gabriel García Márquez and the Poetics of Early Globalization," my goal is to give García Márquez, who has been out of vogue in critical circles for nearly two decades, a fresh approach. I focus on his role as literary icon and international commodity of Latin American literature for export and offer an updated reading of *One Hundred Years of Solitude* that considers the text as progenitor to a poetics of early globalization. In this chapter, I define the *Gabo Paradox*, a term that seeks to capture the conflicting relationship that García Márquez has with the literary world. He both put Latin America on the cultural map and created a vision of it as a romantic and rural backwater. In this chapter, I put into context the Colombian 1960s and the impression this moment had on García Márquez. Emerging from the devastation left behind by the coffee boom and bust, Colombia was in the midst of opening itself to the world for the second time. Picking up where Ericka Beckman leaves off in *Capital Fictions: The Literature of Latin America's Export Age*, this chapter offers fresh insight into *One Hundred Years of Solitude* by reading it as a snapshot of this moment of early Colombian globalization. The novel turns on the tension between rural romanticism and a Colombia that is in the midst of great changes brought on by mass urbanization and the arrival of multinational companies. I analyze this anxiety as one of García Márquez's fundamental artistic impulses, though it is regularly surpassed in focus and critical attention by formal studies of magical realism. By digging beyond the superficial tone that has both made García Márquez famous and turned him into an easy target, I attempt to bring him back into critical parlance by placing his intellectual and poetic concerns in the trajectory of Colombian letters.

This treatment of García Márquez at the aesthetic border continues in chapter 2, "Literary Shipwrecks: Colombian Aesthetic Citizenship after García Márquez." In this chapter, I offer a sociological reading of the way Colombian literature has been marketed on a global scale in a publishing culture that has cultivated oversimplified tastes that left authors who did not fit into the global narrative by the wayside. According to my reading, those who had to deal with the taste created by the cultivation of a new Latin American novel in the Boom and an aesthetics of magical marginality by a handful of publishing houses in Spain during the Franco regime felt the early limits of global aesthetic citizenship. With these authors, we encircle Pascale Casanova's theorization of a world literary system that creates a global political stage in which aesthetic battles can be won under the sign of symbolic capital, where perhaps they could not be won within the framework of economic capital. For the mid- to late twentieth-century Colombian author, however, the experience of world literature presents one of many moments in the national literary canon in which the author runs aground between the nation and the world. Casanova's theory creates a fascinating, and many times empowering, framework that applies a world-systems economic analysis, in the vein of Immanuel Wallerstein and Fernand Braudel, to the aesthetic analysis of the novel carried out in Franco Moretti's

Distance Reading and, in reference to Latin America more precisely, Héctor Hoyos's *Beyond Bolaño: The Global Latin American Novel*.[21] But the theory does not always account for the literary fallout that takes place in spaces such as Latin America alongside the success of figures such as García Márquez whom Casanova uses as quintessential examples of the revolutionary capacities embedded in the novel, a group that, at least according to her nomenclature, effectively shifted the Greenwich Meridian of literature. Here, I highlight the other side of the novel, the side of its limiting capabilities and of major publishing houses, traditionally located on separate continents entirely, to fully capture the literary production of a sociocultural space as complex as Colombia.

In chapter 3, "Narrating Disruption: From the *Novela de la Violence* to the *Narco-Novela*," I historicize the long Colombian twentieth century and the literature that attempts to capture it. This chapter presents the notion that both the socioeconomic context and literary style of narco-literature do not mark a rupture so much as a continuation of a style developed as early as the 1930s in urban Colombia. What in the 1990s and 2000s is the urban resonances of the cocaine industry finds a parallel in the fluctuation in coffee and rubber commodity prices throughout the twentieth century. This study of a dissonant moment in the aesthetic border traces the literary trajectory from the *novela de la Violencia* to the narco-novel. Beginning with Gustavo Álvarez Gardeazábal's *Condors Aren't Buried Every Day* and cataloging its influence on early urban texts, such as Luis Fayad's *Esther's Relatives*, this chapter presents the aesthetic precursor to contemporary urban literature in Colombia. The crux of the chapter develops a catalog of the most impactful and salient examples of the contemporary Colombian urban novel as artifact of the aesthetic border. It further presents an analysis of the subsections of the urban novel, such as the narco-novel, the competing aesthetics of what I refer to as the Cali and Medellín schools, and the development of the "somatic metaphor" that resists the banalization of an otherwise overwhelmingly violent urban milieu. I present an analysis of the way Colombian urban novelists, both from older movements, such as Gustavo Álvarez Gardeazábal, Luis Fayad, and Miguel Torres (1942), and more updated writers of the same genre, such as Laura Restrepo, Mario Mendoza (1964), Andrés Caicedo (1951–1977), Antonio Caballero (1945), and Alonso Salazar (1960), write in the context of the debased standing of the conventional symbolic pillar of the lettered city. With a *Ulysses*-like air, these narrators meander through Colombian cityscapes, often Medellín, offering an ad hoc elegy that attempts to resuscitate symbolically the urban space through narrative and, in doing so, to take on a philosophical problem that looms large in the pan–Latin American intellectual and literary tradition; one need not strain too hard to come up with numerous examples in twentieth-century Latin American literature alone in which the writer attempts to forge an identity based on the geographical shift between multiple spaces.

In chapter 4, "Recasting the National Story after the Inrush of the World," I turn to the present and bring the Colombian global relationship full circle by arguing that, as the dust settles on the two sets of Latin American literary clichés for which Colombia is known, magical realism and the narco-novel, a new towering literary figure has emerged who acts as a synthesis while moving beyond the gravitational pull of the nation's two aesthetic axes, in Juan Gabriel Vásquez. In his novels, Vásquez methodically works through the tropes associated with the Colombian national narrative, recasting them for the post-narco, postglobalization, renovated-national twenty-first century. The chapter presents Vásquez as a literary icon who is both out of step with contemporary Colombian literature and his Latin American peer group and a figure who perfectly encapsulates the conflicting cultural flows of the present. As Vásquez sidesteps his Gen X peers and harks back to the older literary trajectory of nineteenth-century figures such as Silva, one must wonder if he retraces the journey of his forbearers, attempting not to run aground. This is not just a personal but an aesthetic concern. I argue that the text that put Vásquez on the world literary map, *The Sound of Things Falling*, is the first novel in the Colombian canon to attempt to capture the post-Escobar era by working through it in a way that is frontal yet avoids melodrama. Vásquez uses this anomalous innovative-throwback in both style and intellectual formation to gesture toward what I refer to as a *literature of national reconstitution*. He attempts to resuscitate the national narrative, exposing it to but not allowing it to be overcome by mass cultures, technological innovation, and global expectation of the Colombian national brand. The melding of the nineteenth and twenty-first centuries is an aspect of Vásquez's work that Aníbal González considers an attempt to remain globally relevant, while keeping national literary formation at the forefront of poetic concern. This rendering of the aesthetic border has a flavor of both contemporary literature and of Silva himself. González argues not only that the original title of *The Sound of Things Falling*, *El ruido de las cosas al caer*, is itself a verse written in "endecasílabo," one of the many "alusiones a la poesía del modernista colombiano José Asunción Silva" (allusions to the poetry of the Colombian modernist José Asunción Silva), but moreover that there is a shared link "con la memoria histórica, al tema del tiempo y a la búsqueda de verdades colectivas e individuales" (with the historic memory, with the theme of time, and the search of collective and individual truths).[22]

Also in chapter 4, I address Vásquez's individual novels within the context of the meta trends in his work. The section of the chapter turns on his calculated attempt to gesture toward the major clichés of Colombian literature, while reframing them in a high literary register. The analysis of reframed cliché and melodrama continues, as I offer national literary and sociological context, before returning to the individual novel and offering an exegesis of another of Vásquez's prominent works, *The Informants*. Ending the chapter, I focus on Vásquez's attempt to put Colombian diaspora in context by focusing on the World War II era, when immigration flowed inward. By recasting migration, a Colombian trope worn to cliché, and historicizing it conceptually by reminding the reading public that it was not long ago that people fled *to* Colombia, Vásquez evinces his best impulses. He strips back the symbolism of the nation to its studs and then puts it back together, depicting Colombia as bigger than its complicated national narrative and brand yet still very much a product of it.

During the writing of this book, Colombia has experienced the wild sociopolitical swings described in my historical analysis. There have been bright moments of hope and nadirs in which the gravity of historical cycles clashes with idealism. In the interest of letting events breathe and avoiding "hot takes" or comments more apt for journalism than *longue durée* academic monographs, I have stopped my analysis in the year 2017. As I make these final, topical edits in 2021, Colombia finds itself in the midst of ongoing soul searching, in which the country buffets against the bounds of nationhood. In an echo of the history laid out in the following chapters, practically every Colombian demographic has taken to the streets for wide protests in ways that do not fit neatly into traditional political narratives. This is not unique to Colombia; but as is described throughout this project, Colombia is a country that is fascinating because it tends to be exemplary of the pan-American experience, while also offering a hyperbolic version of the agony and ecstasy of the American experiment. It has not been all bad. A heartening phenomenon during the writing of this book has been the increasing interest in Colombian literature and culture on the international stage. From Pablo Montoya's 2015 Rómulo Gallegos Prize for *Tríptico de la infamia* (2014) through the controversial pop hit *Narcos*, the continued success of Colombian artists on the international stage, and the recent cinema verité documentary about J Balvin, *The Boy from Medellín* (2020), one might venture that Colombia is in the beginning of a third wave of cultural globalization. No doubt, entire books could and will be written on these topics. I have chosen not to include them here, along with many other young Colombian writers, because this study is meant to be a jumping-off point to analyze Colombian letters as a product of its relationship to globalization, rather than a catalog of Colombian literature in and of itself. While contemporary Colombian cultural production looks more and more every day like a movement fitting of the narrative of the aesthetic border, those cultural products will have to be focuses of future study, ones that I will very much look forward to reading. For the meantime, what follows is a story of Colombia running up against the world: one filled with families as complex as nations, decades of tumult condensed to a single body, and artisans trying to put it all back together again, while they themselves are catapulted through the labyrinth of world.

1

Gabo against the World

Gabriel García Márquez
and the Poetics of
Early Globalization

Few writers transcend the typical bounds of literature quite like Gabriel García Márquez. His work, especially *One Hundred Years of Solitude*, is the starting place of canon formation. A member of the literary world's innermost of circles, García Márquez is synonymous with world literature. Yet, more than most larger-than-life writers who take on an iconography that resonates as much at the level of myth and commodity as actual word on the page, García Márquez connects with readers on an individual level. From *One Hundred Years of Solitude*'s publication date in 1967, readers as wide ranging as Fidel Castro and Bill Clinton have been able to identify in García Márquez a kindred spirit. To formalists, he made famous a tone that would become one of the most salient of the twentieth century, in magical realism. For advocates of world literature, he, along with William Faulkner, set the very example for how to rewrite the literary map. For agents and publishing houses, he is the author whose sales rival God's, since he falls just short of the Bible in terms of circulation. For critics, he is by turns an avant-garde, a revolutionary, a con artist, a sell out, a North Star of literary production, and a once-in-a-generation genius. For lay readers, he looms just as large. From the adolescent school rooms of his home Aracataca in rural Colombia to the governing halls and offices the world over, the depth of García Márquez's work is perhaps only rivaled by what he means reader to reader. He is romantic, realist, transcendental, political, and mystical. To highlight the fervor that his readers feel, I offer the anecdote that one of my university professors encouraged our class to read *One Hundred Years of Solitude* while on LSD, the way he had when the novel originally came out. We declined his suggestion and read the novel clear-eyed, though I cannot imagine an experience more profound. This pushing and pulling at the heart of García Márquez's work, the feverish reactions and strange-bed-fellow acclaim it engenders, the sort of literature that makes someone in the Amazon feel connected to the culture world and makes a professor do something that could lose him his job, is what I refer to as the *Gabo Paradox*. It is an aleph-like quality that allows him to be transcendental and resonate acutely, to inspire critical diatribe and floral praise in every hue.

Many critics have tried to decode García Márquez's enigmatic success. This criticism falls into the subcategories of biography, close reading, and impact. Unsurprisingly, García Márquez's work has generated a dizzying amount of scholarly work. This chapter draws on much of the overwhelmingly large corpus dedicated to his life and work. In the interest of avoiding an encyclopedic indexing of criticism dedicated to García Márquez, I consider it beneficial to list the most influential to this chapter's conception. Gerald Martin's biography *Gabriel García Márquez: A Life* (2008) has become a classic in its own right. A current in the biography is the notion that much of García Márquez's success is oddly owed to his provinciality. It has now become widespread lore that García Márquez cited his grandmother, who was illiterate, as one of his greatest literary influences. This notion acts as a metaphor for the larger truth that Martin illuminates in his biography, as he draws on comparisons between Macondo, the fictional town now synonymous with magical realism, and Aracataca, where García Márquez grew up trying to square the multilayered histories, mythologies, and religions that imbued his daily life. He grew up amid a symbolism in which shipwrecked sailors founded nations, civil war disappeared neighbors, and syncretic religion ran up against the high structure of Catholicism. It is within the scene set by Martin that the cosmopolitan critic's cynicism melts away when reading quotes by García Márquez that claim that in reality everything that occurs in *One Hundred Years of Solitude* is true: that the novel is both autobiography and national history.

This reading places García Márquez among fine company within both Latin America and the Global South. Pablo Neruda, Faulkner, and Flannery O'Connor are often lauded for similar innovation. There is novel insight in observing multiple cultural flows at the aesthetic border, the place where disparate forms of perception converge. This was what drove the tonal melancholy that somehow betrayed deeper joy for Neruda. This was the horror that haunted gentility in Faulkner's and O'Connor's realism. It is transcendent narrative that tries to unite the mélange of disparate subjectivities in New World nations, especially Colombia, for García Márquez. Gene Bell-Villada's close-reading of García Márquez in *García Márquez: A Man and His Work* (2010) and *Gabriel García Márquez's One Hundred Years of Solitude: A Casebook* (2002) offer close-reading analyses of García Márquez and his seminal work. Important in these texts is the reminder that what occasionally gets lost in the analysis of García Márquez as icon, magical realism as movement, and *One Hundred Years of Solitude* as hit novel is the formal sophistication of the work at hand. Setting sociological approaches to literature aside, García Márquez produced master-works with regard to more traditional ways to read literature. His prosody is well structured. His metaphors are rich. His narrative construction is arguably second to none. This is part and parcel of the Gabo Paradox. There is so much to analyze in his work that it is easy to get lost in particularities. It is simple to forget when thinking of his narrative structure that García Márquez is more than a neo-Baroque writer, akin to his fellow Caribbean writer Severo Sarduy. By the same token, it would be natural to get lost in his biblical imagery and claim that García Márquez is a spiritual writer. One might argue that it is similarly too facile a rendering to let García Márquez stand in as metonym for magical realism and vice versa. These formal dissections of his work and careful unpacking of imagery and sentences remind us that much of what makes García Márquez so complex is that there can be whole novels in a single paragraph, or occasionally sentences that themselves could be novels.

One would be tempted to think that García Márquez's revolutionary form, his celebrity status that goes well beyond that typically afforded to even hit authors, and his dense yet readable style would be enough to make him unique. While true, this would preclude the fact that his meteoric rise onto the world literary stage, one that is arguably unrivaled by that of any author in history, itself presents a case study in the sociological circulation of letters. How did a young man from not just a provincial continent, not just a provincial country, but a provincial place within these latter two so quickly become an emblem of global high culture? In the twenty-first century, analysis of García Márquez has tended to focus as much on his place within the global canon and his rise onto the literary scene as his form. In fact, analysis of magical realism or in-depth reading of García Márquez's work in its own right witnessed a decline during this same period. This analysis of his reception and impact owes much of its popularity to the fertile field of postmodern readings and critical cultural capital. Studies such as Pascale Casanova's *The World Republic of Letters* (2004), which I discuss within the context of García Márquez in Chapter 2, James English's *The Economy of Prestige: Prizes, Awards, and the Circulation of Cultural Value* (2005), and David Damrosch's *What Is World Literature?* (2003) have led to a veritable boom in the reading of literature as social commodity. Given, as I argue, the paradoxes inherent to García Márquez's place in the literary world, he has acted as a mainstay in studies of cultural capital. These socioeconomic-driven studies draw on him to explain the machinery of the cultural world. What interests economists if not the outlier?

The trouble with García Márquez's enigmatic quality is that it can tempt critics to project their framework onto him. He occasionally runs the risk of acting as a hollow signifier, into which ideologies can be poured. Part of the paradoxical nature of García Márquez is that his work neither shrugs off these readings nor wholly affirms them. Fredric Jameson wrote as early as 1986 on García Márquez's presentation of "third world allegory" and as recently as 2017 on his cultural resistance to global superpower absorption.[1] While the vocabulary of the former reading has not aged well, the recent updating of terms shows that there is still something to García Márquez's strange place as both resister to global culture and champion of it. Within the field of the study of Latin American literature, Ericka Beckman's *Capital Fictions: The Literature of Latin America's Export Age* (2013) carries the torch of themes established previously by Jameson. Beckman localizes the study of García Márquez as cultural commodity by placing him in the context of his national tradition. With García Márquez, we see the continuation of Colombian *modernismo*, according to Beckman, as much as anything entirely new. There had long been an understanding of Colombia's place within the world of commodities, according to this argument. In a sense, playing on its comparative advantage by capitalizing on its perceived exoticism, Colombia has a tradition of selling its "un-," if not "anti-," "modern" status. Beckman traces this back to the export of rubber and the notion of what she refers to as "export reverie" as a quasi-foundational national narrative for Colombia. The parallel with the Colombian *modernistas*, such as José Asunción Silva, comes with their paradoxical relationship to global modernity. Silva both benefited from the avenues of capital established by the trade of Colombian commodities and wrote of a modernism that was resistant to the market's instrumental reason. In a similar vein, García Márquez writes a highly romantic rendering of provincial life at a time when economic globalization was gaining speed in Colombia. A case in point of Beckman's export reverie comes famously in the section of *One Hundred Years of Solitude* that offers a historical fiction rendering of a massacre of union workers by the United Fruit Company. All the while, García Márquez benefits from a glossy tone and cosmopolitan taste for this hinterland-style narrative. Even the acute moment of social realism that points a finger is couched by a narrative logic that has already established that death is really not that meaningful an event. García Márquez both revolutionizes global narrative through his unique style and talent and simply picks up the torch of an old national philosophical question. These are compounding contradictions that only a work such as *One Hundred Years of Solitude* can help a writer transcend. This chapter is not about the muddied waters in which García Márquez criticism treads, after all, but his ability to be bigger than those competing readings of him. In short, it is about the Gabo Paradox.

My contribution to this and many other threads of García Márquez criticism is to place it in the context of my argument that Colombia's relationship to the socioeconomic world has poignant representation in narrative. In the case of García Márquez, this narrative representation is often overlooked. Despite the vast amount written on García Márquez, few scholars, Beckman marking a rare exception, have tended to place his work strictly within the Colombian context. This chapter aims not only to place García Márquez within the national story but to show that his work, and *One Hundred Years of Solitude* specifically, marks an inflection point in one of the world's most compelling entrances into globalization. I argue that García Márquez's paradoxical relationship to the literary world is reflective of Colombia's early engagement with globalization—or that the Gabo Paradox is reflective of the Colombian Paradox, in their mutual inherent contradictions. Just as in chapter 3, in which I argue that the Colombian literary canon evolves to capture the violent cityscapes associated with an uneasy postnational status in the global economy, and just as in chapter 4, in which I argue that in the twenty-first century there is an attempt to reconstitute nationhood through narrative, trying to memorialize recent trauma while simultaneously moving beyond it, here I argue that García Márquez presaged the national rupture, in the first instance.

This chapter is broken into two sections. The first offers a close reading of *One Hundred Years of Solitude*, through which we observe the anxiety of the opening up of economic borders in Colombia. The odd attempt to write a local story that became a regional story that became a global story perfectly captures this anxiety. Was García Márquez not trying to simply write a story about his surroundings from the local perspective? The strange global success of *One Hundred Years of Solitude* could easily be treated as a metaphor for the narrative's governing structure. There is a tension, I argue, within the expansive desire to allude to the global mythological canon, to try to capture the entirety of world letters in a single novel, and the fact that it takes place on miniature scale by every measure. García Márquez's history of everything, so to speak, takes place in a small town, is traced through one family and back to a single origin. It marries the rural to the national, the national to the global, and the particular to the whole. In this section, I argue that narrative's polyphonic maximalism challenges its weighty undergirding. It is as if García Márquez, in writing *One Hundred Years of Solitude*, set a competition between expanse and structure, between wanderlust and the Heimlich, and between romance and realism. Or, perhaps better for his readers, he always knew that he would somehow find a way to transcend these binaries.

The second section of the chapter focuses on García Marquez's attempt to write the national story within the frame of the history of humanity. With allusions to Western mythology and the coming together of the modern and altern, García Marquez invites us to understand Macondo as stand-in for Colombia and Colombia as stand-in for the world. This wide theme frames the linear structure of the novel that charts the evolution of Colombia from "jungle" to emergent modern space. There are two forces that underpin both of these themes within *One Hundred Years of Solitude*: that of edifice and that of oblivion. Age-old philosophical questions undergird these structural developments. Is the linear development in the novel from isolation to global modernity a progressive telos that is a natural path toward development? Is the novel's otherwise cyclical structure indicative of a natural order, destruction, and rebirth? Does the attempt to square these two readings of history divulge a belief by García Márquez that Colombia, or at least the Americas, would be the place where such philosophical riddles would be solved? Both thematically and structurally, García Márquez uses this small-town novel as a case study for these universal questions.

García Márquez transcends so many particulars because he was writing at the aesthetic border. He had a privileged position, despite his otherwise provincial status, to witness clearly the unfolding of global culture. This was a sort of double consciousness that allowed him to witness the coming together and clashing of cultural canons and archives from a unique perspective. He was both provincial citizen to the world and the very standard against which world culture is set. He was a figure that tried to write a national novel and ended up writing a global one. One might imagine him wearing the club jacket of world literature but not wearing shoes.

Perhaps the biggest paradox of all is that until his death in 2014, critics had stopped talking about García Márquez. It had become unfashionable to address a writer whose work had been so exhaustively explored for the past twenty years. In a scholarly community in which a critical theory that privileged urban realism and identity studies had splintered into more topically driven projects, there was little room for romantic rural spaces or big authors, much less the biggest of them all. Here I hope to do a small part in breathing new life into García Márquez criticism by taking a fresh approach to his most famous novel. No doubt, García Márquez saw through his dip in critical popularity. The very cyclical nature of *One Hundred Years of Solitude* makes clear that he understood that perhaps the oldest story of all is that embedded in nature: everything has a season.

Colombia Pushes against the World

Bearing in mind all of the lore that García Márquez had the story structure of *One Hundred Years of Solitude* in mind long before he knew how to begin it, the novel proved to be worth the wait. The work is large by every measure. It is lengthy in pages and sprawling in time. The pace of the novel is unrelenting, and the characters stack up. García Márquez knew that he was about to embark on a major literary undertaking and needed an opening line that would befit the hundreds of pages that would follow. One could begin small. García Márquez's fellow Boom writer Julio Cortázar prescribed the now famous maxim that novelists could win over the reader by points, whereas the short-story writer had to strive for a knockout. It is of little surprise that García Márquez opted to sublate Cortázar's binary and have it both ways. He was going to win by knockout and by points.

Few opening lines in the history of literature are as well known, oft quoted, and artfully crafted as that of *One Hundred Years of Solitude*. It transports the reader to the world of Macondo and announces that the governing order will be realism with a sense of otherworldliness. It immediately draws the reader into a space that the more familiar vocabulary of surrealism cannot quite describe. To borrow from Mario Vargas Llosa's description of it: "se agota el mundo, y se agota con él" (it exhausts the world and itself along with it).[2] So the story goes: "Muchos años después, frente al pelotón de fusilamiento, el coronel Aureliano Buendía había de recordar aquella tarde remota en que su padre lo llevó a conocer el hielo" (Many years later, while facing the firing squad, Coronel Aureliano Buendía would remember that distant afternoon in which his father took him to discover ice).[3] The line holds up to the expansive structure of the rest of the novel. It introduces the reader to the jumps in time that will be the novel's syncopated rhythm, with the "many years later" and use of the preterit and historical past all rooted in the present. It highlights that this will be a story of violence, but that violence will take place in spaces and times distant enough in feel to be viewed through the prism of the otherly, with the temporal distance between the reader, the firing squad, and that "distant afternoon." It announces the wondrous awe that surrounds the mundane, with Aureliano Buendía's apparently dying thoughts focused on what any reader in the late twentieth century would consider the prosaic household object of ice. The ice will also introduce the reader to the currents of alchemy that will run throughout the novel. The patriarch of the Buendía family, José Arcadio, will tirelessly attempt to convert base objects into precious metals, and it is important not to lose sight of the alchemy inherent to the novel itself. García Márquez wants us, as readers, to look at the everyday through his tonal lens. He wants us to look at rural Colombia and the way that he transforms it into a different physical state without losing its composition. He wants us to observe Macondo with the same awe and amusement that Aureliano Buendía would, the first time his father took him to discover ice.

The line is so good that García Márquez knew he had to use it more than once. He repeats it throughout the novel, in what acts as a centering force within the expansive and Baroque structure of the novel. These themes of repetition that are set against the complex time signature, the maximalist energy, and sweeping vistas of the novel are what I consider to be allegorical of mid-twentieth-century globalization in Colombia. Part of García Márquez's drive to write a small-town national allegory, to square wonder with science, magic with the market, was the ahead-of-the-curve sense that the world was coming. This artistic prescience, I argue, is part of what makes *One Hundred Years of Solitude* so widely read across the globe still. As economic and cultural globalization undergo a reexamination the world over, García Márquez's early consideration of the alchemy that was going to be necessary to meld the universal and the particular feels relevant, if not cutting-edge, still. In what follows, I analyze themes of repetition and structural expanse in *One Hundred Years of Solitude* and argue that it is allegorical to and reflective of Colombia's commitment to and anxiety over socioeconomic globalization.

When García Márquez was in the process of conceiving *One Hundred Years of Solitude*, Colombia was in a moment of expanse. Yet this expanse is, in the lightest sense, complicated. From Colombia's foundation, a set of paradoxes has been more foundational and long lasting than any institutional or governing force. National constitutions have come and gone, but the energy that simultaneously binds the geographically, linguistically, and racially diverse space into the single nation and the outward-facing nation that felt destined for global inclusion has been present from inception. In some of the first iterations of a Colombian nationhood, Simón Bolívar spoke of a country that would expand north until it joined ranks with the United States and south until it blended with the national movements of the rest of South America. Colombia and the Americas would not just act as theater to the latest revolutionary movements, according to Bolívar. It would auger a new humanity altogether. Colombia, as is written into its founding charter, is a place with its collective eyes on the horizon. It was set to be a country that expands. Certainly, neither Bolívar nor any major Colombian political figure since expected Colombia's relationship to the wider world to encompass the vicissitudes to which it has borne witness over the past two hundred years. Nor would they have predicted that the notion of national expanse would come in the form of diaspora, rather than ideological and subjective normalizing. Bodies are what traveled, not the border.

Much of Colombia's history is a tale of commodities. That Colombia would be an American rather than simply a national project never required a great leap of faith. It is the only country in South America with access to both the Atlantic, by way of the Caribbean, and Pacific Oceans. It is an easy synecdoche for the metaphor of the Americas as fertile new frontier employed by Enlightenment and Romantic philosophers. Most simply, moreover, it is geographically in the middle of the Americas. It was bound to be an outward-looking export nation. The issue, as modern economists have struggled to come to terms with, is that being in the perfect position is oftentimes a macroeconomic hindrance.[4]

At any given moment in Colombia's history, its national economy has always had a strong commodity. In the period of independence, it dominated in rubber. In the late nineteenth century through the mid-twentieth century, it dominated in coffee and bananas, as García Márquez refers to in the "United Fruit Scene" and is tactfully chronicled in Lucila Inés Mena's article "La huelga de la compañía bananera como expresión de lo 'Real Maravilloso' americano en *Cien años de soledad*."[5] From the mid-twentieth century to the present, it has dominated the production of cocaine. That the first three of these commodities were prone to boom and bust economics and that the latter is an illicit product highlight the antagonistic tensions within Colombia's relationship to the wider economic world. It is coffee, not cocaine, that perhaps best captures the national story of boom and bust. The 1880s, a period that, as I describe in chapter 3, marked a moment of (controversial) national renaissance, was underwritten by the "coffee craze." The paradox at the root of the coffee export's rise and fall is that it was Colombia's very entrance into the market that led to the bust. As Charles Berquist describes in *Coffee and Conflict in Colombia, 1886–1910* (1986), there is a lag of five years in getting coffee to market from initial cultivation. During the 1880s, as global coffee prices rose and rail transportation within Colombia made coffee cultivation more attractive to investors and major landholders, there was a mad rush to production. The bubble in production did not register until it had effectively spiraled out of control. This surplus in production led to a crash in the commodity price of coffee, and Colombia was so invested in the coffee trade that it took the national economy with it. As Bergquist writes, "During the mid-1890s coffee accounted for well over half of the value of Colombia's total exports, and for the peak years of 1895 and 1896 coffee made up about 70 per cent of the value of total exports."[6]

The boom and bust in coffee production does not only represent the Colombian national story in the metaphorical sense. The actual institutions and policies that governed everyday life were tied up in it, as well. Railroads, the nineteenth-century symbol of progress and development, had been built to accommodate coffee production and exportation. The Regeneration cultural and political movement, including a rewriting of the national constitution, was predicated on the economic optimism brought on by the coffee expansion. Most important to the cavernous socioeconomic hole left in Colombian society and governance by the coffee bust, however, is the intermingling of debt and the national movement. Following independence, the Colombian government issued land titles to families that they considered to be ideologically in line with the national project. This simultaneously was intended to populate large and difficult-to-govern spaces and give an influential class an economic incentive to sustain Colombian nationhood. Any radical shift in government, so the incentive plan would imply, could lead to the nullification of their land deeds. This was not an unsophisticated governing tactic, and it was also not out of step with the colonial history of the area. Spanish conquistadors had issued land as payment to their troops, who many times accompanied them to the New World on spec, in a de facto commission payment structure known as the "encomienda system." The problem was that, over two centuries, those landowners had slowly taken on their own identity as a "criolla class" and decided to rise up against the Spanish Crown. It was precisely these landowners who became the liberators and intellectuals who would be the driving force behind nationhood.

Compounding the unstable relationship between governance, land, and coffee as global commodity was that the large landowners used their real estate as collateral for bank loans. They used the borrowed capital, secured against their large landholdings, to finance most aspects of the national development of the nation-building era. They invested in urban infrastructure, railroads, and agriculture, all with debt set against the notional value of land that recently had seen a boom due to speculative coffee prices that themselves had an inherent flaw in pricing due to their lag value.[7] Put more simply, a class of people with ties to the national project were granted large swaths of land. The value of that land was assessed on its importance to the global trade of coffee. This class used the perceived value of that land to borrow money to invest in national infrastructure. The economy of this system is not without its own internal logic. The incentives that run throughout it make sense and could use the dynamism of the market to create an urban infrastructure that would benefit everyone. The crucial flaw is that it is all hinged on a single commodity in coffee. This overreliance on a single commodity on the Colombian scale was large enough to lead to a surplus in global inventories and a subsequent crash in prices, taking the national economy and its entire socioeconomic logic with it. When coffee prices crashed, there was a multitiered negative effect for the Colombian economy. A recklessly inordinate level of the national economy had become reliant on the global coffee trade, meaning there was a sharp decrease in local capital flows, an abrupt increase in unemployment, and a quick devaluation of land. This caused a squeeze from every direction. Members of the investor class experienced margin calls from their lenders at a time when their investments were beginning to underperform. Infrastructure projects slowed or were unfinished. Balance sheets went red and loans nonperforming. The Colombian nation and its coffee state had become too big to fail. Yet it failed, and it did so on a practically unimaginable scale.

The fallout of the coffee crash is difficult to overstate. Arguably, it was the last time until the present that the Colombian government actively tried to govern the entire country. It set the stage for the splintering of Colombian society that would quickly see itself divided into warring factions that would spread into competing guerilla and paramilitary groups. It would become a struggling state, and it would do so through its engagement with the world economy.

While Colombia has a sustained trajectory of commodity export, it left such a historically resonating sting that it was not until roughly seventy-five years later that Colombia would seriously open itself to the economic world in a meaningful way again. Three generations of citizens, governing officials, and entrepreneurs came and went before the next attempt to take advantage of what had seemed originally like a strategic position in the pan-American mercantile system. This moment, the 1960s, happened to be when García Márquez was writing *One Hundred Years of Solitude.* The '60s were a time of contradictory energies in Colombia. The shadow cast by the coffee crash and United Fruit Company crisis not only lingered but hit a climax in the Violence and Bogotazo. While I go into further detail about this history in chapter 3, it is worth noting broadly that literature followed suit. Aesthetics became urban, gritty, and focused on failed national promises. The countryside existed, within the realm of national letters, as a place from which to flee. Yet there was an underlying optimism that the worst had passed. For a country that had been in civil war since its inception and was in the midst of its most violent and disorderly period, there was the sense that perhaps the nation had reached an inflection point. This optimism was both local and global. The '60s, of course, presented a fresh vigor in Europe and the United States as well, and the generational notion that rules were being rewritten buoyed all manner of cultural and political projects. In Colombia, the avant-garde poetry group the Nadaistas, led by Gonzalo Arango, best typifies this desire to abandon the past or to set the nation on a new path. If aesthetics and commodities were the guiding stars for the nation, perhaps it was time to reset both. While there is a constant listlessness to the Nadaistas, the desire to break with the institutions that had governed the previous 150 years of Colombian history had its own edifying principles. Though dissimilar in form, a similar logic undergirded the entrepreneurial paradigm of the moment.

The '60s in Colombia also marked an attempt to reenter the global economy with diversified agricultural commodities. A fertile land of abundance, the lesson had been learned, was ripe for more than a single commodity. As John Crow describes, the '60s in Colombia set the stage for a diversification of the local economy, one that has made for a comparative success story in its own right: "Colombia was the only Latin American country to maintain positive economic growth every year during the decade 1980–1990. Over 700 international companies do business in Colombia, with the United States in first place.... Foreign investment is encouraged, and Colombia is no longer a one-crop country. Besides coffee, exports in other areas have grown rapidly: cotton, sugar, bananas, flowers, cacao, fish and crustaceans, textiles, garments, oil, natural gas, chemicals, precious stones, coal, gold, books, and a huge black market in drugs."[8] In the list of commodities listed by Crow lies the competing forces within Colombia as it reimagined nationhood. On the one hand, a generational desire to reignite the national project, and to do so through global economic engagement, was being put into practice. The list highlights the lessons learned by the coffee crash. A stronger economic system had emerged in Colombia, and raw goods were not the only export. It is the last item on the list, narcotics, however, that, as we now know, would haunt Colombia's presence in the global economy over the next four decades. Despite the successful diversification of the economy and the spirit of national reemergence, the fallout of the coffee crash still loomed large. Factions outside the government's control had taken hold of the countryside, which led to paramilitary groups, ideological guerillas, and cocaine producers. During market downturns, the fracturing of the nation in actual practice went so far that guerillas in many ways supplanted the state. Bergquist writes,

> This is the situation that the guerrillas found in all the zones of colonization in which they were active and became a peripheral local power. In the so-called Independent Republics of the 1960s, the colonists were on the brink of ruin because of poor market conditions and the absence of government aid. They did not lose their land, however, because the guerrillas helped them, and to an extent, this help prevented large landowners from acquiring and concentrating the land into large tracts. Insofar as the guerrillas were able to create defenses for the colonists they tended to control the roles of the merchant and the intermediaries and to provide for or attend to the population's most basic needs, such as education, health and justice. Economically, the guerrillas' power was based on contributions or taxes from the colonists paid either in cash or commodities or with labor. The colonists' obligations usually were fulfilled through collective work, either "organization farms" or on the private property of others.[9]

Colombia, a country that had always been at war with itself, was in a moment of simultaneous idealism and fracture. As Andrea Fanta Castro, Alejandro Herrero-Olaizola, and Chloe Rutter-Jensen point out in their introduction to *Territories of Conflict: Traversing Colombia through Cultural Studies*, the national project was alive as idea but lacked coherence in practice.[10] This was the milieu in which García Márquez conceived *One Hundred Years of Solitude*. He was surrounded by practical and symbolic contradictions. His nation attempted to recharter itself through global engagement, and, in doing so, it faced the headwinds set by the last time it had attempted to do just that. It tried to bridge the large experiential gap between the urban and the rural. It hoped that market dynamism would help to fund the building of national infrastructure, but it did so as illicit products began to grow in economic influence. This was the backdrop against which García Márquez wrote. He tried to capture the experience of contradictory flows. He was trying to take a snapshot of the energy produced by fission. When he wrote, he did so in the face of the threat of collapse and the hope of new expanse. García Márquez was the right icon at the right time; his many inherent paradoxes marked an encapsulation of the Colombian Paradox itself.

In its structure, *One Hundred Years of Solitude* is a novel of competing energies. I refer to its explosive tempo, its neo-Baroque interweaving of story lines, and its multiplying characters as its inherently maximalist style. This maximalism presents an outward thrust that challenges the bounds of narrative. In its centrifugal force, the abrupt shifts in time and the constantly expanding cast of characters push the novel up against the limits of what it can achieve. Yet there is a counterpoint to the work's outward movement in that there are persistent themes of repetition and rebalancing throughout *One Hundred Years of Solitude*. The previously alluded to repetition of the opening line of the novel acts as a lifeline for the reader caught in its vertiginous pace. The line presents its own internal contradictions, however. In its repetition, it allows the reader and narrative to return to the beginning and offers a reminder of where the story began. It also provides a snapshot of the entire novel in a single line. It both foregrounds and backtracks. The line, all the same, operates at a dizzying pace. That the stabilizing force within the structure of the novel is so complex captures the double movement, both inward and outward. The opportunity that García Márquez presents the reader to reestablish balance and begin anew is tempestuous and fleeting in and of itself.

The metaphor imbedded within the structure of *One Hundred Years of Solitude* acts as allegory not merely for the nation at the time in which García Márquez wrote but for the contradictory energy intrinsic to Colombian nationhood. Founding a modern nation-state in the metaphorical and actual jungle is a theme that runs throughout the Colombian canon, José Eustasio Rivera's *La vorágine* being the most prominent example. García Márquez adds a layer of complexity to the national metaphor. Here we do not only have a group of explorers trying to orient themselves in unfamiliar territory. For García Márquez, that is not complicated enough. The truer metaphor would be for the symbolic founders of the nation to be in the jungle guided by a compass, but the compass is spinning.

The allusions to trying to read order in chaos are constant in the novel, adding a layer to the complex metaphor at the heart of the novel's structure. The clarifying repetition itself is difficult to understand. That another repeated theme is the attempt to read through the static of the unknown both encourages and confuses the reader. It is this struggle to impose order on chaos and believe in it enough to make it true that García Márquez invites the reader to experience. His characters go through similar leaps of faith. When the novel's patriarch, José Arcadio Buendía, leaves his workshop where he thinks he has a grasp on the world and confronts reality, he is met with the complexity of actual

Colombian experience: "José Arcadio Buendía tardó mucho tiempo para rees-tablecerse de la perplejidad cuando salió a la calle y vio la muchedumbre. No eran gitanos. Eran hombres y mujeres como ellos, de cabellos lacios y piel parda, que hablaban de su misma lengua y se lamentaban de los mismos dolores." (José Arcadio Buendía took a long time to compose himself when he went out to the street and took in the masses. They were not gypsies. They were men and women, just like him, with dark straight hair, that spoke the same language and felt the same pain.)[11] Trying to make sense of the faces around us as the characters pile up, when José Arcadio Buendía leaves his home and is confused by the rushing multitude around him, the reader sympathizes. García Márquez invites the reader to identify with José Arcadio Buendía. That which makes sense in the Heimlich—for José Arcadio Buendía, his home and workshop with comfort-able surroundings and singular understanding—is challenged by the inrush of the world. There is the tone of the levies breaking and trying to fight the engulf-ing waves, as the reader, José Arcadio Buendía, and, as García Márquez under-stood, Colombia tried to come to terms with the vertiginous clashing between local and global cultural and economic flows. Luckily, the three tiers of the metaphor—the nation, the character, and the reader—have a guiding map. Unluckily, the map has never worked before.

This repetition flies in the face of futility, and the novel plays on the shift-ing sands of framing. What will win out: the persistent attempt to reinstate order on the world or the world's constant supply of uncoded terrain? García Márquez's characters ask this question as they try and fail time and time again. El coronel Aureliano Buendía, whose firing squad opens and then repeats throughout the novel, best encapsulates this battle: "El coronel Aureliano Buendía promovió treinta y dos levantamientos armados y los perdió todos. Tuvo diecisiete hijos varones de diecisiete mujeres distintas, que fueron exter-minados uno tras otro en una sola noche antes de que el mayor cumpliera treinta y cinco años. Escapó a catorce atentados, a setenta y tres emboscadas y a un pelotón de fusilamiento." (Coronel Aureliano Buendía incited thirty-two uprisings and lost them all. He had seventeen male children with seven-teen women, all of whom were killed one after another the night before the oldest turned thirty-five. He escaped fourteen assassination attempts, seventy-three ambushes, and a firing squad.)[12] One could argue that Coronel Aureli-ano Buendía, one of the novel's more centrally located characters, frames the meta-allegory of dueling energies through the paradigm of fertility and futility. He is both a constant failure and productive, and reproductive, to the extent that it seems as if nothing will ever deter him. Despite his thirty-two failed armed uprisings, he is unrelenting. Despite his incredible fertility, the seventeen children he had with seventeen women, all died before they reached the age of thirty-five. Despite the fact, as is repeated throughout the novel, that he faced a firing squad, he escaped. This duality layers on the complex metaphor running throughout the novel that what is at stake in the narrative is the force of order and chaos, governance and anarchy, and life and death. Death always slips just out of the reach of life, and life just outside the reach of death.

Coronel Aureliano Buendía has seventeen children named Aureliano in the novel. Given this great fertility and persistent attempt to maintain his name, one would think that Macondo would be populated by his offspring. On the contrary, Coronel Aureliano Buendía marks the only Buendía lineage that dies out. His abundant re-creation proves to be futile, and his children all die before they can reproduce. Adding to the competing energy metaphor, the seemingly stabilizing repetition that Coronel Aureliano Buendía engenders does not bear fruit. Adding more complexity to the theme is that the last character born in the novel is named simply Aureliano, despite the fact that the name does not come from his direct lineage. The novel's competition between repetition and rupture begs the question that one may follow the map as strictly as possible, but what if it leads to a dead end? This complex metaphor captures the energies of the Colombian national project in the 1960s as intellectuals and entrepreneurs sought to reset the nation, both enthusiastically and cautiously, knowing well that the model that they followed to engage the world had failed spectacularly last time.

The duality could simply feel philosophical and reminds the reader of Borges's rendering of the world as competing forms in unending battle. If the nodes in the binary are predicated on their adversarial relationship with each other, any vanquishing of the other would implicate erasure for both. This philosophical problem is present in the novel. It would be too removed from García Márquez's context as a Colombian writer in the 1960s and as someone who attempted to write the Colombian novel by writing a global novel to read it as philosophical game alone, however. Colombia's paradox, that it had attempted to define its nation through globalism, makes the novel feel much more of a national allegory than Borgesian abstraction. The alpha and omega aspects of the Colombian story make one wonder when successful development will finally arrive. Just as one wonders if the story of the Buendía family will have a happy ending, so to speak, that will make all of the tragedy along the way seem worth it, one wonders if Colombia will learn from past failures and this time engage with the world in a more productive way. Does *One Hundred Years of Solitude* and its legacy present, as María del Carmen Porras argues, "la pérdida, mas que la construcción, de una familia, de una identidad, de un país y de un continente? (the loss, more than construction, of a family, an identity, a country, and a continent?).[13] At battle with itself, *One Hundred Years of Solitude*, like the history of Colombia that García Márquez attempted to capture, examines questions as much as it answers them. No matter the perspective, *One Hundred Years of Solitude* captures the competing energies within Colombia when García Márquez undertook his ambitious novel. The expanding maximalist energy is virtually uncontainable. With the novel's themes of repetition and recentering, however, García Márquez attempts to tie a band around the expanse. He tries to harness the energy of complexity and use it to imbue a simple, singular structure. Allegorical to Colombia's attempt to charter the nation by using the dynamism of the international marketplace, García Márquez pulls from competing energies in order to create a literary classic.

Shipwrecks across Generations: Gabo's Polyphonic Simplicity

One Hundred Years of Solitude is a novel that attempts to embody everything. It aims to capture the existential notion of being between indigenous, Afro-Caribbean, and Spanish Catholic cosmologies. It strives to be both historical and mythic text. It is a novel of the nation as told through the persistent failure to found a society in the coastal South American jungle. The poetics of expansion set against structural resistance, as explored in the previous section, has a parallel in the novel's linear structure that faces the headwinds of persistent amnesia. Like the snapshot of the competing socioeconomic energies of Colombia's place between the nation and world while García Márquez was writing *One Hundred Years of Solitude*, there is the notion that the novel is really a simple tale. Many of the actions within the novel are foretold by earlier figures. It is simply the reader's, and indeed characters', narrative and historical amnesia that keeps development and stability from ever arriving. Among the most readily posited notions about magical realism is that it captures the experience of being between oral and written histories. It is, according to this argument, a form of semi- or peripheral development. I argue that in a novel that is at once so complex and, from the zoomed-out view, so simple, the text argues for the need of a strong national story, or a letters of the nation, before successfully moving forward. While I go into the largely failed national project of founding a lettered Colombian nation in the late nineteenth century in chapter 3, here I posit that García Márquez uses themes of repetition and rupture, as well as amnesia, to argue for the need of a well-founded cultural nation that will foster development. In the midst of Colombia's second wave of globalization, he argues for a new national culture that will buttress the nation against the coming waves of global culture. In true García Márquez fashion, this proposition arrives embedded within the antidote itself. The people of Macondo are doomed to repeat history, due to their persistent neglect of it. Colombia, on the verge of a new commodity wave, may be about to repeat the coffee boom and bust. What better way to buttress the cultural nation than through a literary classic?

Three themes run throughout *One Hundred Years of Solitude* that structure a simple story line in an otherwise polyphonic text. The first is that the novel places emphasis on the concept of origin. With allusions to the origin stories and myths that are both biblical and national, the novel announces from the start that this is a story about beginning. By the same token, the novel's matriarch and patriarch, Úrsula Iguarán and José Arcadio Buendía, mark a new foundation in the Colombian jungle and foretell the story that will follow. The problem is that their offspring do not heed their prophecies and, as such, are plagued by interrupted development. The second theme is the novel's broad structure of point, repetition, and rupture. The early pages of the novel place a heavy focus on new beginnings, of the founding of a new society, and how this will be embryotic to a new humanity. The novel's middle section is a study in repetition. Scenes and character names repeat, and what was, in its early pages, imagined to be a fertile nation bound for development ends up being a place of incestuous insularity. The third and last part of the novel places emphasis on themes of rupture and rebirth. As the mythical origin story and advice given by José Arcadio Buendía and Úrsula Iguarán finally take hold, the novel's characters are freed to move beyond the titular solitude that haunts Macondo for well over half the novel.

The use of the metaphor of family to define nation is so explored that it is difficult to imagine a novel that acts as national allegory being presented in any other way. Within Latin American literature, both the forebearers and latter champions of this style are prominent. The nineteenth-century national romances that Doris Sommer has so successfully described in Gertrudis Gómez Avellaneda's *Sab* (1841) and Jorge Isaacs's *María* (1867) do not just act as allegory but take an active role in the founding of Latin American nationhood.[14] The 1990s and early 2000s saw the likes of Cristina García and her novel *Dreaming in Cuban* (1992) and Juno Díaz with *The Brief and Wondrous Life of Oscar Wao* (2007) use the family metaphor to examine the nation after its members had been generationally and diasporically spread throughout the Americas. One could similarly read *One Hundred Years of Solitude*, in its distilled form, as simply a family story. It marks a moment of complexity between the other two family-nation allegorical models. The 1960s in Colombia do not present a moment in which the nation was originally formed and could be captured through a simple romance. Nor is this a moment that can be distilled to three generations, in which the grandparents represent the home nation, the parents the new nation as experienced by diaspora, and the coming-of-age protagonist as the in-between new national subject. This is a novel about the world rushing into a not fully or successfully formed Colombia, not Colombia rushing out. As such, it takes seven generations to do it justice, and the linear development is only evident in the macro view. It is somehow an antinational and still national novel, all of which captures the energy of the incipient postnation.

The first section of the novel could be read as an all-encompassing origin story that opens itself to both optimistic and pessimistic renderings. On the one hand, it is the story of the founding of Colombia, with its implicit connection to the Bolivarian notions of a new humanity. It is a recasting of the beginnings of the national story, not as one of a violent uprising that ended in a despotic leader and civil war but as a mythical quest through a bucolic hinterland. The Spanish conquistadors who explored the area harbored similar visions of themselves, as romantic visionaries seeking the perfect place to build a new society. José Arcadio Buendía and his desire to found Macondo begins when he stumbles upon a shipwrecked galleon. In what will begin the metaphor of globalization, the mere presence of the galleon is enough to indicate to José Arcadio Buendía that Macondo is both an idyllic garden and close enough to mercantile ship routes to be connected to the world. He had found the perfect place between an off-the-beaten-path space with its natural beauty and one in touch with major thoroughfares. That he based this notion on the presence of a shipwrecked galleon will begin the alchemic theme that will run throughout the novel. José Arcadio Buendía tries to make something of nothing, to transform the properties of a space and found an idyllic city. This is a lot of faith to put in the presence of an old ship run aground, and the double way to read this section begins with this icon of the world and its floundering in the local space. Did this make Macondo the perfect place to found a new city, or does the fact that the ship was never recovered not imply that this was a place bound for isolation and abandonment? This tension begins early when José Arcadio Buendía celebrates the presence of the galleon and what it implies: "¡Carajo!—gritó—Macondo está rodeado de agua por todas partes" (By God!—he yelled—Macondo is surrounded by water on all sides).[15]

Macondo, so the icon of the ship implies, will be both a place of ideal, isolated beauty and open to the world. His optimism is haunted by moments of doubt, however: "'Nunca llegaremos a ninguna parte,' se lamentaba ante Úrsula. 'Aquí nos hemos de pudrir en vida sin recibir los beneficios de la ciencia.' Esa certidumbre, rumiada varios meses en el cuartito del laboratorio, lo llevó a concebir el proyecto de trasladar a Macondo un lugar más propicio." ("We will never get anywhere," he lamented to Úrsula. "Here we will be left to rot without ever receiving the benefit of science." This certainty permeated the small room that was his laboratory for months, until it dawned on him to move Macondo to a more promising setting.)[16] José Arcadio Buendía at moments was certain that Macondo was perfectly placed and at others insisted on finding higher ground. Could he really refound global culture and science in his personal laboratory? Could the lettered city really exist in such an isolated place? It is Úrsula, the true marker of origin in the novel, who decides that they will stay. She does so not because of the location but because they have had a child there: "—No nos iremos—dijo. Aquí nos quedamos, porque aquí hemos tenido un hijo.—Todavía no tenemos un muerto—dijo él—. Uno no es de ninguna parte mientras no tenga un muerto bajo la tierra. Úrsula replicó, con una suave firmeza:—Si es necesario que yo me muera para que se queden aquí, me muero." (—We are not going anywhere—she said. We are staying here, because this is where we had our son.—No one has died here yet—he said. No one is anywhere until they have put a body in the ground. Úrsula responded, with sophisticated firmness:—If it takes my death to convince you all to stay, I'll die.)[17]

The stage is set early in the novel for the competing forces that will run throughout it. Present are the tension between fresh starts and insularity, the intergenerational relationship necessary to create the historical and folkloric repetition that creates histories and mythologies, and the at-odds drives of life and death. Úrsula's refusal to budge challenges José Arcadio Buendía to follow his plan to the letter. Macondo will be the place of new origin, and it will be the matriarch, Úrsula, who makes that decision. This origin story compounds the biological and mythological senses of origin. It also includes the foundational icon of the shipwrecked galleon. The origin story will be set in the key of a failed opening to the world. That it is the presence of Aureliano Buendía, even as a baby, that leads Úrsula to insist that they stay and charter Macondo on the grounds in which they had Aureliano shows that this will be a story of foundations and new beginnings. A Buendía has been born in that space, and to quote José Arcadio Buendía, "No serán casas de vidrio sino de hielo, como yo lo soñé, y siempre habrá un Buendía, por los siglos de los siglos" (The houses will not be made of glass but of ice, as I dreamed it, and there will always be a Buendía, one century after another).[18] This is an origin story that will only be consecrated, according to Úrsula, once she is dead. Yet, even as death surrounds her, she lives for an improbably long time. It is a place whose houses are chartered to be built with ice. Yet they defy physics and hold up. There is the notion that Macondo, in its very foundation, will be a place that survives in the face of it all. It is a place founded in the image of a shipwrecked galleon, an icon of failed participation in international waters, and life and transcendence defy the odds.

The second section of the novel is marked by the attempt to reconcile Macondo with the world. While the first section imagines a proximity to the global order, the second actively allows it to rush in. For one, foreigners begin to arrive, bringing with them the imagined, and real, high culture of elsewhere. Occasionally, they are seduced by the mystical perfection of Macondo, as the founders José Arcadio Buendía and Úrsula envisioned it, and occasionally they reject it. Bookending the middle section are the characters Rebecca and Gastón. Rebecca is an orphan who is adopted by the Buendías and later marries José Arcadio. This would make for a perfect nation-founding romance. José Arcadio, the first person to be born in Macondo, is the reason for its charter. He is the biological tie to the land and mythology of Macondo. Rebecca, by contrast, has no known past or lineage and infects Macondo with a bout of insomnia. As is the case throughout *One Hundred Years of Solitude*, this superficially nationally reconciling marriage is a study in contrasts. Every foundational or progressive moment will be offset by death, disease, or sleeplessness. As Rebecca's story line progresses, she is increasingly enclosed and cut off from society. There is a parabolic arc to her presence in the novel. She arrives an orphan, only to become a foundational character for Macondean society. While she is not of known lineage, she tries to reconcile her biological lack by eating land. Yet, after José Arcadio's death, she cloisters herself off in a ramshackle hut in Macondo and wiles away her days in virtual orphanage.

That Macondo is an idea and space that rifles through characters in a revolving set of competing ideas is confirmed by a character who is similarly foreign to Macondean society and who shows up at the end of the novel's middle section. Gastón marries into the fifth generation of the Buendía family, when he moves from Belgium to be with Amaranta Úrsula. The presence of Gastón marks a nod back to Europe. Amaranta Úrsula meets him when she travels to the Old World in a conventional action of the child of a prominent Latin American family. Gastón and Amaranta Úrsula bring with them the high cultural ideas of the modern European nation. They are here to affirm the original idea that Macondo can be a place that mixes the bucolic beauty of the rural Americas with the high arts and sciences of Europe. Amaranta Úrsula, however, is seduced by her place of origin and eventually abandons Gastón for her nephew, the second of seventeen Aurelianos. The contrast between Rebecca and Gastón is well structured. While Rebecca marks an early attempt for the family to branch out and expand Macondo, she feels a lack to the extent that she devours the local land. Gastón tries to change the sociocultural structure of Macondo but is rejected by a turn to incest. Rebecca's early presence assures that the Buendía family is founded beyond the realms of incest, yet she is eventually abandoned. In parallel, as Gastón attempts to assure that local culture is not incestuous, he is rejected in parallel. This contrast of characters marks the similar need and rejection of the outside, as the local Macondo attempts to feed off and reconcile itself with the world.

This section of the novel moves beyond the focus on origin and exhibits a multilevel competition between engagement with the wider world and the entropic gravity of the local. Foreigners begin to show up more quickly, including the arrival of multinational companies. At the same time, civil war continues, and the body count in the novel piles up. This cyclical conquering and reconquering, edifying and destructing, inrush of new ideas and subsequent devouring of them marks the cyclically refounding nation that enters and exits the global socioeconomic theater. On the one hand, the Buendía family continues to dominate local society. On the other, it is simultaneously announced, following a temporary conquest, that the local infantry should lay down its arms and burn the local archives, and younger generations begin to imagine Macondo as a place of modern technology and industry.

By the time Aureliano Segundo's daughter Meme, also known as Renata Remedios, arrives, we have traveled very far from houses made of ice. Macondo is now a place with multinational companies and international travelers. Meme grows up in a global Macondo, where she "aprendió a nadar como una profesional, a jugar al tenis y a comer jamón de Virginia con rebanadas de piña. Entre bailes, piscina y tenis, se encontró de pronto desenredándose en inglés" (learned to swim like professional, to play tennis and eat Virginia ham with sliced pineapple. Between dances, swimming, and tennis, she found herself holding forth at length in English).[19] In many ways, Meme marks the Macondo dreamt up by José Arcadio Buendía and Úrsula. The premonitions brought on by the presence of the Spanish galleon had come to fruition. In short, the world had arrived. Yet the world also demanded things of Macondo. There is the mechanical reproduction inherent in Meme's modernism. Her very name implies the sameness that in many ways Macondo was supposed to move beyond. Her presence is also undercut by the most violent section of the novel. While civil war plays in the background of the majority of the novel, the most acute moment of historical violence ties into Meme's modernity. Macondo is increasingly cosmopolitan and international, because multinational companies are industrializing the production of local commodities, in this case fruit. Her international friends are there because their parents work for companies such as the alluded-to United Fruit Company, which had a violent encounter with a group of striking workers. The scene is usually discussed as a moment in which social and historical realism break through the gloss of García Márquez's magical tone. Yet there is a deeper placing of the moment of violence within the frame of global engagement that is telling in its support of the metaphor of cyclical global engagement and rejection. Any attempt to complete the vision originally laid out for Macondo, to make it an ideal place that both offers local natural beauty and takes advantage of its centrality to the pan-American mercantile system, is set against a backdrop of violence and abandonment. Eventually Meme, the very emblem of Macondo modernism, departs for a convent, where she is silent for the rest of her life. As the engagement with the outside, exemplified by Rebecca and Gastón, ends in abandonment, in the case of Meme, what begins as an eruption of new form turns to silence. Macondo may be a place where characters can defy gravity, but if there is a governing physics, it is that that which goes global must return local.

The third and final section of the novel furthers the theme of competing forces. While the first focuses on the complexities of new beginnings set against isolation, and the second on opening up to the world versus the force of cyclical history, the third marks a rupture from the repetition. Yet it also brings with it the hallmarks of the first two sections in that it is rife with themes of amnesia, abandonment, and insularity. It is a section focused on rebirth and fresh starts but one that is plagued with the titular solitude.

By the end of the novel, oddly all of the forces set against each other have sublated and completed all of the foretold promises. Macondo is a new center through which goods, foreigners, and cultures have flowed. It is, at the same time, a place of incestuous inward-looking cultural practices. It has been the site of revolution and decay. It has created culture, history, and mythology and forgotten those very social buttresses. By the time we reach the seventh generation and the final Aureliano, we have passed through the rise and fall of a civilization. That the novel ends with an Aureliano is telling. This is the twenty-second iteration of an Aureliano. Yet repetition itself, the consecrating and embedding force, has hollowed out its own meaning. Aureliano's parents, Amaranta Úrsula and Aureliano Babilonia, one would imagine, would be ready to champion the name that goes back to the second of the Macondo lineage. Yet they themselves, not entirely clear about the origins of Macondo, cannot convince the people around them of their family's history. In trying to find out if they are related, because they are about to have a baby together (it turns out that they are related), they engage with the eventual distortion caught in constant repetition. Speaking with a local priest, the conversation goes,

> Hace muchos años hubo aquí una calle que se llamaba así, y por esos entonces la gente tenía la constumbre de ponerles a los hijos los nombres de las calles. Aureliano tembló de rabia.—¡Ah!—dijo—entonces usted tampoco cree.— ¿En qué?—Que el coronel Aureliano Buendía hizo treinta y dos guerras civiles y las perdió todas—contestó Aureliano—. Que el ejército acorraló y ametralló a tres mil trabajadores, y que se llevaron los cadáveres para echarlos al mar en un tren de doscientos vagones.—Ay, hijo—suspiró—. A mí me bastaría con estar seguro de que tú y yo existimos en este momento. De modo que Aureliano y Amaranta Úrsula aceptaron la versión de la canastilla, no porque la creyeran, sino porque los ponía a salvo de sus terrores. (Several years ago there was a street here that had that name, and back then people had the custom of naming their kids after streets. Aureliano shook with rage—Ah!—he said—so you don't believe in it either.—In what?—Aureliano responded—. That the army rounded up and shot three thousand workers, and that they transported them in two hundred wagons to throw them in the sea.—Oh, son—she whispered—. It would be enough for me simply to be certain that you and I exist right now. And with that, Aureliano and Amaranta Úrsula decided that they would accept their preferred version, not because they believed it, but because it allayed their fears.)[20]

The incessant repetition of the novel has unleashed its own abandonment. As temporal and experiential distance separates the heirs to the Buendía lineage, the repetitive mechanisms set to fight against the natural forces of erasure themselves become routine acts. The street names, part of the logical machinery set to fight against the erosion of Macondo's origin story, themselves eclipse the very founding family, as the town's sages begin to think that younger Buendías are named after the streets, failing to grasp that the streets themselves were named after elder Buendías. The game that García Márquez plays throughout *One Hundred Years of Solitude* is that there are paradoxical forces inherent in the sublation of dyadic opposites. There is forgetfulness embedded in memory, abandonment in new beginnings, and distortion in repetition. The birth at the end of the novel bears all the hallmarks of these competing forces. A final Aureliano is born, and he is born with a tail to punish his incestuous parents. His parents knew their family history but chose to ignore it in the interest of new beginnings. The very inertia of the name Aureliano acknowledges as much.

This had all been foretold by the gypsy Melquíades. If anyone had been able to or taken the time to translate Melquíades's divining archeology of the future, they would have seen that they were bound to fall into the same traps over and over. They would have known that Macondo would travel the familiar trajectory of utopia to abandonment. Aureliano Babilonia, father to the final Aureliano, translates and reads Melquíades's projections once it is too late:

Macondo ya era un pavoroso remolino de polvo y escombros centrifugado por la cólera del huracán bíblico, cuando Aureliano saltó once páginas para no perder el tiempo en hechos demasiado conocidos, y empezó a descifrar el instante que estaba viviendo, descifrándolo a medida que lo vivía, profetizándose a sí mismo en el acto de descifrar la última página de los pergaminos, como si estuviera viendo en un espejo hablado. Entonces dio otro salto para anticiparse a las predicciones y averiguar la fecha y las circunstancias de su muerte. Sin embargo, antes de llegar al verso final ya había comprendido que no saldría jamás de ese cuarto, pues estaba previsto que la ciudad de los espejos (o los espejismos) sería arrasada por el viento y desterrada de la memoria de los hombres en el instante en que Aureliano Babilonia acabara de descifrar los pergaminos, y que todo lo escrito en ellos era irrepetible desde siempre y para siempre, porque las estirpes condenados a cien años de soledad no tenían una segunda oportunidad. (Macondo was already a terrifying whirlwind of dust and debris centrifuged by the cholera of the biblical hurricane, when Aureliano jumped eleven pages to not waste his time on those already well-known facts, and began to realize what he was seeing, deciphering it as he lived it, prophesying himself in the act of deciphering the last page of the parchment, as if he were looking in a speaking mirror. Then he jumped ahead to see the predicted date and circumstances of his death. Yet, before even arriving at the section, he already understood that he would never leave this room again, that it was already foreseen that the city of mirrors (or mirages) would be leveled by wind and banished from the memory of mankind in the instant that Aureliano Babilonia finished reading the scroll, and that everything that was written in it would be unrepeatable since forever and forevermore, because families condemned to one hundred years of solitude did not get second chances.)[21]

In Macondo, history is all already written—even that its citizens are bound to forget, repeat, and abandon it.

Gabriel García Márquez and particularly the novel that propelled him to international fame, *One Hundred Years of Solitude*, are cultural artifacts of early Colombian globalization. Written amid Colombia's second entrance into the global economic system, the novel bears all the hallmarks of Colombia's conflicting relationship to the wider world. A writer who rested heavily on his instincts, as García Márquez wrote, he sensed that Colombia was entering into its second wave of globalization.[22] Yet the nation did so as it wore off the aftermath of the coffee craze and subsequent bust at the turn of the century. García Márquez and the conflicting energies that he represents, which I have defined in this chapter as the Gabo Paradox, as well as *One Hundred Years of Solitude*, mark a cultural snapshot of this important inflection point in Colombian history. As the country opened itself to the world with the coffee bust and United Fruit crisis in its proximate rear view but still not knowing that the cocaine trade was ahead of it, it was a moment of hope and caution, of romanticism and science, in other words of magical realism. These apparently at-odd movements and tones capture perfectly a country that has always, and in the 1960s in an acute way, tried to move beyond itself before it had fully become itself in the first place.

2

Literary Shipwrecks

Colombian Aesthetic
Citizenship after
García Márquez

Among the great paradoxes that surround and imbue Gabriel García Márquez and *One Hundred Years of Solitude* is that he and the novel are Colombia's and Latin America's most successful cultural exports. In writing a national novel that captures the complexities of existing at the threshold of the world, García Márquez went on to become the interface to the world, for not just a nation but a region. This success has not been without its own sociocultural trappings. Latin American authors, both within the Boom that García Márquez typifies and after, have increasingly spoken of the difficulty of writing under the shadow cast by such a successful literary star. Members of the Boom have tended to regard García Márquez with more camaraderie and reverence than malice. They, after all, did benefit greatly as a cohort of regional writers by García Márquez's success. In many ways, he opened a path for Latin American writers to ascend to the world stage, as they did in the '60s, '70s, and '80s. Yet García Márquez also created an expectation of Latin American and Colombian literature that did not resonate with the huge complexities and differences within Latin America. The problem with a regional aesthetic movement being spearheaded by someone with the cultural weight of García Márquez was that it created an environment in which his whims were set to represent those from differing realities and perspectives.

Mario Vargas Llosa, another renowned member of the Boom and the only other to receive a Nobel Prize for Literature, has only recently felt comfortable about breaking with García Márquez publicly. It took being fully consecrated by the apparatuses of world literature itself, in this case through the highest possible prize, before he shed light on the internal tensions working within the Boom. United originally in their love for Faulkner, Vargas Llosa and García Márquez quickly realized that they did not share much else beyond being from the same continent. García Márquez gravitated toward Virginia Woolf, while Vargas Llosa, who lived in Paris at the time, was more interested in Continental philosophy. The Cuban Revolution only augmented the breach. At the time, the most important and meaningful icon of Latin American politics created fault lines within the Boom, and how could it not? Vargas Llosa felt that García Márquez and his routine appearances alongside Fidel Castro were cynical and propagandistic. The notion was that two of the most recognizable icons of Latin America to the world at the time were Fidel Castro and García Márquez in the personified sense and revolution and magical realism in the cultural sense. Not only are these not a natural fit, but Vargas Llosa claims that García Márquez did not have favorable views of the Cuban Revolution until he was drawn to the celebrity of it. Vargas Llosa claims,

Creo que García Márquez tenía un sentido muy práctico de la vida, que descubrió en ese momento fronterizo, y se dio cuenta de que era mejor para un escritor estar con Cuba que estar contra Cuba. Se libraba del baño de mugre que recibimos todos los que adoptamos una postura crítica. Si estabas con Cuba podías hacer lo que quisieras, jamás ibas a ser atacado por el enemigo verdaderamente peligroso para un escritor, que no es la derecha sino la izquierda. La izquierda es la que tiene el gran control de la vida cultural en todas partes, y de alguna manera enemistarse con Cuba, criticarla, era echarse encima un enemigo muy poderoso y además exponerse a tener que estar en cada situación tratando de explicarse, demostrando que no eras un agente de la CIA, que ni siquiera eras un reaccionario, un pro-imperialista. Mi impresión es que de alguna manera la amistad con Cuba, con Fidel Castro lo vacunó contra todas esas molestias. (I believe that García Márquez had a very practical approach to life, which he developed in those early moments, and he realized that it was better to be a writer with Cuba than against it. He avoided the dust storm that those of us that were critical of Castro caused. If you were for Cuba, you could do whatever you wanted; you were never going to be attacked by the truly dangerous enemy of a writer, which is not the Right but the Left. The Left is what has wide control over cultural life practically everywhere, and to antagonize Cuba, to criticize it, was to take on a powerful enemy and moreover have to explain yourself in the face of constant criticism to show that you were not a CIA agent, that you weren't even a reactionary, or pro-imperialist. My impression is that in many ways his friendship with Cuba, with Fidel Castro, inoculated him from these problems.)[1]

It was García Márquez's relationship to the world and his place within its cultural iconography, one that Vargas Llosa describes as a *border*, where he faltered in Vargas Llosa's opinion. Not unlike Colombia's entrances into the global market place, also not unlike Macondo, García Márquez was going to be a literary figure that would cause wrinkles in the Colombian and Latin American aesthetic economy. In this chapter, I analyze the uneasy publishing terrain that García Márquez, one of the foremost global literary icons, has left for his fellow Colombians.

The Aesthetic Border and the Closing of the Literary World

It may have seemed like low-hanging fruit. It may have been the sort of ironic twist that Fernando Vallejo, a writer with a standing, reciprocal, and highly publicized love-hate relationship with his home country, himself would have considered heavy-handed had it come in prose form. But when the Bogotá stop of the book tour for his most recent work, *El don de la vida* (2010), was scheduled to take place in the Centro Cultural Gabriel García Márquez, Vallejo could hardly help himself: "Estoy muy contento de estar con ustedes en este centro cultural tan hermoso. Lastima que le han puesto un nombre tan feíto: El Centro Cultural García Márquez. . . . No es un escritor, es un burócrata." (I'm very happy to be here with you all in this beautiful cultural center. It's a shame that they gave it such an ugly name: The García Márquez Cultural Center. . . . He is not so much a writer as a bureaucrat.)[2]

Though the comment attracted some nervous laughter, few in the audience were surprised. Vallejo was clearly channeling Fernando, his literary persona and recurring narrator, whose default public setting is snide and premeditatedly divisive. There is reason to believe that Vallejo was even simply playing to the crowd. García Márquez was at the event in name only and had become an easy target for members of a younger generation who have struggled with his far-reaching shadow. And Vallejo, in his homecoming, decided to address the elephant in the room head-on. His own literary career covers and comments on the Colombian cultural canon piecemeal. He is at once Colombia's most intriguing living writer and its foremost, if ad hoc, literary critic. And he is in a generational position, directly following the Boom, that pits him against Colombia's largest cultural export of the late twentieth century, magical realism, without the privilege of Generation X irony, new media, and prize committees and critical cultures that favor diverse literary production.

Vallejo's antitotemic tendencies are at once pioneering and revealing. As an urban novelist in a Colombia that has largely played into narratives of the rural elsewhere for international audiences—the unsullied, spiritual backwater that one day may finish, though not contribute to, European projects—Vallejo struggled for decades to gain publishing and critical attention with a tone and subject matter that depicted his nation in a way that many readers found too harsh: more real human experience than tourist advertisement, more grit than exception, and more urban than rural. While publishing houses and prize committees averted the gaze of willing international publics from the harsh realities of Latin America during the '70s, '80s, and '90s, authors who worked toward a poetics that would represent the lived reality of the time struggled to find an audience, and Vallejo decided to relish the irony in presenting a book to an admiring audience in a building named after a figure who had acted more as obstacle than edifice for him.

One must question how a literary icon as well regarded as García Márquez can hinder rather than foster local literary production. And to understand how we travel from a largely romantic Nobel Prize winner to an enfant terrible like Vallejo in the span of one generation, an assessment of world literary systems and the form of the novel itself is in order. Is world literature a forum through which diverse groups express themselves? Or is it a constricting and aesthetically limiting epistemological framework? Is the novel a revolutionary medium? Or does it simultaneously colonize as much as it emancipates.

In chapter 3, I place Vallejo's work within the context of the Colombian urban novel. Here, I offer a more sociological reading of the way that literary aesthetics circulate globally and how Vallejo and other members of his generation, such as Héctor Abad and, as Annie Mendoza highlights in her book *Rewriting the Nation: Novels by Women on Violence in Colombia*, Fanny Buitrago and Alba Lucía Ángel, have suffered from such large-scale literary machinery.[3] In doing so, I argue that Vallejo, as synecdoche for this group, complicates notions of world literature, a literary framework that has largely been regarded as revolutionary and emancipatory. I explore to what extent current formations of world literature are liberating and to what extent they foster Vallejo's literary bureaucrats who oversimplify spaces of dense literary output. To explore Vallejo's relationship with the celebrated literary styles of the time, I focus on the Boom generation, a group that is regularly celebrated as exemplary by proponents of world literature, and the Colombian urban novelists who struggled to gain acclaim due to a publishing and critical culture that favored, and in many cases continues to favor, the style of García Marquez's most internationally recognized works. My reading of world literary systems and the late twentieth-century Colombian novel through Vallejo's and his contemporaries' experience analyzes the epistemic distortion that a singular literary system causes. Similar to my analysis of the continued sociopolitical and literary ramifications of the lettered city in chapter 3, I examine the ongoing implications of the closure of the literary world during the nineteenth century, in the birth of what Goethe labeled early on as the "market of general intellectual commerce" in *Weltliteratur*.[4] I analyze the theoretical development of world literature and point to the shortcomings of using "peripheral" figures such as Boom writers to justify an emancipatory reading of both the novel and a singular literary epistemology. This topic has enjoyed renewed analysis since the publication of *Beyond Bolaño* by Héctor Hoyos and *América Latina en la "literatura mundial,"* edited by Ignacio Sánchez Prado.[5] This study, however, traces their augmented foci back to the root of perhaps the biggest literary distortion caused by the Boom generation.

There is, of course, no shortage of irony at play when antitotemic figures like Vallejo become widely regarded literary icons themselves. It presents a series of literary challenges that forces us to question if literary personae like Vallejo can survive the process of becoming canonized representatives of their home regions in their own right. Since Vallejo's ascension within the literary scene, the tone and poetics that he represents have gained attention with international audiences and favor with publishing houses and prize committees. This has led to a mixture of further distrust for major Latin American literary publishing houses on behalf of local authors, questions over whether Latin American urban and realist representations are any less marginalizing than the taste for magical and rural tones and settings already in circulation, and highlighting by advocates of a singular literary system that the system itself corrects its own aesthetic blunders.

Fernando Vallejo, the Urban Novel, and Aesthetic Citizenship

On May 6, 2007, Fernando Vallejo renounced his Colombian citizenship in an act that simultaneously came as little surprise and was a total shock to the Latin American literary world. The bildungsroman of the five-novel series *El río del tiempo* (1985–1993) had come to a stand-off, and the two main characters—Vallejo, fictionalized in the recurring character of Fernando, and Colombia—were going their separate ways. Vallejo had legitimate cause for concern over his country. He had long been underappreciated as a writer whose style did not match the expectation the world had of Colombian literature, and the Catholicism-guided sociopolitical discourses that surrounded him candidly disapproved of his open homosexuality. Still, Colombia, especially members of the conservative press, may also have had reason to question the way he treated local, still touchy, subject matter, namely, the long history of violence, revamped in Vallejo's narco-cartel-run Medellín. Consider the way in which he communicated to the nation that he was about to leave his citizenship behind in favor of a new life in Mexico, for example: "Desde niño, sabía que Colombia era un país asesino, el más asesino de la tierra. Cuando reeligieron a Uribe, descubrí que era un país imbécil. Entonces, solicité mi nacionalización en México." (Ever since I was a kid, I knew that Colombia was a nation of assassins, the biggest in the world. When they reelected Uribe, I also discovered that it was a nation of imbeciles. That was when I applied for Mexican citizenship.)[6]

The statement is overblown, haughtily simplistic, and perfectly attuned to the key of Fernando, a narrative voice that seeps into Vallejo's interactions with the media and always mixes bombastic statements with intrigue. Yet, while we suspect that there is more behind Vallejo's public statements, we wonder if conservative members of the Colombian press understood that they were playing to Vallejo's gambits when they retaliated in a similar register. In the run-up to the premiere of the film adaptation of Vallejo's most acclaimed novel, *La virgen de los sicarios* (1994), Germán Santamaría, a critic for the conservative lifestyle magazine *Diners*, claimed unequivocally, "Vamos a decirlo de manera directa, casi brutal: hay que sabotear, ojalá prohibir, la exhibición pública en Colombia de la película *La virgen de los sicarios*" (We are going to say it directly, almost brutally: one must sabotage, hopefully even prohibit, the public exhibition in Colombia of the movie *La virgen de los sicarios*). He continues,

> Y no puede ser paradigma de la creación quien niega la vida, la misma posibilidad de la continuidad de la especie humana. Esto no se le ocurrió ni a Nietzsche, D'Annunzio o Sartre, apóstoles de la desesperanza. Grandes artistas de Colombia son un García Márquez o un Fernando Botero. El primero, que jamás habla mal de Colombia fuera de sus fronteras, que participa en los planes de ciencia, educación y cultura para la juventud colombiana; y el segundo, que le acaba de hacer al país, en obras de arte a Bogotá y Medellín, el regalo más generoso que jamás colombiano alguno haya tenido para su nación. (And it cannot be of the same paradigm to deny life and ponder the continuance of the human race. This never occurred to Nietzsche, D'Annuncio or Sartre, apostles of hopelessness. Great Colombian artists are people like García Márquez or Fernando Botero. The first of these never spoke badly about Colombia outside of its borders; he helped develop science, education, and culture for Colombian youth; the second just made for the country, through works in Bogotá and Medellín, the most generous gift that Colombia has ever received.)[7]

Santamaría, no doubt, reveals more in his diatribe than he intends, highlighting precisely the lack of critical appreciation that led Vallejo to leave Colombia in the first place; in the subtext of his argument, we read that Vallejo was never actually a citizen of Colombia in aesthetic terms to begin with. He did not play the game of potboiler magical realism, and he did not pay lip service to the abstract nation. While he did donate the entirety of his Rómulo Gallegos Prize (US$100,000) to animal shelters in Caracas, an act of actual infrastructural benefit to a local country, he did not go through symbolic gestures that propped up the nation in world literary systems. For many readers,

Vallejo was too materially real and too light on gloss to have ever been a late twentieth-century aesthetic citizen of Colombia to begin with.

The contemporary Colombian critic Mario Armando Valencia addresses the terms of Vallejo's departure when he writes, "[Vallejo] renuncia a una *cultura política* dominada por el monstruo bicéfalo del bipartidismo liberal-conservador, la renuncia a una *mentalidad coercitiva y represiva* expresada en los *patrones de conducta* derivados de un catolicismo rancio e hipócrita, cuñado por los *códigos de valor* procedentes del narcotráfico, y renuncia a *una cultura estético-literaria* entregada mayoritariamente al realismo mágico" ([Vallejo] renounces a *political culture* dominated by a monstrous two-headed, liberal-conservative bipartisanship. He renounces a *coercive and repressive mentality* expressed in the *codes of conduct* derived from a stale and hypocritical Catholicism, coupled with of an *honor code* derived from narco-trafficking. And he renounces a *literary-aesthetic culture* dominated by magical realism).[8] When Vallejo leaves Colombia for good, an *ida* [departure] without the implicit *vuelta* [return] so common in Latin American narrative, he renounces his aesthetic citizenship, giving equal treatment to world literary systems (and the fallout they imply), conservative media, and the Catholic Church, a combined target that few people would typically take on at once.

Yet an analysis of the genealogy of the contemporary Colombian urban novel sheds light on Vallejo's disdain for world literary systems, going back to the *novela de la Violencia* and a time when aesthetic debates over how to treat themes of national trauma were largely split between a gritty urban realism based in major cities—places of both failing urban infrastructure due to massive migration and lived political violence—and the provincial literature of the magical exception. In an analysis of one of the *novela de la Violencia*'s strongest proponents, Rory O'Bryen traces the resuscitation of this hardly celebrated form to the doctoral dissertation of Gustavo Álvarez Gardeazábal (1945–), written in 1971, in which Gardeazábal laments the fact that Colombia does not have a structural equivalent to the Mexican *novela de la revolución*.[9] Gardeazábal found it hard to believe that, despite the fact that there was a great amount of urban literary production that grappled with the themes relevant to Colombia directly after the Bogotazo and during the onset of the Violence, predominantly written between the years of 1951 and 1970, the literature failed to garner any lasting support with international publishing houses and, as a result, was largely left out of international literary debate.

The logic of publishing houses appears to be threefold. First, they felt, one might presume, that literature that dealt with issues such as violence and failing infrastructure head-on would be considered shameful on the national scale in Latin American countries that continued to struggle to produce functioning states. Second, the Cold War created a taste for unpsychologized marginality in places that were considered geopolitical battlegrounds without sociopolitical agency. And third, at a time when nineteenth-century novels appeared to have exhausted the realism and the global avant-garde pointed to "new" realities, no matter how much magical realists became the cause célèbre of global socialist institutions, distancing oneself from social realism was good politics in a publishing culture based largely in Spain, northern Europe, and the United States. Indeed, politics through the lens of escapist distancing was much easier to sell to a public of all political stripes, even in a highly politicized era, than a literature that would force a mass readership to deal with material issues head-on. With the privilege of forty years of hindsight and the theoretical tools that world literary theory provides, obvious answers begin to arise to the questions that Gardeazábal presented in his thesis. Anadeli Bencomo writes about world literature's celebration of the Boom, the Latin American publishing culture's leveling of dense literary production, and the singularity of global tastes when she writes,

El *Boom* narrativo latinoamericano figura como un momento clave para la modernización y la proyección en el mercado internacional de la novelística hispanoamericana alrededor de la década de 1960. La consagración de esta novelística latinoamericana iba ligada con la imagen de Barcelona como una suerte de meridiano de Greenwich decisivo para su promoción y visibilidad, junto al impulso suplementario de premios como el Biblioteca Breve, el premio Formentor y el Prix Internacional de Literature que actuaron en su momento como plataformas idóneas de lanzamiento de los nuevos prestigios narrativos. Dentro de la conversión de la narrativa latinoamericana al marco más amplio de las letras hispanoamericanas resultaron igualmente decisivos ciertos procesos de *literaturalización* e *internacionalización* que actualizaron en su momento cierta lógica particular del Hispanismo. (The Latin American narrative Boom comes at a crucial moment of modernization and the projection in the international market of the Hispanic American novel around the decade of the 1960s. The consecration of the Latin American novel was tied in with the image of Barcelona as a sort of Greenwich meridian, which was decisive for its promotion and visibility, alongside Biblioteca Breve's knack for creating literary prizes, such as the Formentor Prize and the International Literary Prize, that acted as platforms to launch new avenues of literary prestige. Within the conversation of Latin American narrative in the wider frame of Hispanic American letters, equally important were the processes of *literalization* and *internationalization* that molded their own understanding of Hispanism as digestible icon.)[10]

A reduced concept of Hispanism and a Latin American experience manipulated by both international critics and publishing houses followed the "shifting of the Greenwich meridian of literature"—the success story for proponents of world literature—leaving in its wake simplified concepts of Latin American literary production and a demand for the performative repetition of the same aesthetic, alienating urban fiction, especially in García Marquez's Colombia, that did not fit into the new narrative of twentieth-century Latin American modernism.

The Colombian writer and critic Harold Alvarado Tenorio (1945–), himself a figure for whom world literature has done few favors, adds to Bencomo's and Gardeazábal's criticism, going so far as to write out a list of authors who directly suffered García Marquez's success in Colombia. His list of authors who would fall under the purview of Gardeazábal's *novela de la Violencia* include Eduardo Caballero Calderón (1910–1993), Manuel Mejía Vallejo (1923–1998), Próspero Morales Pradilla (1920–1993), Héctor Rojas Herazo (1921–2002), and Manuel Zapata Olivella (1920–2004). He adds to this list a group of writers whose work would fall after the period of the *novela de la Violencia*, authors who wrote and published subsequent to the publishing of *One Hundred Years of Solitude* (1967): Gardeazábal, Luis Fayad (1945–), Luis Caballero (1943–1995), and Fernando Vallejo. And Alvarado Tenorio is, perhaps, less diplomatic than most people when he offers a thesis of the underdevelopment of Colombian urban narrative, pulling no punches when he writes, "Pero lo cierto es que los verdaderos promotores de los narradores y poetas hispanoamericanos, a nivel mundial, fueron dos *aristokrátos* catalanes, miembros de una célula subversiva conocida como Grupo de Barcelona: Carlos Barral y Jaime Gil de Biedma. . . . En torno a ellos se desarrollaría, a medida que Barral se arruinaba como editor, el prestigio de nuestros escritores posteriores al Modernismo" (8). (What is certain is that the true promoters of Hispanic American writers, on the world stage, were to Catalonian *aristocrats*, members of a subversive cell known as the Barcelona Group: Carlos Barral and Jaime Gil de Biedma. . . . This is the axis around which our postmodern authors turn.)[11]

According to Alvarado Tenorio's and Gardeazabal's firsthand laments of the machinery of world literature, the literary prizes that were predominantly set up in Barcelona to consolidate a Latin American cultural capital that would project Latin American literature onto the world stage in a moment when an easily marketable Spanish cultural commodity was in crisis under Franco must be treated, at least, as a Janus-faced undertaking. The author's movement from Wallerstein and Braudel's periphery to the literary center or nodal point—a cultural equivalent to the traveling of a raw material to be processed in the metropolitan core—at once develops a literary icon that does a great deal to develop *and underdevelop* the Latin American literary space. That world literature's "bureaucrats" chose one of two clearly distinct styles in a highly politicized Colombia brings with it a series of ethical dilemmas.

While it is difficult to fault García Márquez, not least because *One Hundred Years of Solitude* is, in fact, a literary master work, the contemporary critic must wonder why he insisted on such sleepy, rural settings and why the cultural industry so quickly embraced him, given that in precisely the moment when García Márquez took off, Colombia was in the midst of one of the most violent periods of its otherwise-not-serene history; and this moment in history, arguably more so than any other period, presented largely *urban* problems. Far from the romanticized figures who resonate in Colombian history in a magical setting, Marco Palacios discusses actual political citizens and their migration to the city in search of new opportunities in the years preceding García Márquez's magical realism when he writes, "En un ambiente inseguro, buscaron protección entrando a las redes caciquiles y de compadrazgo, supletorias de las instituciones estatales. Este campesino migratorio, ora colono, ora peón de obras públicas, tuvo en la Violencia una opción perversa." (In an uncertain atmosphere, they sought protection by entering into despotic kinship networks that supplemented state institutions. The rural migrant, sometimes a tenant farmer, sometimes a pawn of public works, had in the Violence a perverse set of choices.)[12] And on the new problems of urban migrations and a mass popular culture, unrecognizable in Macondo-based novels, he writes, "La cultura, más ruralizada y heterogénea, creó una cultura de masas que colonizó las culturas regionales. Se esfumó la hegemonía de la cultura letrada y elitista, laica o religiosa. A la formación de la cultura urbana concurrieron otros factores como el menor aislamiento del país a partir de la posguerra, el aumento de las tasas de escolaridad y la integración de los colombianos a una matriz de comunicaciones centrada en la radio y la televisión." (The culture, more rural and heterogeneous, created a mass culture that colonized regionalisms. It blew away cultural hegemony, be it lettered and elitist, lay, or religious. The formation of an urban culture also went hand in hand with the country's incremental integration after the Second World War, increased grade-school attendance, and the integration of Colombians into a media network centered around radio and television.)[13] While García Márquez theorized a new aesthetics of Colombian rural life and Spanish-based publishing houses celebrated a new revolutionary form, Colombian cities presented unprecedented cultural issues that required literary exploration and working through. New forms of mass culture challenged old aesthetic norms. Violence and crime erupted in city centers as a release for increasingly unbearable living standards. And cyclical national violence became centered around urban spaces.

Though the publishing and critical cultures that operate under the logic of world literature would lead international critics to believe that there is a hole in the Colombian archive, or a failure to account for these urban experiences and polemics, as Gardeazábal and Alvarado Tenorio point out, a large amount of literary production that grappled with mid- and late twentieth-century Colombian issues was simply overlooked in favor of glossier representations. Subsequent critical and writing generations have picked up where the *novela de la Violencia* left off, recognizing the short shrift that international literary prizes and easy marketing answers had long given its authors. In *La dimensión crítica de la novela urbana contemporánea en Colombia* (2009), Mario Armando Valencia offers a list of writers who have, effectively, resuscitated, or at least inherited, the form of the *novela de la Violencia* in the updated context of late twentieth-century and present-day Colombian cities such as Bogotá, Medellín, and Cali. Armando Valencia lists writers whose work shows an aesthetic and intellectual indebtedness to Alavardo Tenorio's list of writers who suffered García Márquez shadow, including contemporary writers such as Antonio Caballero (1945–), Jorge Franco (1962–), Mario Mendoza (1964–), Efraím Medina Reyes (1967–), and Alonso Sánchez Baute (1964–)—a writer who appears on both lists is Fernando Vallejo.

Vallejo's literary battles with the publishing and critical industries that surrounded García Márquez started early. And to the extent that the tone and literary persona of "Fernando" condensed and took shape after a long series of negative tit for tat with the national media, one might venture that Vallejo's iconoclastic style still bears the weight of García Márquez's shadow, in that Fernando is born from the aesthetic rupture with his popular forebear's literary time signature. Valencia writes, "La literatura de Vallejo rompe y ataca toda forma literaria romántica, inclusive en los episodios literarios en los que deviene melodramático y hasta cursi; pareciera que ello hace parte de la trasgresión estética que se propone y con la que encaja armónicamente siguiendo el propósito último de su transgresión, transgresión que se hace estéticamente concreta en una suerte de *hiperrealismo crítico* en el que devienen sus novelas" (73) (Vallejo's literature attacks and breaks all notions of romantic literature, including his episodes that dabble in tacky melodrama; it would seem that it all forms part of an aesthetic that ultimately finds harmony in transgression, a transgression that congeals into a sort of *critical hyperrealism* in his novels).[14]

In Vallejo's recurring narrator, we find a character whose world could scarcely be further from the largely nonmaterial settings of Macondo. And while his work is still based on a poetics of hyperbole, Vallejo's unfiltered, id-heavy ramblings give testimony to the cultural clashes and violence of late twentieth-century urban Colombia. One of the more interesting contrasts that Vallejo draws arises through his rants about the growing popular register and the distortion that it causes when set against Fernando's insistence on a high grammatical and communicative level. Nowhere is this more evident than in Vallejo's best-known novel, *La virgen de los sicarios*, a ranting narrative about the controversial and unlikely affair between Fernando and the young *sicario* Alexis. Despite the fact that the novel itself does not skimp on melodrama, the interaction between Fernando and Alexis offers a densely packed urban, cultural polemic. Vallejo forces the Colombian tradition of transcendental grammarians—Antonio Caro and Rafael Nuñez, for example—to interact with popular rhythms. He places the grammatical precision of the Caro y Cuervo in the context of the sights and sounds of urban dwellers from down-market barrios, leading to a destabilizing dissonance that would parallel the symbolic crisis and attempt to establish new representative aesthetic forms in urban Colombia during the late twentieth century.

Vallejo is not alone in exploring this urban cultural problem. Fellow urban novelists, spanning three generations, deal with similar issues. Andrés Caicedo uses music to represent the destabilizing presence of a new form of urban popular culture in *Que viva la música* (1977). Jorge Franco alludes to an aesthetics of the narco–nouveau riche in *Rosario Tijeras* (1999). And Mario Mendoza draws parallels between the hardboiled detective novel and popular radio shows in *Scorpio City* (1998). All of which—and, of course, this is more the case for members of earlier generations, such as Vallejo and Caicedo—represent an actual, massive, lived Colombian experience rather than pandering to the celebrated international tastes of the rural marginality. Though Vallejo's work brings with it its own ethical problems, and despite marketing and critical pressure in the '80s and '90s to do otherwise, he unarguably represented the pressing issues that Colombia faced much more than the magical realism that the international public demanded at the time did. Valencia continues, "Vallejo subvierte todos los órdenes morales que la sociedad colombiana había conocido hasta entonces. Una defensa a ultranza del homosexualismo y una crítica feroz a las instituciones de la iglesia, la familia, y la sociedad, acompañan ese impulso incontenible de afirmación individual sobre la base de la desobediencia en todos los órdenes." (Vallejo disrupts all moral order that Colombian society had known up until then. An unapologetic defense of homosexuality and a ferocious criticism of the institutions of the church, the family, and society in general accompany this uncontainable impulse to affirm the individual by way of unruly disobedience.)[15] In keeping with his iconoclast and subversive literary persona, when Vallejo renounces his Colombian citizenship, he, in turn, renounces his aesthetic citizenship, delinking from the singularization of taste created by the infrastructure of world literature in favor of a more complicated and nuanced look at the real cultural issues in his far-from-Macondo Colombia.

Colombian Urban Literature and the Political Economy of Prestige

In Héctor Abad's acclaimed memoir of the death of his father at the hands of paramilitary groups during the Colombian Violence, the author plays a game with the reader and his critical audience that reminds us that neither his story nor his style are anything new. He, along with other Colombian urban novelists who have written in order to work through the trauma of the Colombian midcentury for decades, are not going to let publishing houses that swoon over them, critics that rush to praise them, or international audiences that act as if they had been there all along get away without at least a few barbed lines. Abad describes a fictional writer whom his narrator tries to track down in a novel that projected Abad himself onto the Latin American literary scene, *Basura*, when he writes, "El problema es que nadie puede escribir después de muerto; de ahí que la solución sea vivir como si se estuviera muerto y seguir escribiendo, pero nunca publicar nada. Más aún: sin siquiera tener la menor intención de publicar nada." (The problem is that no one can write after dying; so the solution must be to live as if one were dead, writing all the while, but not to publish anything. Moreover, one should write without even the slightest intention of publishing).[16] Given his situation, as a writer born in the Colombian '50s, Abad describes not only what he would consider an ethical yet paradoxically silent author but also the publishing milieu of his generation. He, along with generations of urban novelists on either side of him, wrote as if they had no audience, because, until recently, they scarcely did (some exceptions on the national level, at least, would include Gardeazábal and Franco). We can read allusions to Davanzati in the novel as a way of coping with a lack of readership or, ironically, *Basura* as a text that itself panders to a prize committee—striking remarkable resemblance to the early work of Roberto Bolaño, the novel won the first ever Premio Casa de América de Narrativa Americana Innovadora (2000), on which Bolaño sat as a judge. Regardless of how we read *Basura*, there is an uncomfortable irony behind the increasing recognition that Abad's generation receives. On the one hand, this is a group that, as the title *Basura* implies, has been swept to the dustbin of history by the success of glossier alternatives; and on the other hand, the lag time in the evolution of taste between cosmopolitan critics and the Latin American prize committees that act as their feeders has many times shown complete disconnects in the framework of world literature.

Abad's latest text to be translated to English, *El olvido que seremos* (2006), highlights precisely the problem of "peripheral" awards and "core" reception. Despite his real tone, sparse prose, and urban setting, Abad cannot shake off specters of what Colombian literature is *supposed to be* for cosmopolitan critics. While London's the *Independent* put the translation of *El olvido que seremos*, *Oblivion: A Memoir*, in its "Top 10 Indy Book Choices," the critic could not resist both alluding to García Márquez and describing the book with affective hyperbole in his three-hundred-word summary. It may be the twenty-first century, but Colombia is still a place for armchair emotional extremes, according to London's press: "This compelling memoir of the man, written by his son Héctor Abad, is a chronicle of a death foretold in which the frequent reminders of the father's eventual fate lend the narrative a near unbearable pathos."[17] The *Independent*'s critic is not alone. Though Julius Purcell's review in the *Guardian* goes into detail about the measured reserve of Abad's tone, he too cannot resist the inevitable comparison to García Márquez, who has absolutely nothing to do with Abad's work: "Abad's fellow countryman Gabriel García Márquez famously began his novel *Chronicle of a Death Foretold* with the words 'On the day they were going to kill him ...' In *Oblivion* Abad employs a similar effect, only revealing the details of the murder towards the end of the book, its inevitability making the almost artless outpouring of filial love all the more unbearable."[18] Beyond both texts involving a death and both authors being from Colombia, at no point does *Oblivion* show any signs of García Márquez's *Crónica de una muerte anunciada* (1981). And if there is anything remotely magical about the relationship between Abad and García Márquez, it is that the latter's ghost simply will not die. His specter resonates and appears everywhere a Colombian writer is mentioned by name. And, having been awarded some critical traction and attention in publishing circles, Abad recognizes the irony behind his generation and, more precisely, his particular situation, writing in *El olvido que seremos*, "Es una de las paradojas más tristes de mi vida: casi todo lo que he escrito es para alguien que no puede leerme, y este mismo libro no es otra cosa que la carta a una sombra" (It is one of the saddest paradoxes of my life: almost everything that I have written is for someone who can't read it, and this book is nothing more than a letter to a shadow).[19]

Abad clearly does not consider the act of writing to be futile, and by the time that he writes about a lack of an audience, he knows that his work will enjoy a wide reach. What we witness through Abad and contemporary Colombian urban novelists, including Vallejo, however, is the growing attempt to laud and embrace a literary style whose authors pull largely from their negative experiences with world literary functionaries and publishing systems for inspiration. They straddle the line of aesthetic citizenship and publish with one foot in and one foot out of the publishing economy. Critics may call them sellouts. In fact, some originally fervent supporters have already begun to question their moral fortitude now that it appears that they will inherit the club jacket of world literature. Harold Alvarado Tenorio, who has been the great critical advocate of the urban novelists swept away by the machinery of world literature, has not viewed these authors' burgeoning success favorably. If they become the new icons, whether or not they are openly critical of the very aesthetic system into which they enter, should we not also critically attack them? Wondering if the generation of urban novelists does not reproduce an oversimplification of Colombian letters, Alvarado Tenorio writes about the group's recent world tour in *El País*,

> Gracias a la cooperación de las multinacionales de espectáculo y las agencias inmobiliarias, una de las sucursales de los Hay Prisa Festivals y Abadfaciolince Apartmens & Condos, diez agraciados reporteros e insidiosos, y dos novelistas,

han recorrido cuarenta y tres pequeños municipios belgas y franceses donde han perorado en igual número de minúsculas librerías donde trabajan otros tantos colombianos exiliados y abandonados de la suerte y la fortuna, acerca del odio que profesan al recién abolido gobierno de Alvaro Uribe Velez, financiados, eso si, con el dinero que la prosperidad democrática de este último, ha permitido que el Ministerio de la Cultura, les financie los pasajes y las profusas libaciones. (Thanks to the cooperation of multinational companies dedicated to spectacle and real estate, one of the branches of the Hay Festival and Abadfaciolince Apartments & Condos, ten ingratiating and insidious reporters, and two novelists have visited forty-three small regions of Belgium and France, where they have held forth in the same number of tiny bookstores where it so happens the staff is filled with exiled Colombians who have been abandoned by fortune and fate, about their professed hate for the recently abolished president, Alvaro Uribe Velez, all funded, air travel and copious libations included, by the money that Uribe's government generated.)[20]

Months after Alvarado Tenorio published articles attempting to resuscitate these very urban novelists, he wrote a sardonic critique of their growing prominence, and critics must question the obvious paradox. We can read Alvarado Tenorio's response one of two ways. Not being a literary agent, publicist, or member (be it because he rejected the offer or was not invited) of the touring caravan, Alvarado Tenorio possibly feels that he does not receive the credit that he is due. On the other hand, and more likely, however, he articulates the very mixed literary message that Colombian urban novelists represent. If they straddle the aesthetic border and epistemological line that the machinery of world literature creates, then they must send two messages. In Alvarado Tenorio's journalistic about-face, we read the style of a generation condensed. We witness the political economy of prestige both embraced and satirized, world literature's facilitating avenues both populated and ironized, and the form of the novel both celebrated and challenged.

For James English, the problem lies in the very nature of global circuits of prestige. In his book *The Economy of Prestige: Prizes, Awards, and Circulation of Cultural Value* (2005), English examines the origins and development of world literature through the focal point of prizes and awards. He highlights the economic interests behind cultural awards and ceremonies, ranging from the Nobel Prize for Literature to local competitions for best new novel. For English, prizes do not simply account for a system of monetary exchange but, moreover, in a similar vein to Casanova's world republic of letters, follow an international market of cultural exchange. English focuses on the limiting effects of such a system. He finds that many prize committees that tie into the interests of publishing houses, as is clearly the case in the buildup of the cult surrounding the Boom, simply shadow economic markets, both fiscal and prestige markets that level cultural diversity in equal measure. While literary prizes are capable of empowering authors, even at the local level, and can lead to dynamic shifts in literary trends, for English, the overall schema of such systems forces literary aesthetics to pass through a reductionist focal point—the political economy of prestige reifies literary aesthetics, glosses tones and trends, and then exports them to a global market. Even the Noble Prize, an award whose six Latin American recipients have unarguably done great things for Latin America's cultural weight on the international scale, is not beyond reproach, for English. He describes the terms of Goethe's *Weltliteratur* in the twentieth century, using exactly the moment when magical realism began its ascension on the international scene, when he writes,

> As the pace of economic and cultural globalization has accelerated since the 1970s, this tendency of prizes, festivals, and related forms of competitive cultural events to facilitate exchange of symbolic capital between the indigenous [taken to mean local] and the metropolitan market-places—often by circumventing strictly national institutions—has become much more pronounced. Though still capable of exerting powerful symbolic effects through their own proper systems of reward and penalty, the national fields of cultural productions have seen their significance seriously diminished. This is now, however, simply because they have been subsumed within a vast transnational field on which an artist's national prestige is recalculated according to ever more disadvantageous (or Disneyfied) rates of exchange. It is, even more critically, because the "local hero," the artist celebrated at the subnational level of indigenous community, can now be fed directly into a global market for indigenous cultural production without any reference to a national standard of value. Indeed, as regards prizes and awards, the national honors which used to serve as prerequisites for "Nobelization" now themselves often trail behind global consecrations serving merely as post-facto adjustments or corrections of the domestic symbolic market; the global awards, meanwhile, depend on a particular sifting of local or "fourth world" prestige as a basis of eligibility for global celebration.[21]

The text that did as much as any other to simultaneously gain regional prestige and reduce the breadth of Latin American literary aesthetics for at least three generations, *One Hundred Years of Solitude*, followed a shift from regional recognition to the center of the world republic of letters to the largest literary award in the world in the Nobel Prize. García Márquez's text won the second-ever Venezuela-based Premio Rómulo Gallegos in 1972 (he is straddled by fellows members of the Boom on either side: Mario Vargas Llosa's *La casa verde* won the prize in 1967, and Carlos Fuentes's *Terra Nostra* won it in 1977), the French Prix de Meilleur Livre Étranger in 1969, and the Noble Prize in 1982, all while the *novela de la Violencia* and the *novela urbana* failed to gain international attention. At over thirty million copies, *Cien años de soledad* has sold more than all of the works of the Colombian urban novelists combined. And places as geographically distant from coastal Colombia as Buenos Aires now have cafés and bars in their tourist districts called Macondo in an attempt to produce the regional expectation of foreign tourists. Cultural prestige clearly does not come without its cultural price.

In this publishing atmosphere, Abad's reluctance to recognize his own reading public is understandable. Alvarado Tenorio's mixed message to a generation for which he has acted as spokesman is fitting. And Vallejo's typically heavy-handed tendency to lay into the beneficiaries of the political economy of prestige at a moment when he himself is gaining prominence is apt. When basing a literary style on the struggle for agency, headlines in global newspapers and prizes awarded by star-studded committees sit uncomfortably. And the generation of Colombian urban novelists responds with a poetics that accounts for the epistemological dissonance that the form of the novel and the economy of prestige cause writers in a place on the periphery of world literary systems. It is doublespeak, of course, when Abad claims that no one has ever really read him in a book that is bound for a large audience, when Vallejo attacks published authors from the bully pulpit of Alfaguara-sponsored events, and when Alvarado Tenorio argues on behalf of urban literature in the local press while criticizing the same authors in an international forum (*El País* owns Alfaguara, it is worth adding). But by engaging with the system, it is a poetics that also alludes to the need for alternatives. It is a literature that simultaneously benefits from world literature and calls the system's bluff. And given that Colombian urban novelists and other Latin American authors who have been openly critical of the publishing culture surrounding the Boom now gain large amounts of international attention and win prizes themselves—Bolaño won the Rómulo Gallegos in 1999 for *Los detectives salvajes*, Vallejo won it in 2003 for *El desbarrancadero*, and William Ospina won it in 2009 for *El país de canela*—they are challenged with alluding to a literature that delinks from the singular aesthetic system that world literature and the economy of prestige imply. In turn, they have responded with a poetics that sends mixed messages about the tension between local and global aesthetics and at once contributes to and undercuts the world literary system.

Perhaps the greatest irony surrounding the relationship between Colombian urban novelists and the framework of world literature is the fact that new generations in critical and publishing cultures have begun to look at urban and gritty aesthetics favorably. Roberto Bolaño (1953–2003) has most famously undone the aesthetic map left by the likes of world literary stars, such as García Márquez, with his own overblown mythology and suspect marketing decisions in tow. And Vallejo has also won international prizes and is something of a bourgeoning star himself. Oddly enough, in renouncing his aesthetic citizenship, Vallejo has helped shift the international aesthetic palate, forcing critics to wonder if the global taste for marginality has simply changed geographies, moving from the rural to the urban, and if escapism has been replaced by what María Helena Rueda refers to as a "comercialización de la marginalidad" (commercialization of marginality).[22]

As the world literary system appropriates new figures and styles, Erich Auerbach's worries about the reductionism and "difference obliterating" tendencies that a singular literary time implies, no matter who is in a position to radicalize it, hold true. Just as Immanuel Kant's shift from multiple aestheses to a particular aesthetics, Goethe's labeling of *Weltliteratur* marks the closing of the literary world, which plays out clearly in late twentieth-century Colombian narrative. As is seen in the case of Vallejo and, in a larger context, the Colombian urban novel, a singular modernism is too narrow an approach to literary production, and its proponents ignore the difficult literary terrain that the internationalization of literary icons leaves in its wake. Within the framework of world literature, critics who argue in favor of the emancipatory properties that larger-than-life literary personae present when they move from the "periphery" to the "core" many times ignore the fact that the same figures they celebrate are considered highly reductive, if not altogether kitsch, by their home regions. And while Vallejo's literary delinking certainly runs up against its own set of problems, and his *maldito* persona risks becoming a caricature for international consumption, one can hardly blame him for complaining, even if so bombastically, about world literature's bureaucrats.

3

Narrating Disruption

From the *Novela de la Violencia* to the *Narco-Novela*

The opening shot sequence of Victor Gaviria's 1990s social-realist film *La vendedora de rosas* (1998) pans a squalid river and scene-setting Medellín skyline that is interrupted by the sound of sporadic gunfire. Luis Fayad's novella about a family's repeated failure at social ascension, *Los parientes de Ester* (1978), depicts a systemically inhumane Bogotá where governmental infrastructure is arguably worse than total chaos. Gonzalo Alvarez Gardeazábal offers a Colombian microcosm in which supposed civic and spiritual leaders are serially assassinated by a local hero-cum-sniper in *Cóndores no entierran todos los días* (1971). Mario Mendoza's *Scorpio City* (1995), Laura Restropo's *Delirio*, and Santiago Gamboa's *Perder es cuestion de método* (1997) all revolve around the attention-grabbing and uncanny appearance of a mutilated body. Alonso Salazar treats Medellín as a source of trauma that needs to be worked through rather than a stabilizing symbolic pillar in *No nacimos pa' semilla* (1990). Antonio Caballero's Bogotá consists of an undecipherable labyrinth with a low-glass ceiling rather than a clear civilizing map in *Sin remedio* (1984). Andrés Caicedo's young characters take a cultural tour of Cali in an urban road trip that ends in a bloodbath in *Que viva la música* (1977). And Fernando Vallejo gives a lament to a Medellín whose only civic code is immediate gratification and conspicuous consumption in *La virgen de los sicarios* (1994).

If late twentieth-century Colombian narrative is any indicator, the lettered city, the wholesale importation of an aesthetic global system long taken to be a civilizing outpost supposed to comprise logical, Cartesian urban design in the New World, has never looked so bad.[1] The lettered city cultural model, as I detailed in the introduction and continue here, has a long history with a literary parallel in Colombia. It presents the nation's organizing principle as intertwined with the aesthetic border, or put another way, as convergence of the global and local through a governing and constitutional logic. With evolution from the lettered city to the narco-state, we witness an embodiment that straddles local cityscapes and global cultural and economic flows in the very schema of quotidian existence. The roots of this symbolic "border citizenship" has a long history in Colombia. Arguably, no other country in the Western Hemisphere took the notion of lettering its citizenry more seriously than the Colombian "founding fathers" did.

In a period of high Latin American modernism, the Colombian presidency of Antonio Caro emphasizes to what extent global aesthetic epistemology and politics had become intertwined in Colombia. Caro's late nineteenth-century government laid out maps of the evocation of the citizen by way of aesthetics through a political framework that operated under a paradoxical inclusive and exclusive paradigm. For Caro, and indeed the governmental framework surrounding him, a government steeped in *modernismo* attempted to create a unified cosmopolitan lettered citizen while at the same time using the consolidation of cosmopolitan knowledge among the governing elite to create a state of exception. José María Rodriguez García puts the exclusivity of the self-perpetuating aesthetic government best when he writes, "Caro articulates a definition just as narrow of Colombia as a nominally democratic nation, in which there is no longer room for the daily plebiscite fostered by the de-essentialized liberal state. Rather, identitary orthodoxies are enforced, including the need for even the large indigenous population to identify with the Spanish language, the Catholic religion, and the institutions of paternalist, semi-feudal domination administered by the educated creole elite."[2]

Here, I discuss the theoretical implications that surround the lettered city in modern and contemporary Colombia. In doing so, I explore the origins of the Colombian urban novel, following current critical trends that trace the form back to the *novela de la Violencia*. In the Colombian urban novel, I argue, we witness an aesthetic alternative to the turn-of-the-century modernist writers who embraced the logic behind the lettered city.

To a large extent, the urban novel unletters and then reletters the city, taking literary aesthetics out of the hands of the governing elite and to the streets, where its writers seek to capture the failing infrastructure and many times extreme political reality of cities such as Bogotá, Medellín, and Cali. Many times its writers depict the violent scenes of post-Bogotazo and drug-cartel-run city life in a way that pervades the lives of their protagonists. In other moments, they focus on the cultural polemics instigated by the lettered city, depicting the actual urban mapping of aesthetic distance through contrasts of the upper-class space where citizens have a great deal of symbolic capital with areas where popular culture threatens the "pure" standard. Through these contrasts and in addition to my focus on the urban novel, I further allude to the two cinematic styles that gained traction in Colombia in the '70s, '80s, and '90s: the social-realist aesthetic of the Medellín school and the cosmopolitan and philosophically brooding Caliwood, two styles that complement the literary evolution of the urban novel and offer contrasting philosophical approaches to a similar genre.

Among the urban novels that I explore, Fernando Vallejo's *La virgen de los sicarios* presents the most interesting and open allusions to the undermining of the lettered city. Vallejo's insistence on exploring the nation's history through Medellín leads to a national lament that, at least through the narrator's eyes, the nation is on its last legs. The protagonist, Fernando, makes direct references to the Colombian lettered tradition when he claims to be the "último gramático de Colombia" (Colombia's last grammarian) and leads the reader through a tale in which a metonymic extension of Caro himself dwells in the streets of drug-cartel-infused Medellín, mixing with popular sights, sounds, and rhythms. Arguably the Colombian urban novel at its most distilled, *La virgen de los sicarios* presents a contrast between high literary modernism and new approaches to Colombian realism that present the aesthetic state in a harsh light. I use contemporary criticism of Vallejo's best-known novel to situate him within the tradition that attempts to debunk high grammarians, in favor of a rounder aesthetic representation of Colombia's institutional shortcomings, leading to an exploration of what Jean Franco has recently referred to as the "decline and fall of the lettered city."[3]

Through allusions to Colombia's canonical modernists and the many times ironic insistence on portraying "purity" in popular urban Colombia, authors of the *novela urbana* expose the exclusivity in universalizing aesthetic registers, set to the key of European modernism. This literary experimentation and evolution mark a cultural hologram of the bucking and braying at the aesthetic border: an attempt to shrug off the tension inherent to the place where global and local aesthetic and cultural flows converge.

Violent and Urban Letters

With migration increasingly flowing and a stable social ecology perilously buckling, the populist leader Jorge Eliecer Gaitán sensed the rise of a new urban subjectivity earlier than most people. Entrenching himself in a politics that would challenge the transcendentalist Catholic ethos of his Conservative rival

Laureano Gomez, Gaitán confronted the existing order by appealing to the unrepresented masses in mid-twentieth-century Bogotá: "El pueblo urbano, que sentía día a día los azares de la reproducción de sus condiciones de vida, y aspiraba a mejorarlas, captó al instante los registros morales del discurso gaitanista que castigaba los excesos del capitalismo salvaje y el apareamiento de los grandes negocios con las cúpulas del Estado" (The urban masses, who felt the day-to-day swings in their living conditions and aspired to improve upon them, instantly understood the moral registers of a Gaitanist rhetoric that chastised the excesses of an unleashed capitalism and the presence of major corporations in the halls of governance).[4] But for all of Gaitán's political fervor, he knew that the entrance of a new urban subjectivity into the national order would not go unchallenged, especially by groups that had dominated cultural life in Colombia for centuries. With his eyes firmly fixed on the writing on the wall, he offered apocalyptic premonitions. "¡Si me matan, vengadme!" (If I am killed, seek my vengeance!), he was regularly known to instruct his growing swaths of followers.[5]

On April 9, 1948, Gaitán's foreshadowing proved not to be in vain; and his supporters retaliated in kind. Gaitan's followers, now known to some people as the *nueveabrileños*, decimated the city, destroying as much as one-third of the *centro* and causing three thousand deaths in a matter of days.[6] Unruly masses, sensing a power vacuum, attacked the presidential palace, set free prisoners, and burned down civic and religious buildings, both of which they considered to be symbols of a conservative government that had done little to represent them for well over a century. While the panic and absence of state were quickly replaced by the heavy-handed presidency of Gaitán's rival, Laureano Gómez, the Bogotazo did not consist of an acute and isolated rebellion. The rioting of April 9, 1948, would go on to cause similar uprisings to ripple throughout the countryside and spill over into other cities, leading to one of the most violent eras in Colombia's history: the Violence—a period that would eventually see more than two hundred thousand deaths and little governmental representation beyond authoritarian-hued measures.

The lettered city had been strongly challenged and was now in a state of mediation. The challenges to governing bodies brought along with them challenges to the literary archive. It would be hasty to argue in favor of the *nueveabrileños*, a group that led to destruction and disorder to the extent that the Bogotazo caused, but it would also be difficult not to consider that the rioters of the Bogotazo were not simultaneously reacting to an ongoing social symptom in a way that breached a largely unrepresentative symbolic and political order. The literature that had been used to prop up an unrepresentative government rather than to challenge it followed suit, and Colombian letters experienced a pronounced tonal and thematic shift, increasingly representing the problems surrounding urban Colombia in these moments of political and migratory flux. Literature in mid-twentieth-century Colombia increasingly became a tool to work through the failure of political systems and national infrastructure rather than a distancing governmental platform that propped up a state of exception that superficially filled a national cultural archive. While there is no shortage of Colombian cultural fragments that explore representational problematics prior to the mid-twentieth century—some canonical examples would include the works of José Asunción Silva, the poetry of Porfirio Barba Jacob, and José Eustasio Rivera's antinational classic-national classic *La vorágine*—for the first time in the history of Colombian literature, entire genres began to address the distortion between aesthetic orders and lived experiences in Colombia, many times calling into question the livability of the Colombian city, postmigration, postlettered credibility, and post-Bogotazo.

As Colombian political infrastructure continued to roundly underrepresent Colombian masses and heterogeneous cosmologies after the Violence—the authoritarian regime of Laureano Gómez, governing between 1950 and 1953, and the power sharing between Liberals and Conservatives during the National Front—challengers to national discourses found a representational outlet in alternative aesthetic forms, where we witness the birth of the *novela de la Violencia* as a genre, a form that, as I argue, evolves into the *novela urbana*, which also finds a branch in the social-realist cinema of the Medellín School.

The first person to refer to the genre of the *novela de la Violencia* as such is a writer who would go on to write one of the style's classics. In his 1971 doctoral thesis, Gustavo Álvarez Gardeazábal discusses the rich literary output in Colombia between 1950 and 1970, over thirty novels that challenged preconceptions of the nation and its relation to culture. He found that the genre was scarcely celebrated on either the national or pan–Latin American scale, however, due in large part to its tendency to deal frontally with difficult themes that challenged preconceptions about the relationship between the government, literature, and violence. Despite the genre's lack of international and local recognition, Gardeazábal found that it was a highly important literary form, whose poetics was part of a larger cultural project that addressed crises in subjectivity and representative systems in Violence Colombia in a way that lent itself to a framing and working through of lived tumult. Rory O'Bryen summarizes Gardeazábal's thesis and the genre that he coined when he writes, "It refers as much to a constative process of producing memory and recording history as to a performative process of burial, and an attempt to give closure to the past *as* past. Thus, at a 'constative' level, the novel can be read as an attempt, not only to counter censorship and amnesia, but also to narrativize and make sense of *la Violencia*."[7]

For Gardeazábal, the genre tended toward representations of violence and tremendous experiences, many times in urban Colombia. Tones harden, and, in contrast to the literature of magical exceptionality with which mid- to late twentieth-century Colombia is readily associated, realism prevails as a medium. To understand the lasting legacy of the *novela de la Violencia*, it is best to turn to Gardeazabal's most famous work, *Cóndores no entierran todos los días*, a novel that he published in the same year as he finished his doctoral thesis. Written during the National Front, the novel acts as a stark contrast to both García Márquez's treatment of a cyclical governmental underrepresentation and lived political violence and the regime of letters that had previously prevailed. While García Márquez frames violence through hyperbole and exceptionality, Gardeazábal's poetics asks the reader to confront the systemic problems of Colombia's major institutions head-on. Gardeazábal's Colombia presents no refuge, no rural backwater, and no coarse reading of history to distract his public from the weight of the Colombian experience. It is no surprise that he did not enjoy the same international prestige as the Boom writers, be it from the perspective of North American reading publics, European prize committees, or the Casa de las Americas. It is also of little surprise that Colombia's major institutions do not come out of *Cóndores no entierran todos los días* unscathed.

Cóndores no entierran todos los días drops the reader in, in medias res, in a moment when the members of the town of Tuluá are coming to terms with the political reality of post-Violence Colombia. The civil war between Conservatives and Liberals, exacerbated by the recent assassination of Gaitán in the 1949 of the novel, demands that the inhabitants of Tuluá take sides in a battle that to them makes little immediate sense. The first line of the work foreshadows the theme and announces a hallmark rupture with the already-not-peaceful past: "Tuluá jamás ha podido darles cuenta de cuándo comenzó todo, y aunque ha tenido durante años la extraña sensación de que su martirio va a terminar por fin mañana en la mañana" (Tuluá has never been able to realize exactly when everything started, although for years it has had the strange sensation that its martyrdom would finally come to an end tomorrow morning).[8] The novel does not go on to simply lament the death of the populist leader, nor does it tell the tale from the perspective of a liberal uprising. Conversely, Gardeazábal follows, and to a large extent deconstructs, the psyche of a conservative and prominent businessman of Tuluá. He forces the reader to examine the social fabric and institutional makeup of the Colombian nation through the micro example of the seemingly innocuous cheese-shop owner Leon María Lozano, whose relationship with the nation in miniature, through Tuluá, presents a distillation of the ongoing civil war and the bodies that resonate in its competing political discourses. With the assassination of Gaitán, something is born in Lozano, something that turns him irrevocably violent—Gardeazábal employs the metaphor of a "cóndor" that is sparked inside Lozano and takes over his rational political drive. While Lozano was already conservative, before the politically divisive Bogotazo, he was still functional within the symbolic community. Though many readers may not agree with his politics, his right-wing affectations were hardly extreme: "León Maria como buen godo nunca dejó de asistir a misa y ser un católico reconcentrado y un conservador fanático que como dice el dicho 'El que peca y reza empata.' No leía sino *el Siglo* y escuchaba *la Voz Católica* que solo hablaban del partido conservador." (He who sins and repents ends in a draw. He did not read *el Siglo* but instead listened to *la Voz Católica*, which only talked about the conservative party.)[9] Yet with the birth of the "cóndor," Lozano takes a radical turn, quickly descending into psychopathy. As the novel progresses, we witness Lozano alternately increase his stake in the local community—purchasing land and forging political connections, usually through the collective referent of Catholicism and social posturing— and convert into a mass murderer.

There is something darkly quixotic about Lozano's rapid descent into madness. As the novel's body count rises, so does Lozano's level of self-assurance. More and more, we gather that Lozano feels that he is engaging with a universal project, one that spans ages. His determination and insistence on winning *tierras* and instating authority many times approaches an uncanny resituating of chivalric literature, and we wonder if Lozano is what El Cid would have looked like in the twentieth century, more serial killer than foundationally mythic hero. If we want to distance ourselves from the violence that Lozano represents, we struggle to do so. At the end of the novel, the reader hardly blanches when a rivaling sniper kills Lozano. While we never quite lose perspective of the extremities of violence in Gardeazábal's Tuluá, we remember Pecaut's "banalization of violence" as the bodies pile up.[10] One may refuse to take sides, but a philosophical dilemma arises when Lozano is killed: Is it not for the better? If so, where does the cyclical violence stop? Gardeazábal places the reader in the frame of the overwhelming decision-making process of *Violencia* Colombia, depicting extremities that challenge the limits of representation, and at the same time forces the reader to address the "cóndor" within.

The "cóndor" metaphor, and the narrative in the larger sense, explores the unease that saturates the *novela de la Violencia*. Gardeazábal ventures that with the intensification of violence that would follow the assassination of Gaitán, we observe a hardening of the literary form that would radically break with the high governmental letters of fifty years prior. And he presents the subject matter in a way that does not readily lend itself to the taking of sides. Gardeazábal's presentation of violence roundly accuses all political institutions as a collective culprit that has led to precisely the political violence that is born from April 9, 1948. He does not depict Lozano as a natural psychopath so much as a figure with political leanings and religious practices who is psychologically derailed by the sociopolitical flux of the Violence. The narrative resists any progressive reading of violence, regardless of whose side the reader favors. The use of the "cóndor" stands in contrast to a Nietzschean phoenix that, according to Nietzsche's reading of Greek mythology in *The Birth of Tragedy*, would rise from the ashes of destruction, in this case, of the civil war. On the contrary, Gardeazábal's Tuluá and Lozano's "cóndor" present a Dionysian embrace of the death drive without the Apollonian return at the end. It is a death that is senseless and escapes the frame of philosophical and political discourses. And the situating of Lozano as a subject turned psychopath blurs the positive edges of the civilizing discourses and aesthetic registers that would accompany violence in Colombia and arguably in the larger framework of Latin America. O'Bryen asserts, "Along these lines 'El Cóndor' would represent another figure such as Rosas in Sarmiento's *Facundo* (1845), and *la Violencia*—like the cycles of civil war and violence recounted in said text—an anachronistic continuity in the present of a 'deep' cultural past that had consistently exceeded the 'civilizing' process of nation-formation."[11]

In hollowing out the city and state, Gardeazábal leaves a ruin of lives and untestimonialized trauma. He skirts social realism and presents a dark shadow of civilization that makes the reader feel implicated in the ongoing saga that frames violence through a poetics that is clearly influenced by the texts he surveyed for his doctoral dissertation. The formal structure of the work, in the words of Harold Alvarado Tenorio, makes for "una dualidad de planos narrativos donde el silencio de un pueblo se expresa en los chismes que van y vienen entre sollozos y los gritos de las viudas y los huérfanos. El *Verfremdung* brechtiano que produce en la novela es un alejamiento de la mimesis prodigando otra realidad, otro estado, que denota una postura ética ante la crueldad de la existencia" (a duality of narrative planes, in which a town's silence is expressed through rumors that come and go amid the wailing of orphans and widows. The Brechtian *Verfremdung* that the novel produces is the distance from smoothed-over mimesis, from another form of state, which takes on an ethical posture in the face of cruel forms of existence).[12] With Alvarado Tenorio's quote in mind, the natural inclination is to read shades of Rulfo's Comala in Gardeazábal's Tuluá, a reading that gains credibility when considering Gardeazábal's self-reflective impetus to create a genre that would mediate the relationship between mass publics, collective trauma, and political systems. As early as his dissertation, Gardeazábal encircles a founding question: Why had Colombia not developed a formal equivalent to the Mexican *novela de la revolución*? In turning to another example of the *novela de la Violencia*, Luis Fayad's *Los parientes de Ester*, I explore to what extent Gardeazábal was successful in answering his own questions and doing just that.

While Alvarado Tenorio reads resonances of Brecht in *Cóndores no entierran todos los días*, it is easy to speculate that he would see more Lukács in Luis Fayad's *Los parientes de Ester*, a novel that, like *Cóndores*, escapes the bounds of standard-issue social realism. Still, all the ingredients are there. In Fayad's Bogotá, society is presented as a totality; all levels of the sociopolitical order—governing, colonized, fledgling, aspiring, bureaucratic, bare, lettered, and unlettered—are depicted as an intertwined system, where authoritative capital coercively maintains the status quo. Perhaps nowhere else in the Colombian canon is Aníbal Quijano's "colonial matrix of power" more clearly represented.[13] *Los parientes de Ester* presents a Colombian infrastructure in which social ascension, or even basic survival, is for all intents and purposes impossible. Economic, subjective, gender, and authoritarian orders are all rigidly maintained by social norms, and we read a counterfoundational national story in which bodies that attempt to enter into the lettered system, or to achieve the promise of lettered civilization, are routinely denied entrance into the exclusive order.

Los parientes de Ester follows the trajectory of Angel Callejas, also known as Tío Angel in the novel, and Gregorio Camero. Gregorio, having been left out of work for years, along with almost everyone he knows, looks for room for maneuver in the economic system—on one occasion, Gregorio says to Angel, "Tú por lo menos tienes un trabajo y eso en este país es como ganarse la lotería" (At least you have a job, and in this country that is like winning the lottery), to which Angel ripostes, "Cuando te entregan el premio la única sensación que te queda es la de que te han estafado" (Yes, but when they give you the prize, your only sensation is that you have been conned)—and he buys and manages a café.[14] Far from an example of venture capitalism, and even the subtler undertaking of Lozano's cheese shop in *Cóndores no entierran todos los días*, in Angel and Gregorio's café, we witness a humble attempt at day-to-day survival. The choice of a café, of course, is not incidental; it is a space tied into the national psyche, both for the tradition of the public spectacle of café life and the weight that coffee holds in promises of economic progress and the marketing of a national image. While Gardeazábal offers a representation of the lives that get lost in the competing political discourses of the incipient Violence, Fayad points to the failure of the National Front and its peace-and-prosperity-promising power share to lead to any form of progress. Coffee acts as a paradoxical marker. While coffee prices steadily grow as multinational companies come into Colombia under the National Front, no meaningful socioeconomic structure builds around the commodity.[15] In parallel, Fayad ties coffee, the public sphere, the continued low glass ceiling for the majority of Colombia's citizens, and postmultinational investment into a narrative in which the four are inextricably linked.

Los parientes de Ester is set up in a cyclical structure, with opening and closing scenes that both point to a lack of historical teleology and the dialectics of the National Front. In both scenes, Gregorio and Angel sit pensively, drinking coffee and smoking cigarettes, trying to find a way out of the Bogotá that, despite promises of collective progress, feels more like a disordered maze than a logical social map. By the closing scene, as readers, we are sick of coffee. Along with the characters, we have practically drowned in it. It is the only thing that is of abundance and readily available in the novel. Everything else of substance, even the most basic necessities such as food, lead to political squabbles among Bogotá's underbelly and remind the reader of Gregorio and Angel's failing business venture. The state is notably more hindrance than help. One bureaucratic functionary, from the comfort of a state position, muses disdainfully to the new café owners, "Casi todos van a pedir que les fíe. . . . En estos negocios los únicos que ganan son los clientes. Aparte de que no pagan, se roban las cosas. Mire—el hombre le mostró una cucharita agujereada—, hay que hacer esto para que no se las roben, y sin embargo se las roban. Y mire—le indicó a Angel Callejas para que observara al otro lado del mostrador—, este cajón está lleno de vales que con seguridad no van a cancelar nunca." (Everyone is going to ask to pay on credit. . . . In these sorts of businesses, the only people who win are the clients. Not only do they not pay, but they also steal. Look—the man showed him a spoon filled with holes—, you have to do this to the cutlery so they won't steal it; and even then, they'll probably steal it. Look—he pointed to the other side of the counter—, this cash register is full of IOUs, and no one will never pay them.)[16] Fayad creates a situation in which lettered and unlettered citizens stand face-to-face, with Gregorio and Angel in the middle, acting as potential representatives of a socially mobile middle class that would make a leap from one to the other. At this point in the novel, however, we realize that it is unlikely that the café is going to do anything to help their social standing or personal independence. And Fayad gives an ironic treatment to both state workers and the lumpen. Like Gardeazábal and notably Fernando Vallejo, whose first novel followed *Los parientes de Ester* seven years later, Fayad subtly derides the systemic social problems of Colombia, pointing to its largely underprivileged place in the global economy as a source of ongoing problems. Far from the idyll imagined in the lettered city, Fayad renders the Colombian capital into a failed project where, for Alvarado Tenorio, the city "acompaña a sus personajes por la vida misma, siguiéndoles en sus vicisitudes y desgracias, haciendo de los protagonistas el lector, con sus miserias, hambres, imposibles sueños, odios, carencias, humillaciones, maquinaciones, mezquindad, maledicencia y arribismo" (accompanies its protagonists throughout life, following their ups and downs, highlighting for the reader their miseries, hungers, unrealizable dreams, hates, lacks, humiliations, machinations, cruelties, slanders, and snobbery).[17]

With Fayad's *Los parientes de Ester*, we are not far from the modern-day *novela urbana*, and especially the branch of the *narco-novela*. Fayad's broad implication of all levels of society in ongoing cultural polemics has a clear influence on Jorge Franco's celebrated *Rosario Tijeras*, and his refusal to let the novel veer into the waters of maudlin or exotic renderings of Bogotá's lumpen neighborhoods still feels fresh largely due to Fernando Vallejo's recently revamped approach to a similar style. Fayad depicts bare and unlettered lives as part and parcel of larger geopolitical problems than the microsuffering we see in the novel. We approach Fayad's characters with sympathy, because we witness the decision-making process that they go through, searching for tactics of survival at the level of the day-to-day. When their projects fail and the characters run up against the low glass ceiling of National Front Colombian society, we blame the economic and representational system rather than taking agency away from the urban characters by thinking "they need our help"; nor do we feel emotions evoked through a poetics of poverty porn. As in Gardeazábal's *Cóndores no entierran todos los días*, we feel implicated and alienated when the political system is laid out explicitly before us and when, in *Los parientes de Ester*, Gregorio and Angel follow the social guide espoused by the political discourses of the time to the letter, making earnest attempts to become functioning political, economic, and aesthetic citizens, the reader cannot help but wonder what more they could do to meet with the state's superficial standard. The breach between the messages that the state sends and the lived reality of the mass public is made obvious, and it is clear that Colombia's urban populace has no infrastructural outlet under *Violencia* and National Front governments.

Considering Gardeazabal's depiction of a society in which rational political citizens are derailed by the intense trauma of the Violence and Fayad's illustration of the ongoing underrepresentation and lack of opportunity for the Colombian masses during the National Front, it is retrospectively of little surprise that an alternative socioeconomic order was about to take hold in both rural and urban Colombia, one that the government would be able to do little to control or suppress. Colombia was about to enter into a phase of globalization mediated by the otherwise anomic groups that were kept at bay both economically and symbolically for almost two centuries. The power vacuum left by the Bogotazo was about to evolve into an alternative economic order that would restructure Colombian economies, urban aesthetic registers, and literary representation permanently.

By the last quarter of the twentieth century—around the time Colombian letters entered into a stage of mediation—groups that were until then neglected by the lettered city and its national regime of letters came back to haunt the government on a more lasting scale than was experienced during the *Violencia*. Anomie slowly became a social norm, and having been denied opportunity on every representational level for generations, wide swaths of the population turned to guerilla groups for governance and to the drug trade for economic support. An alternative social order, parallel to the state, developed that challenged the symbolic primacy of the lettered idyll. Alfredo Molano describes the alternative socioeconomic orders that replaced the state when he writes,

> In the so-called Independent Republics of the 1960s, the colonists were on the brink of ruin because of poor market conditions and the absence of government aid. They did not lose their land, however, because the guerrillas helped

them, and to an extent, this helped prevent large landowners from acquiring and concentrating the land into large tracts. Insofar as the guerrillas were able to create defenses for the colonists they tended to control the roles of the merchant and the intermediaries and to provide for or attend to the population's most basic needs, such as education, health and justice. Economically, the guerrillas' power was based on contributions or taxes from the colonists paid either in cash or commodities or with labor. The colonists' obligations usually were fulfilled through collective work, either "organization farms" or on the private property of others.[18]

The alternative social orders set up around guerilla groups, their paramilitary alternative, and the drug trade make for a dense story with little clarity in regard to right and wrong, positive and negative. And the national government increasingly began to weave in and out of the history of these alternative groups, many times illicitly—several members of the Alvaro Uribe government still have pending investigations regarding economic ties to the drug trade, and under the Ley de Justicia y Paz (2005), Uribe effectively co-opted paramilitary groups, paradoxically causing the government to enter into warfare parallel to the state. But in aesthetic terms, unarguably, we witness the simultaneous rise of new forms that debase the high poetic registers of the lettered city and sociopolitical orders that challenge the state's primacy. New genres emerge that, for the first time in Colombian history, mediate the lived experience of large portions of the Colombian population and the literary archive, giving literary representation to the watershed Bogotazo, the subsequent birth of the narco-industry, and the urban experiences that accompany both. New lived reality demands a new poetics, or a new way to articulate life at the aesthetic border, and the *novela de la Violencia* continues to evolve into the *novela urbana*.

The Contemporary Colombian Urban Novel

By the 1980s, urban Colombia would have been entirely unrecognizable to the vision held by idealists who viewed the city as a beacon of universal civilization roughly a century earlier. The '80s bears witness to the taking up of arms by more than one-third of young men in Colombian urban spaces and the birth of the *sicariato* as a profession—by the '90s, 190 separate branches of gangs and *pandillas* will be identified in Medellín alone.[19] Battling paramilitary and guerilla groups also fail to lend prolonged stability to urban subjectivities. So-called death squads, or *escuadrones de la muerte*, continue to operate in Cali and Medellín, in Palacios's terms, working to "extirpar los llamados *desechables*: 'gamines,' pordioseros, prostitutas, homosexuales y pícaros callejones (annihilate the so-called disposables: street kids, beggars, prostitutes, homosexuals and urban ruffians).[20] Along with challenges to the civilized idyll, the regime of letters slowly turns into a regime of arms, and the violence implicit in the exclusionist lettered state becomes manifest when, after the Violence, the government and its "social cleansers" begin to call their non-citizens by name. Marginality becomes manifest around the time that it becomes clear that the state of exception has failed, and in the name of ongoing war, figures considered *desechables* (disposable) become the new enemies of the state.

Formal representation evolves to capture the updated terms of violence, urban experiences, and massive clashes with the government. The *novela urbana* distills as a genre and branches into subcategories. Varying film aesthetics in two different cities, Medellín and Cali, consolidate to form a poetics of Colombian social realism. The Colombian noir novel takes off, beginning with Gonzalo España (1945–), who explores the *novela policiaca* as a way to situate violence in urban Colombia, and matures into the noirish aesthetics of Mario Mendoza and Santiago Gamboa, who use the hardboiled detective novel to represent the Colombian citizen's search for the root cause of ongoing violence. And authors of the *narco-novela* attempt to capture the affect and cultural registers of urban Colombia's unofficial economic systems, many times focusing on youth, popular culture, and the ideology (and lack thereof) that has built up around the drug trade. It is an atmosphere that, for Palacios, challenges old institutions, rethinks the conditions of the lettered citizen, and updates the relationship between subjects and official representational registers: "Las cohortes de niños y adolescentes parecieron más dúctiles a los lenguajes y símbolos de la radionovela, la telenovela, el cine, el deporte y la música. Allí se fraguaron nuevos significados culturales, creencias y modos de expresar los afectos, que rompieron con la estrechez y rigidez del catolicismo entonces prevaleciente, como se vio, por ejemplo, en el campo de la sexualidad y de la formación de la vida de pareja." (Cohorts of kids and teenagers seemed more adaptable to the language and symbolism of radio-novels, soap operas, cinema, sports, and music. They forged new cultural signifiers, beliefs, and modes of expressive affect that broke with the strict rigidity of then prevalent Catholicism, as was seen, for example, in the field of sexuality and how romantic life changed.)[21]

The most lasting examples of the Colombian film industry come in the form of two directors, both of whom, I argue, are chroniclers of the aesthetic border: Víctor Gaviria of the Medellín School, whose *Rodrigo D no futuro* and *La vendora de rosas* have gained attention, praise, and criticism on both the national and international scale, and Luis Ospina, a representative of the socially minded half of the politically bipolar Caliwood—Ospina, in contrast to Andrés Caicedo, with whom he founded the first Colombian cinema journal, *Ojo al cine*, is notably more concerned with the tumultuous existence of marginalized figures, falling in line with the literary aesthetics of Luis Fayad, than is Caicedo, who always pushes for a philosophical exploration of the semi-cosmopolitan upper-middle classes. Both Gaviria and Ospina work toward an imagery and cinema that captures the novel subjectivities born out of the aesthetic border in '80s and '90s urban Colombia and the marginal and underdeveloped situation that many of the youth experience. They search for a poetics that gives agency to until-then-underrepresented subjects, while grappling with the ethical dilemmas of exporting an aesthetics of poverty to a global intelligentsia. The cinema of both directors works to capture a subjectivity that is somewhere between Enrique Dussel's *potentia* and marginalized bare life, a double political movement that is caught between an empowering challenge to underrepresenting institutions and the risk of being continuously left out of social systems. Juana Suárez and Carlos Jáuregui describe the cultural tension that Ospina and Gaviria's generation attempts to represent when they write,

> Entre los discursos cotidianos sobre la marginalidad y la criminalidad urbana emergió con renovadas fuerzas una imagen: la de la ciudad como un lugar contaminado no por los ruidos y la polución industrial de la modernización periférica, ni por los residuos petroquímicos de los motores que la cruzan, sino por una "polución humana". Para la *ciudad letrada* de las últimas décadas del siglo pasado, el malestar por la ciudad fue frecuentemente un malestar de lo nacional frente a las muchedumbres democráticas, la plebe, los inmigrantes, y la abigarrada heterogeneidad lingüística, étnica y política de la multitud. En las últimas décadas del siglo XX, ese imaginario se renueva con las constantes referencias a una ciudad *sucia de humanidad*, asediada, infectada e infestad de "elementos indeseables." (Between everyday discourse about marginality and urban crime emerged a new forceful image: that of the city as a space contaminated not by noise, industrial pollution of peripheral modernization, or chemical residue of traffic, but by a sort of "human pollution." For the *lettered city* of the last few decades of the last century, what was bad for the city was frequently bad for the nation in the face of democratic masses, the *folk*, immigrants, and multitudinous linguistic, ethnic, and political heterogeneity. In the last few decades of the twentieth century, this imaginary had constant references to an urbanism that was *polluted by humanity*, and besieged and infested by "undesirable elements.")[22]

While a wide-scale challenge to the primacy of the lettered idyll successfully debases the preeminence of high literary modernism in Colombia, there is a shift from the semantics of the "unlettered" to the "disposable" body. Allusions to order over chaos and universal aesthetic civilization over the perceived squalor of the lived urban experiences of the Colombian masses undergird both political discourses. Literature, however, increasingly becomes a tool with which to work through and mediate cultural problems, rather than a cultural anchor that lends governing bodies a credible aesthetic distance. In the films of Gaviria and Ospina, we find a poetics that works through social problems on the popular scale. The violence already perceptible in Gardeazábal's works and the attention to the socioeconomic vulnerability of the urban masses in Fayad's complex renderings are taken to the screen and projected alongside images of Colombian urban youth who attempt to piece together a meaningful existence, figures who are almost always left to the social alternatives of the drug trade and *pandilla* violence.

While there are well-founded discourses that point to the Latin American city and urban space in general as the representational heart of the dissonance inherent in Latin America's foundational binaries, hybridities, and representational polemics, the rise and fall of the lettered city is perhaps nowhere more pronounced than in Colombia.[23] Though the Latin American urban novel finds its inspiration in Roberto Arlt's Southern Cone, the cultural problems that spring from Colombian cities arguably make for the genre's most poignant expressions. It is in Colombia that the author's desire to rethink, reorder, and reletter the city is set against the backdrop of a socioeconomic order not officially recognized by the Colombian government. It is also in Colombia where the rise of a popular culture and "mediated" literature contrasts most starkly with the idyll espoused by the regime of letters a century prior. Indeed, in a state as precariously up against the brink of collapse as '80s and '90s Colombia, the importance of literary intervention in urban spaces could hardly be overstated.

We can read the literary intervention of the Colombian *novela urbana* in its broadest context—the division into the subgenres of the noir novel and social-realist cinema notwithstanding—as exhibiting three tendencies: (1) the exploration of violence through somatic metaphors; (2) the reordering of the city by representations of walking and dwelling in urban spaces; and (3) the depiction of affective registers not otherwise represented in the literary archive.

The Colombian hardboiled detective novel has lent itself most readily to the use of soma as a metaphor for violence. And the tendency to open a novel with a crime scene and the shocking exposure of a dead body plays most prominently in the works of the current renovators of Colombian noir, Santiago Gamboa and Mario Mendoza. Both narrate from the perspective of a down-and-out figure, a detective and a journalist, respectively, with literary tendencies. A post-authoritarian governmental functionary and a post-high-aesthetics writer, the protagonists offer examples of Fayad's state representatives and Caro's aesthetes in an updated 1980s and '90s "mediated" Colombia. In Mario Mendoza's *Scorpio City* (1995), for example, we explore the day-to-day street life of Bogotá and the role that violence plays in relation to the psyche of the average citizen. Mendoza explores the ways in which the appearance of a dead body weighs on one of the government's "desechables." Not unlike the Catholic-come-off-the-rails in Gardeazábal's *Cóndores no entierran todos los días*, Mendoza's serial killer, The Apóstol, has a deep religious bent. The Apóstol is a ritualistic killer who only goes after society's underbelly. In implied coordination with the "death squads," we, as readers, uncomfortably witness the relationship between religious fervor, social order, and violence along with the detective protagonist, who tries to piece together the crime scene. Mendoza writes, "Te fijas en los rostros de las prostitutas y travestías que caminan por los andenes esperando la caída de un cliente. Te parece increíble que haya un grupo de fanáticos religiosos encargado de exterminarlos. Y otros, como El Apóstol, pensando en exterminar a los exterminadores. Así es el país, piensas con tristeza, ésa es nuestra forma de sentirnos colombianos, negando y aniquilando al que está a nuestro lado." (You fixate on the faces of the prostitutes who walk around the sidewalks looking for clients. It seems incredible to you that a group of religious fanatics wants to exterminate them. And others, such as The Apostle, are thinking about exterminating the exterminators. That's the state of the country, you think sadly; that is our way of feeling Colombian, denying and annihilating what surrounds us.)[24]

Mendoza calls the state of the nation into question by representing its competing political discourses in microcosm and transposing them into an urban crime narrative. On the one hand, the detective, Sinisterra, grapples with the flagrantly unacceptable death-squad discourse. Yet on the other—and here the philosophical dilemmas of *Cóndores no entierran todos los días* return—he cannot accept the ritualistic killing of the killers themselves. Sinisterra attempts to come to grips with the cognitive dissonance that the competing political discourses, his job as a detective, and his own intuition imply. Along with him, the reader explores the nuance and micropsychological problems that blunt institutional responses cause for Colombians—the "desechables" in the eyes of paramilitary and governmental groups, the police force, the average urban citizen—and ends up questioning all obvious answers. Sinisterra touches on the failure of Colombia's political discourses to represent lived reality when he rants, "Entonces, desde los esquemas tradicionales, un homosexual ecologista, ¿es conservador o liberal? Una lesbiana mística, ¿es liberal o de izquierda? Regina 11, la hechicera espiritista con gran respaldo popular que llegó hasta el Senado de la República, ¿es de izquierda o de derecha?" (Then, from the perspective of traditional politics, a gay ecologist is liberal or conservative? A mystic lesbian is liberal or conservative? Regina 11, the spiritualist with a huge following who made it as far as the national Senate, is she left wing or right wing?)[25] He continues, "Entonces, un travestí místico con cuenta en Miami, ¿es un burgués opresor o un proletario oprimido? Un abogado con apartamento en el norte de Bogotá, en el mejor sector, que sin embargo tres días a la semana amanece en los expendios de bazuco del sur de la ciudad, en el peor sector, en medio de sus propios excrementos después de fumar hasta la saciedad papelas de bazuco, ¿es un arribista despreciable que vive en la riqueza y la comodidad, o un drogadicto miserable víctima del sistema?" (So, is a trans mystic with a bank account in Miami a bourgeois oppressor or a member of the oppressed proletariat? What about a lawyer in the north of Bogotá, from the nicest neighborhood, who nonetheless three days a week wakes up amid his crack paraphernalia in the south side, covered in his own feces after smoking himself silly? Is that a member of the elite, a lowlife living in comfort, or a victim of the system?)[26] Mendoza uses Sinisterra to connect to the reader. Through him, we feel connected to the social problems that, by way of Sinisterra's rants, we come to realize have, as much as anything, to do with the application of awkward political discourses to the body politic. Mendoza depicts average citizens who are caught between social anomie and a political inclusion that implies its own violent terms. Through the crime novel, he explores the causes and meanings of mass violence. The appearance of cadavers and the mutilated body stand in for the disfigured nation, and like a sleuth, along with Mendoza and Sinisterra, the reader considers the implications that this trauma has on Colombia as a collective subjectivity.

In a second instance of the use of soma to metaphorize the crises of a nation, the raw image of a dead body drives the narrative of Laura Restrepo's *Delirio*. The primary theme of *Delirio* is not simply death, although it is the presence of a cadaver that causes the protagonist, Agustina, to reimagine her childhood and to induce the titular delirium. Agustina's mental collapse, along with the revisit she pays to her past, opens up the larger theme of decline in the novel and paints Colombian violence in entropic hues. While in *La vorágine*, whose frenetic, visceral tones come to mind when reading *Delirio*, a harsh reality breaks through a fragile imaginary and is metaphorized through images of heat and fire, political confrontations in *Delirio* focus on images of impotence that firmly contrast to themes of libidinal drive. Impotence reminds the reader of the failings of a state that has spent a long twentieth century trying to come to grips with its populace. The most overt representation of impotence arises through the character El Araña and his desire to prove to his friends that he can become sexually aroused despite his physical handicap, which makes it impossible for him get an erection. El Araña's sexual decline is more subtly paralleled by the German immigrant Nicolás and his intellectual and existential impotence as he is faced with the inability to make a living out of music, while the theme is even further complicated by the character Agustina's mental deterioration. In all of these cases, we witness grotesque and mentally violent clashes between the two realities—decline and health, *destrudo* and libido— as the crude reality that has been set aside as aberration returns to haunt the characters' respective ideological and social imaginaries.

The narrative dedicated to El Araña and his desire to prove his sexual potency is cast as a brutishly virile bet among a group of upper-class middle-aged men who have made a game out of one of the principal tenants of superficial masculine honor. As El Araña moves away from the sexual and masculine norm, he slowly strays from socially acceptable fetish into the waters of squalid sexual fantasy. In the scenes that ensue in the back room of The Aerobics, their social club, the reader witnesses a gradual decline into the sinister, resulting in the eventual death of the aptly named Dolores. El Araña stages a scene in which he almost reaches arousal as a woman is violently bludgeoned, during a moment when pain and pleasure come together, erasing the social boundary, even in the macho sense, that separates the two. The spatial representation of Dolores's death accentuates this point. The Aerobics offers a space of masculine bourgeois fantasy, a privatized space of leisure and superficial appearances of health. But just as El Araña's sexual desire quickly delves into the sinister, another character, Midas, uses the back room, or the space that is not readily visible, to set up perverse sexual shows.

Restrepo's installment to the national saga adds a psychoanalytical element to the complexities surrounding the mixed messages sent by the state and its subsidiaries. It layers Freudian drives over the violent power struggles waged in '80s and '90s urban Colombia and uses a single body to help readers quantify the violence. It goes to lengths to resist Pecaut's banalization of violence and the remote distancing of large, unfathomable numbers; and the tension between a small junta-like elite and the larger public continues to be a prevalent theme. Restrepo accentuates the disposability of the peripheral body in the minds of a select group, as they play with Dolores's body as if it were a rag doll. Restrepo further explores the breach established between the lettered government and its evolution into the political paradigm of the meaningful and disposable citizen. Instead of the late nineteenth century's regime of letters, operated by a select group of functionaries with lettered weight, we witness a late twentieth-century update through a group of men in a private club who manipulate social reality to fit their designs. The scene change and time shift make the relationship between a governing elite and a mass public appear even more drastic when layered over the virile drive, and the presence of the mutilated body in the club takes the dead body out of the run-down *barrios*, countryside, and "feral" mountains and places it at the feet of the party responsible for its mutilation. While Restrepo's work and the genre of the *novela urbana* use popular registers to challenge the primacy of the literary archive, the exposure of the raw body reminds the reader what is at stake in political discourses that subtly espouse concepts such as the trumping of order over disorder through "social cleansing."

A prototype of the Colombian "dwelling" and "walking novel" that will be an important contribution to the *novela urbana* comes in the form of Andrés Caicedo's *Que viva la música*. As early as the first page of his only completed novel, the Cali-based Caicedo's protagonist, María del Cármen Huerta, confronts the existential problem that will both haunt and drive her throughout a drug-induced flâneuring that frames the entire work. María discusses how her "whiteness" and hair color lead other *caleños* to associate her with cultural icons from a freshly available international and cosmopolitan register, when she energetically claims, "Pero me decían: 'Pelada, voy a ser conciso: ¡es fantástico tu pelo!' Y un raro, calvo, prematuro: 'Lillian Gish tenía tu mismo pelo,' y yo: 'Quién será ésta,' me preguntaba, '¿Una cantante famosa?' Recién me he venido a desayunar que era estrella del cine mudo. Todo este tiempo me la he venido imaginando con miles de collares, cantando, rubia total, a una audiencia enloquecida. Nadie sabe lo que son los huecos de la cultura." ("But they would say to me: Girl, I'm going to get to the point: your hair is fantastic!" And a strange prematurely bald man: "Lilian Gish had the same hair," and me: "Who is that," I wondered, "a famous singer?" Only recently did it dawn on me that she was a world-famous actress. All of this time I had imagined her with thousands of necklaces, singing, total blonde, to an enraptured audience. No one really understands these holes in culture.)[27]

Que viva la música is about speed, youthful energy, and the inevitable comedown from earnestness experienced in the context of a young group of friends from Cali, with whom we spend a week in the life under the haze of a sex, drugs, and rock-and-roll frenzy. Caicedo takes us along for a ride in his 1970s Cali, a time and place in which multinational corporations began to make great headway in urban Colombia, largely resignifying the urban symbolic order and bringing a string of cultural problems along with them.[28] And through María and her friends, (another) María and a practically unending flow of gringos and libido-driven twenty-somethings, Caicedo, a cinephile, invites the reader to experience, arguably for the first time, Colombia at twenty-four frames per second.[29]

More than speed, however, the novel is about the "holes in culture" (los huecos de la cultura) that María alludes to in her opening exclamations. Along with the new wave of cultural referents that life in Cali brought in the 1970s, a new cosmopolitan border opens up for a young generation that grew up with access to international popular culture on a scale until then unprecedented, causing a clash between a local, many times folkloric, sense of nationality and a new cosmopolitan cultural register. Caicedo uses music and urban dwelling to explore this cultural problem, going so far as to include a discography, or sound track, at the end of the work. Music is the impulse that keeps his characters riding a high whose comedown is threatened cyclically, giving way to a largely standard bildungsroman pattern. The protagonist leaves home, on the microspatial scale of an outing and multiday bender, experiences a new cultural form that would symbolically kill her parents (in this case through the international narrative of rock music and more specifically through the Rolling Stones), considers, though refuses, a return home (represented by salsa within the musical metaphor), and then seeks out a third place, in this case without grounding in the city.

In the case of *Que viva la música*, however, the bildungsroman does not occur seamlessly, at least to the extent that the protagonist does not grow, mature, and successfully carve out a place of her own, but is trapped by the need to continue to move; she is caught in an errancy that parallels her and her peers' growing dependency on drugs. Through María's constant motion, we witness signs of both an attempt to reorder the city by walking and dwelling in the urban space and resonances of Franco's "decline and fall of the lettered city." We watch as a protagonist attempts to mediate and reorder the city according to her new cultural register but bumps her head against the city's structure repeatedly until she gets lost in the urban space.

An updated version of María makes for one of the genre's most interesting urban dwellers in Antonio Caballero's protagonist, Ignacio Escobar Urdaneta, from Caballero's best-known work, *Sin remedio*. Ignacio falls in line with many of Latin America's most intriguing, existential urbanites. In him we read shades of Horacio Oliveira (Cortázar's *Rayuela*) and José Fernández (Silva's *De sobremesa*). Moreover, part of the cult that has built up around the character stems from his resistance to clear readings. As Ignacio spends his time searching for the meaning of literature and political reality through a combination of high and low media, we ask ourselves if he is a naval-gazing picaro who uses literature as a way to keep meaningful relationships at arm's length or if he is a virtuosic neo-Enlightenment thinker whose insight and resistance to social norms inspires soft revolution. Is he a mediated urban subject, in whom we view the clashes between an elite governing body and lived urban reality condensed into one character, or is he an updated version of late nineteenth-century modernists without a purpose in late twentieth-century Bogotá? Regardless of how we read Ignacio, Caballero uses him to challenge the city's social ordering, which, if we take Fredric Jameson's understanding of the literary implications as a guide—the city creates "a situational representation on the part of the individual subject to the vaster and properly unrepresentable totality which is the ensemble of society's structures as a whole"—must be read as politically involved.[30] Ignacio's trajectory as a walker and dweller reveals the social stratification that would have occurred in major Colombian cities as the dust of the National Front settles. He uses literature and cultural artifacts as motivation and guides as he brings the asymmetrical distribution of cultural capital among Colombia's urban citizens to the surface. In an inversion of the spatial exploration in Caicedo's Cali from *Que viva la música*, Ignacio moves from the iconic and folkloric yet downtrodden city center to the upper-middle-class north of the city. All the while, he is in search of a "truth" or "deep meaning" in art and literature, creating a double representation of literature and culture: as an inspiring guide, a tool with which to explore the cultural problems of the moment, and as a sociopolitical mechanism that has contributed to the very stratification that Ignacio examines. This walking and dwelling in the city take on an updated twist, as the narcotics industry washes up on its shores.

The Narco-Novel

Perhaps nowhere in the genre of the *novela urbana* is the use of popular registers more broadly prevalent than in the *narco-novela*, a form that deals with weighty subject matter about a group of urban, largely *pandilla* groups that themselves use popular cultural consumption as a social measuring stick. It is problems in agency and form that call for a poetics that uses a popular medium to represent the consumption of popular forms themselves, all set against the ethical dilemmas of representing a hyperviolent social milieu for an external audience. How does the writer capture the socioeconomic tension at the aesthetic border in a popular way without glossing the tremendous political situation of the urban subject? Two varying responses that come out of Medellín in the 1990s narrate the narco-city and its infrastructure: *Rosario Tijeras* by Jorge Franco and *No nacimos pa' semilla* by the former mayor of Medellín Alsonso Salazar.

Jorge Franco's *Rosario Tijeras* interestingly straddles literary tendencies in a way that allows the author to give an innovative narrative voice to a violent socioeconomic ambience in postglobalization Medellín without losing the interest of readers who expect a fast-paced, cinematic novel. In a sense, the world that Franco creates in *Rosario Tijeras* accomplishes as much as would a neorealist, almost Gramscian, account of the difficult existence in a drug-based infrastructure with a rigid class differential, but he does so in a way that would be appealing to a youthful audience, giving a grittier spin on the most prominent efforts coming out of the McOndo and Crack generations. Franco's most notable indebtedness to popular media lies in the cinematic quality of *Rosario Tijeras*, to the extent that the entire story is set up in flashbacks while the narrator sits in the hospital awaiting news about Rosario's medical standing and offers a sort of voice-over to the cinematic scenes that frame the novel.

As critics, we approach Franco with skepticism, given his exportation of violent subject matter. But *Rosario Tijeras* is notable for the complexity and difficult-to-place nature of the eponymous character, Rosario, who at once exhibits tendencies of the femme fatale, a muse, a dominant strategist, a diabolical schemer, a saint, and most interestingly a narcotic. In contrast to Restrepo's representation of the elite governing body in *Delirio*, in *Rosario Tijeras*, Franco offers a complex reading of the many faces of urban political alternatives, while always reminding the reader of the underprivileged status of those who are caught up in the narco-industries. There is a clear line between those who produce and those who consume drugs, followed by the moral division between those who take part in the narco-industry for recreation and those who are forced into it for survival.

While Rosario's multifaceted existence portrays the nebulous lines of identity in a society based on contradictory social discourses, the theme of Rosario as a drug opens itself to more precise themes of class and the unequal distribution of symbolic resources in Medellín. With class in mind, Franco eroticizes Rosario without ever taking away her agency or place of power. Franco does not simply portray Rosario as the rich kids' muse, but on the contrary, he inverts the class dynamic by portraying Rosario as having a dominating sway over both Emilio and the narrator, two upper-middle-class consumers of the narcotic cultural industry. Throughout the work, one class does not dominate the other wholly, but both are depicted in an interdependent relationship of co-musing. This class relationship plays out spatially in the novel in the emphasis put on the way that the city is laid out, with the economically dominant class occupying the *cerro* overlooking the city, as is noted by Rosario when she visits Emilio's house. But with regard to social life, this dynamic is inverted. In the *discotecas*, Rosario's old friends, or the *narcotraficantes*, have the best seats and are afforded the primacy of the VIP rooms that overlook the dance floor. They control the terms of popular culture but not of cultural capital. This dominance finds a further parallel in Rosario's early desire, and subsequent failure, to meet Emilio's family standard, on the one hand, and Emilio's failure to acquire Rosario's fidelity, on the other.

While Franco does not portray one social class as entirely dominating another, in a way that could have easily happened by denying Rosario any agency and simply projecting her as an exotic muse for rich kids who are slumming it, he also avoids the pitfalls of romanticizing the drug culture. To portray both subjectivities as unweighted differences, in the postmodern sense, would also be an injustice to an underprivileged class. Franco, instead, uses the metaphor of Rosario as a narcotic, and a representative of the social infrastructure that facilitates a narcotics industry, to show that, despite the fact that all classes are implicated by its existence, for some people, it is easier to distance themselves from violence than for others. Rosario's death, which frames the novel, reminds us that while urban Colombia is in a state of mediation, and the drug culture offers economic alternatives to total social anomie, it is still easier for the narco-industry's consumers to disengage than it is for its producers.

If Franco's novel shows an indebtedness to popular cinema, Alonso Salazar's *No nacimos pa' semilla* (1990) clearly pulls from the politically engaged documentary for inspiration. Salazar, the mayor of Medellín from 2008 to 2011, parallels the social realism of the Medellín School with his collection of first-person narrations of *pandilla* street life. In *No nacimos pa' semilla*, Salazar transcribes multiple accounts from anonymous *sicarios* and gang members, interspersing third-person narrations of the places where gang members will dwell throughout their lives, narrating their home space, the streets, and prison blocks. Salazar is skillfully absent from the collection. He resists the ethical dilemmas surrounding the giving and taking of agency and the depiction of an urban poor—a criticism that has shadowed the films of Víctor Gaviria, for instance—and lets experience speak for itself. Salazar does not condemn the individual perpetrators of violence; yet the violent experiences that the young boys describe do not lack salience. Salazar simultaneously resists the banal depiction of violence and the privileged moral distancing of the reader. The anonymous introduction to the collection, written by a member of CINEP (Centro de Investigación y Educación Popular), the group that funded the project, puts the social problems at the heart of *No nacimos pa' semilla* bluntly: "Cuando lo más importante se ha banalizado, puesto en el mercado, destruido, la tarea de colaborar en la construcción comienza por hacer el diagnóstico. Para esto hay que adentrarse en las motivaciones y la lógica de los jóvenes que pasan matando. Leer su racionalidad y su moral como una legitimación de la enfermedad es ser incapaz de darse cuenta que el problema hay que plantearlo desde dentro para poder superarlo" (9) (When the most important things have been banalized, put into the marketplace, destroyed, the task of collaborating in reconstruction begins with diagnostics. To do this, you have to delve into the motivation and logic behind what makes young people kill. Reading this rationalization and morality as a legitimation of the sickness is to be incapable of realizing we have to get to the root of the problem to be able to overcome it.)[31]

There is a tension in *No nacimos pa' semilla* that points to the representational and aesthetic problems at the heart of Colombia's askew symbolic economy. After years of underrepresentation, when large groups of the population seek out economic and symbolic infrastructure parallel to the state, can anyone actually condemn them for it? The problem, for Salazar, is how we talk about Colombian anomie, where the only constant is violence itself. We must recognize the moral and ethical code and the causes for Colombian gangs and *sicariatos* without romanticizing them or turning them into cultural artifacts for public consumption. The essential question is how to understand without justifying the groups. Salazar does so by spanning the psychological particularities of the experience of killing—in one episode, the *sicario* describes the first time he killed someone when he claims, "Estuve quince días que no podía comer porque veía el muerto hasta en la sopa . . . pero después fue fácil. Uno aprende a matar sin que eso le moleste el sueño" (I went fifteen days without eating, because I saw death everywhere, even in my soup . . . but then it got easier. You can learn to kill without losing a bit of sleep). Salazar describes the ritual and moral code that builds up within the groups—the same *sicario* describes his quasi-religious process of killing, stating, "En esos casos, tengo una costumbre que me ha resultado muy buena: cojo una bala, le saco la munición y le echo la pólvora a un tinto caliente, me lo tomo y eso me tranquiliza" (In those cases, I have a habit that has worked for me: I take a bullet, I take out the gunpowder and put it in my coffee. When I drink it, it calms my nerves). This code is contrasted by the testimony of a Catholic priest who respects, if not venerates, the passion with which *sicarios* and gang members mourn their own dead: "En el cementerio, lo sacaron del ataúd y lo cargaron en hombros, le gritaron cosas delirantes, y le hicieron disparos al aire, hasta que por fin lo sepultaron. En esta vida me ha tocado ver cosas muy extrañas, pero este ha sido el entierro más raro de todos." (In the cemetery, they take the body out of the coffin and carry it on their shoulders, screaming like mad, shooting in the air, until the bury it. I have seen a lot of strange things in my life, but that was certainly the most bizarre funeral).[32] Salazar also describes the cultural syncretism with which these otherwise-anomic figures engage. Salazar argues that in the *sicario*, we observe the cultural crossroads of Colombia's socioeconomic flows: the *sicario* is where *paisa* culture, socioeconomic modernization, and popular registers converge.

In the *sicario*, we witness symbolic anomie and subsequent alternative social formation, the entrance into economic globalization through an officially, though thoroughly consumed, illicit product, a rise of popular media to combat the transcendental aesthetics of Colombian modernism, and the shift in official political discourse from the unlettered to the disposable body. In the *sicario*, we read an essentially Colombian story distilled in a social movement, a group whose complexities present their own dilemmas of representation and whose representational poetics, given its inherent paradoxes, will challenge Colombian, Latin American, and international standards of comfort and acceptability.

Sixteen years after publication of Fernando Vallejo's best-known work, *La virgen de los sicarios*, few critics, at both the local and international level, agree on how to approach it. It is arguably the most controversial and densely packed of the *narco-novelas*. In a publishing culture in which ethical debates tend to revolve around the representation of a marginalized subjectivity for a privileged and international audience, in *La virgen de los sicarios*, Vallejo draws our attention to more immediate issues. In *La virgen de los sicarios*, we follow the eponymous narrator, Fernando, as he experiences a disheartening return to Medellín after several years in absentia. Anyone familiar with the chronicles of the character's (and author's) years abroad leading up to the return from the years embodied in the series *El río del tiempo* expects harsh criticism. They will know that Fernando has the tendency to superficially buy into the idealism espoused by major institutions, to place himself in a position of belief, only to go on to give scathing critiques of their paradoxes, letdowns, and fallacies. Yet even familiarity with Vallejo's literary persona does not prepare the reader for the fact that the boundaries of Fernando's love and hate for his home city are about to overflow. There is something new in this heavy-handed first-person approach:

it creates a sense of insider- and outsiderness that Fernando uses to guide the reader through his hometown but with enough distance to act just as appalled as the reader at the state of his city. He uses this tactic of double agency—it is almost as if his voice got caught off the coast of Colombia in the Boca de Ceniza, like Silva's lost oeuvre—to provide himself enough poetic space to wage a harsh critique of a sociopolitical system of which he forms a part. All the same, the role as guide on his way home creates enough critical distance, we presume, to allow Fernando to critique major Colombian institutions both cerebrally and viscerally. For Fernando, everyone is to blame, except, of course, himself and interestingly the marginal figures on whom, by the '90s, the state had declared unofficial war. Vallejo pits himself and the "desechables" against the rest of Colombian society, in a no-holds-barred act of symbolic sparring.

The narrator Fernando's tactics are troubling. On the surface, at least, it is easy to read him as an unrepentant fascist. Many of his prolonged rants target the impoverished for not pulling themselves up by their bootstraps; women, on whom he blames the perpetuation of the "absurd tragedy of life"; and popular dialects and cultural registers, for which he blames the bastardization of his grammatical and cultural precision. For this reason, critical cultures have tended to read him through an "and/or" lens: Fernando is either ironic or fascist; his rants are either deeply Catholic or anticlerical; he either deeply loves or loathes Colombia.[33] More interesting, however, is the way in which Fernando sifts through superficial political claims and institutional discourses to highlight the actual human lives lost, the bodies that are considered, depending on the political discourse, either disposable or good only as a political tool. In an interesting reading of Fernando as a postglobalization *costumbrista*, Jean Franco claims that regardless of the way in which we approach Fernando, the text acts as a sort of x-ray for Colombian urban life in the '80s and '90s. It brings to the surface governmental claims about the disposable citizen: "In this regime all values other than exchange value melt into air. Does the *desechable* (the garbage) simply extend the logic of globalization until it reaches the end of human history?"[34] Fernando, as polemicist, crystallizes the cultural problems of his times and makes them readily visible. The fact that we are repulsed by his views does not surprise, but, through Fernando, Vallejo does little more than alter the context of the sociopolitical discourses espoused by the government, the day-to-day practices of the Catholic Church, and the opening of the economic border's tendency to reify human experiences; he condenses the rhetoric that weighs on the Colombian psyche into a single, scarcely palatable, human voice in a comedown from an international experience and lets loose on a Medellín in one of its most vulnerable historical moments.

If we think that Fernando is excessively harsh on his home country, we are right. If we think that his hate is too visible and his diatribes too at the ready, we are right. If we think that Fernando's libido is intemperately uncurbed, we are right. But if we think that his motives are easily quantifiable and that his moral compass neatly follows political models, then we are off the mark.

Fernando is a multifaceted character whose ideology shifts with the given moment. He straddles the tendency to disengage politically and the propensity to reproduce both left- and right-wing discourses. His distaste for popular culture mimes both his high-modernist predecessors' aesthetic distancing from the masses and turgid Marxist claims about the perversion of culture in times of globalization. If that does not make us squirm, the pederasty will. The opening of the novel sets the tone and the scene when it begins with a fairy-tale structure: "Había en las afueras de Medellín un pueblo silencioso y apacible que se llamaba Sabaneta" (On the outskirts of Medellín, there was a quiet and peaceful town called Sabaneta).[35] As we zoom in, however, the sweeping tone quickly capsizes; three pages later, Fernando continues to set the scene: "Y para entonces Sabaneta había dejado de ser un pueblo y se había convertido en un barrio más de Medellín, la ciudad la había alcanzado, se la había tragado; y Colombia, entre tanto, se nos había ido de las manos. Éramos, y de lejos, el país más criminal de la tierra, y Medellín la capital del odio." (By then, Sabaneta had stopped being a tiny town and had become more a neighborhood of Medellín; the city had reached it, had devoured it; and Colombia, in the meantime, had slipped out of our hands. We were, by far, the most criminal country on the planet, and Medellín was the capital of hate.)[36]

Fernando makes his appearance in a makeshift whorehouse, where men contract young *sicarios* not as hit men for hire but for sex. Within the space of the first five pages, we travel from an idealized introduction to the author's childhood neighborhood to a close-up on the *sicario*, albeit in a more extreme context than we are used to. Fernando's *sicarios* are not just products of pop-cultural syncretism, extended economic borders, and the failure of the Colombian state, as Salazar's work suggests, but in *La virgen de los sicarios*, they are also highly eroticized. This is where the text usually loses critics. What do we make of a novel that not only addresses the difficult-to-place urban subject of the *sicario* but also adds sexual perversion to the scenario?

Maria Helena Rueda argues that one way to read Fernando's relationship to his young *sicario* lovers, at first Alexis and then Wilmar, is through the lens of narcissism. Fernando eroticizes the *sicario*, using sexualization as a means to take control of a social situation in which he feels politically impotent. And Fernando's libido, having run up against its bounds, turns in on itself, converting him into an oversexed curmudgeon, in what, for Rueda, may be the beginning of a new tendency within the contemporary Colombian urban novel: "Se puede decir que *La virgen de los sicarios* inaugura una tendencia a la erotización de nuevas formas de violencia, que aparecen aquí centradas en personajes marginales, y que son abordadas desde una posición ansiosa por el intelectual" (It could be said that *La virgen de los sicarios* inaugurates a tendency to eroticize new forms of violence that appear centered here around marginal subjects and that mean that any intellectual approach starts from a place of anxiety).[37] There is something to this argument, not least in the way that Fernando clings to a dominant position in the face of social instability; he role-plays the Colombian governing bodies in historical times of upheaval and claims to be the "último gramático de Colombia," while his *sicario* lovers favor what for him is the hissing white noise of popular music, mediated political opinion, and idle chatter.

More than a narcissistic insistence on dominating microrelationships in the face of social impotence, Fernando complicates notions of visibility and agency. He pantomimes the treatment of marginal figures by Colombian aesthetic modernists, the government, and the church. Vallejo's own canonization of himself and his self-placement in national and international literary schemas does not err on the side of subtlety. His first professionally published text, *Logoi: Una gramática del lenguaje literario* (1983), is a highly "lettered" manual that attaches reason to grammatical precision, as well as establishing an intertextual connection to the Greek philosopher concerned with metaphysics and epistemology Heraclitus (circa 500 B.C.), whose most famous work revolves around the concepts of universal reason and its points of conflict based in the *logos*, in addition to other pieces that revolve around the theme of the river of time.[38] In rapid succession, from 1983 to 1985, Vallejo published an updated version of Hercaclitus's philosophy, *Logoi*; an autobiography on Porfirio Barba Jacob, *Barba Jacob el mensajero* (1984); and the first novel of the collection *El río del tiempo, Los días azules* (1984). In the foundation of the voice of Fernando, we read as much performance of both Barba Jacob, who acts as a distorted version of the literary modernists of the end of the nineteenth century, and Heraclitus as anything altogether new. Vallejo writes himself into the Colombian literary canon with a philosophical twist that adds the theoretical problems established by Heraclitus twenty-five hundred years earlier.

Vallejo's detailed biography of Barba Jacob focuses largely on the reasons that Barba Jacob left Colombia for Mexico. He discusses the ways in which his modernism had run aground and to what extent his lifestyle clashed with local social pressures. When framed by Vallejo and the performative prism of Fernando, Barba Jacob himself shows resonances with Heraclitus. In his poem "Espíritu errante," the final two stanzas address epistemological normalization, form, and the resistant subject:

¿Quién sabe en la noche que incuba las formas
de adusto silencio cubiertas,
qué brazo nos mueve, qué estrella nos guía?
¡Oh sed insaciable del alma que busca las normas!
¿Seremos tan sólo ventanas abiertas
el hombre, los lirios, el valle y el día?

Espíritu errante, sin fuerzas, incierto, que trémulo escuchas la noche callada:
inquiere en los himnos que fluyen del huerto, de todas las cosas la esencia
sagrada

(Who knows in the night that incubates forms
covered by measured silence,
what hand moves us, what star guides us?
What an insatiable thirst of the soul that seeks out norms!
Are we just open windows
man, lilies, the valley, the day?

Errant spirit, listless, uncertain, whose vibrating silence you listen to at night:
inquiring into the hymns that flow from the garden, of all things, the
sacred essence.)[39]

Vallejo rolls out the literary persona of Fernando with the precision of a performance artist. He sets the stage for a clash between the local and the global
when he bases his first text on philosophical problems explored by a Greek philosopher millennia earlier. He then takes a literary icon who suffers the tensions explored in both his and Heraclitus's texts from the local context and
follows with a persona who will embody traits of both writers. He, in a sense,
attempts to find the *logos* alluded to by Heraclitus that transcends all partiali-
ties. This is not an uncommon literary trick. Dante employs a similar tactic in
the *Divine Comedy*, for example; he develops his poem with an eponymous narrator guided by an established literary master, Virgil, implying from the outset
that he is the next step in a succession of masters. But there is no paradise on
the other side of Fernando's journey. His interest in the clash between the local
sicario and universal aesthetic reason—Barba Jacob's "himnos que fluyen del
huerto"—are crisis and conflict driven. When Fernando returns to Medellín,
with his grammatical precision in tow, he acts as an agent who flows from the
zero point of universal reason. He takes on the persona of Caro, darkened by
Barba Jacob, and forces them to confront the consequence of their extended
logic. Universal and particular epistemologies clash precisely at the point in
which Fernando and the *sicario* come into contact: the *sicario* as a transmodern, mediated product of urban architecture and Fernando the representative
of the *logos* and the ideal aesthetic citizen. If Fernando continuously attempts
to dominate the *sicario*, unsuccessful as he is, it is because he represents the
extension of Heraclitus's theory; he applies universal standards to the local
body, be it cultural, political, or ethical, and the *sicario* always slips out from
under Fernando's schema. It is Fernando who seeks out the *sicario* rather than
vice versa; and it is Fernando who is fascinated by the *sicario* as urban subject.
For the *sicario*, Fernando is many things, but dynamic sociocultural model is
not one of them.

There is a series of scenes in the *La virgen de los sicarios* in which Fernando's anxiety over his inability to dominate mediated culture plays out. In every instance, he attempts to reestablish a privileged position in relation to the *sicario* and his cultural order—according to the logic of the text, the *sicario* stands in for dynamic media, and Fernando, the rigid standard. The first time that Alexis, Fernando's first *sicario* lover, visits Fernando's house, their tastes clash explicitly. Alexis, whose cultural register grates on the high grammarian, is shocked by the lack of music in Fernando's house. Fernando explains,

> Le compré una casetera y él se compró unos casetes. ¿Y tu te llamas a esta mierda música? Desconecté la casetera, la tomé, fui a un balcón y la tiré por el balcón: al pavimento fue a dar a cinco pisos abajo a estrellarse, a callarse. A Alexis le pareció tan inmenso el crimen que se rió y dijo que yo estaba loco. Que no se podía vivir sin música, y yo que si, y que además eso no era música. Para él era música "romántica," y yo pensé: a este paso, si eso es romántico, nos va a resultar romántico Schönberg. (I bought him a tape player and he bought some tapes. And you call this shit music? I unplugged the tape player, I took it to the balcony, and threw it off: it fell five stories to the pavement and exploded; it fell to silence. For Alexis, this seemed like such an immense crime that he laughed and said that I was crazy. He said that he could not live without music, and I said that I could, and that wasn't even music anyway. For him it was "romantic" music, and I thought: if that is what they call romantic these days, then Schönberg is romantic.)[40]

The exchange is a piece in a thematic thread that runs throughout the interactions between Fernando and Alexis. In their first sexual encounter, Fernando carves out a place of cultural privilege for himself, taking the philosophical and aesthetic high ground, when he explains to Alexis, "Mira Alexis, tú tienes una ventaja sobre mí y es que eres joven y yo ya me voy a morir, pero desgraciadamente para ti nunca vivirás la felicidad que yo he vivido. La felicidad no puede existir en este mundo tuyo de televisores y casetes y punkeros y rockeros y partidos de fútbol." (Look, Alexis, you have an advantage over me and that is that you are young and I will die soon, but it is a shame that you will never experience the happiness in life that I have. Happiness cannot exist in this world of yours of televisions and tapes and punks and rockers and soccer matches.)[41] Any tension that Fernando feels in the presence of a cultural order that he cannot quantify, or that challenges his utility as an aesthetic modernist, the *logos* in Medellín, is quickly explained away with sweeping disdain. When really pushed, Fernando explodes the mediated order, in the first scene actually physically destroying the cassette player. As the aesthetic distance between the two registers, high and low, transcendental and mediated, grammarian and *sicario*, closes, the grammatical master can only respond with violence.

There are two moments in the novel that complicate the relationship between the aesthetic registers that Fernando and Alexis represent. The aesthetic border between the two becomes blurred, yet no less violent, when in one scene Fernando threatens to kill himself and, in another, a conflict with a taxi driver leads to an impromptu assassination. In the first instance, Fernando claims that he is going to attempt suicide and asks Alexis for his revolver. Fernando describes Alexis's response: "Alexis sabe que no bromeo, su perspicacia lo siente. Corrió al revólver y para que no me quedara una sola bala se las vació al televisor, lo único que encontró." (Alexis knows I'm not messing around, he can feel it. So he ran to the revolver and so there would not be a single bullet left, he emptied the chamber into the television, the only thing he could find.)[42] The scene is quickly followed by an altercation, in which Alexis kills a taxi driver who refuses to turn down his radio, presumably, though not specified, on Fernando's behalf. Fernando, who has simply insisted on getting out of the taxi, describes his shock at Alexis's response: "Y [el taxista] arrancó: arrancó casi sin que tocáramos el piso, haciendo rechinar las llantas. De los mencionados hijueputas, yo me bajé humildemente por la derecha y Alexis por la izquierda: por la izquierda, por su occipital o huesito posterior, trasero, le entró el certero tiro al ofuscado, al cerebro, y le apagó la ofuscación. Ya no tuvo que ver más con pasajeros impertinentes el taxista, se licenció de trabajar, lo licenció la Muerte: la Muerte, la justiciera, la mejor patrona, lo jubiló." (And the taxi driver took off: he took off almost before we hit the seat, screeching his tires. As for us, I got out humbly on the right side and Alexis on the left: on the left, through his occipital or his posterior skull bone, is where he was shot to darkness, in the head, and it ended the blurred uncertainty of life. He would never have to deal with difficult passengers again, he had quit, or he had been fired by Death: Death, the final judge, the best boss of them all, had retired him.)[43]

As the aesthetic distance between the two registers that Fernando and Alexis represent narrows, the level of violence in which the scenes result escalates. In what comes close to a role reversal, Fernando is shocked by the level at which Alexis responds to situations involving popular culture. In the first example, he unloads a revolver on a television, dramatically topping Fernando's earlier insistence on throwing Alexis's cassette player from his balcony, and in the second case, he actually takes a fellow citizen's life, when the taxi driver insists on not turning down his radio. The technological artifacts are the constant in the three scenes: the cassette player, the television, and the radio represent the media that stand between Alexis and Fernando. Yet as Fernando attempts to letter Alexis, to bring him into his world of high registers and waspish responses to the background noise of mediated culture, Alexis does not become a functioning lettered citizen himself but is derailed affectively and responds with increasing violence. In the scenes, we read the failed application of the letter, or the universal *logos*, to the particular body in miniature. Fernando as representative of the lettered idyll watches on as the lettered city fails before his eyes, even going so far as to question to what extent he is implicated in the murder of the taxi driver. How did Alexis get it so wrong? Fernando is bewildered as he watches Alexis reproduce his own violence. Alexis takes the epistemic dissonance implied in the application of the universal *logos* to the Colombian body and reproduces it physically. He follows the logic purported by Fernando as representative of the aesthetic ideal and plays it out literally. As it is reproduced in front of him, even Fernando is shocked, confessing, shortly after Alexis unceremoniously murders the taxi driver, "Tenemos los ojos cansados de tanto ver, y los oídos de tanto oír y el corazón de tanto odiar" (Our eyes are tired from so much seeing, our ears from so much hearing, and our hearts from so much hating).[44]

If the logic of the Colombian regime of letters looks bad in the *La virgen de los sicarios*, the relationship between Fernando and Alexis does just as much to highlight the discourse of the disposable body. Through Fernando's dalliances with *sicarios*, we observe the reproduction of both stages of institutional responses, at first the failure of the lettered city to successfully evoke a functioning urban citizen and, after the decline and fall of the lettered city, the discourses of the "desechable" urban subject. Life among the marginal classes in the novel is valued at virtually null. The systemic governmental and economic problems that lead to the foundation of the *sicariato*, the hit-man-for-hire trade, come to the surface. Both Alexis and Wilmar reproduce the logic with a natural air, reminiscent of the interviewees of *No nacimos pa' semilla*. We witness the natural political economy of the *sicario* subjectivity and the sociocultural effects of marginality in '80s and '90s Colombia. The *sicario* is not without a code, perverse as it may seem. Nor do *sicarios* lack a symbolic hierarchy— conspicuous consumption plays largely in the way that *sicarios* place themselves in the visual urban order. It is here that Vallejo alludes to the market's influence on popular culture. While the genre of the *novela urbana* tends to challenge the primacy of the high aesthetic registers that lend the lettered city its primacy, the *sicario*'s high regard for free-market goods also casts the mediated culture in a negative tone. As the novel progresses, and most noticeably after Wilmar replaces Alexis as Fernando's lover, the thematic tendencies move away from the relationship between the high grammarian and the mediated citizen and toward the shifting valuations of human life and the body as commodity, underpinned by the *sicario*, who, according to the logic of the text, is both human being and commodity himself—assigned only temporary value, the *sicario* is hired and valued within the logic of the market and then, once used, goes back to being considered disposable in the eyes of the government and the majority of Colombian society.

There are two telling moments in the novel that reveal to what extent the *sicario* internalizes a combination of market and governmentally endorsed "marginal equates disposable" discourses. One comes when Fernando and Alexis find a fatally injured street dog, and the other is when Alexis informs Fernando that he has killed someone simply for the person's tennis shoes—doubly implicating Fernando, Alexis's killer, Wilmar, is later murdered because it is alleged that he has stolen someone's tennis shoes. In the last moment that Fernando and Alexis spend together—in a dramatic accentuation of this pivotal moment, a fellow *sicario* kills Alexis from the back of a *moto* directly following the street-dog tableau—Fernando and Alexis are confronted with a philosophical problem that exposes their ideological differences. Fernando describes the wounded dog they find: "No va a poder volver a caminar—le dije a Alexis—. Si lo sacamos es para que sufra más. Hay que matarlo." (He is not going to be able to walk—I told Alexis—. If we save him, he is just going to suffer more. We have to kill him.)[45] The scene hinges on the irony of Alexis's response:

¿Cómo?—Disparándole. El perro me miraba implorante de esos ojos dulces, inocentes, me acompañará mientras viva, hasta el supremo instante en que la Muerte, compasiva, decida borrármela.—Yo no soy capaz de matarlo—me dijo Alexis.—Tienes que ser—le dije.—No soy—repitió. Entonces le saqué el revólver del cinto, puse el cañón contra el pecho del perro y jalé el gatillo. La detonación sonó sorda, amortiguada por el cuerpo del animal, cuya almita limpia y pura se fue elevando, elevando rumbo al cielo de los perros que es al que no entraré yo porque soy parte de la porquería humana. (The dog looked at me imploringly with these sweet, innocent eyes that will stay with me as long as I am alive, until the instant in which Death, compassionately, decides to erase it for me.—I am not capable of killing the dog—Alexis said to me.—You have to do it—I said.—I can't do it—he repeated. Then I took the revolver out of his belt, I put the barrel against the dog's chest and pulled the trigger. The detonation was almost silent, muffled by the animal's body, whose pure and clean soul was elevating, lifting toward dog heaven, which I will never get to see, because I am part of this worthless and despicable humanity.)[46]

The scene is central to the depiction of the relationship between the aesthetic government and the disposable body. It is a scene in which the exclusionist grammarian and the disposable body have to look in the mirror and to a large extent reverse roles. Both come to terms with the fact that they value the life of a dog more than they value members of the "porquería humana." Alexis, who at this point has killed without hesitation or regret, knows instantly that he is not capable of bringing himself to kill a dog. The street dog falls out of lettering and developmentalist projects and therefore falls out of both characters' cognitive schema. The dog is not so much unlettered as it is unweighted by the state. It is not assigned a positive or negative value; it is neither lettered nor unlettered, neither of social import nor disposable. Alexis values the dog more than he values his peers, because that is the discursive tendency that he has internalized. He treats the dog with real human sentiment, with pre–governmentally coded affect. Yet he views himself, his fellow *sicarios*, and the taxi driver whom he kills just pages earlier through the prism discourses that mark the unlettered body as disposable. Following the scene, Fernando himself concludes, "El Estado en Colombia es el primer delincuente" (The Colombian state is the biggest criminal).[47]

The market and Colombia's entrance into economic globalization are not spared Fernando's ire, and through Alexis, we witness a foundational problem for the average urban citizen in '80s and '90s Colombia: on one side, there is a free-market system to which subjects like the *sicario* gain access through illicit infrastructure built up around the narco industry, leading to its own devaluation of human life and the overvaluation of commodities; on the other, there is a state that has, since its inception, used the negative example of the unlettered and disposable body to grant itself authority and primacy. Fernando addresses the reader: "¿Cómo puede matar uno o hacerse matar por unos tenis? preguntará usted que es extranjero. Mon cher ami, no es por los tenis. Es por un principio de Justicia en el que todos creemos." (How can someone kill for a pair of tennis shoes, the foreign reader may ask. Mon cher ami, it isn't for the tennis shoes. It is for the principles of Justice in which we all believe.)[48] Fernando's statement sardonically alludes to the justice of the market and the state, while at the same time pointing to the tensions between the local and the global. He addresses the reader, presumably a foreigner, as if he is our guide, there to highlight how wrong our own forms of justice have gone in his home country. He points to the skewed value system at play among Colombia's urban populations and implies that at the edge of economic and aesthetic modernity, universal systems—be they rooted in a Kantian aesthetic *logos* that will develop into civilized lettered polis or in a liberal economic model that will lead to a bucking economy and a global narcotics industry that is not recognized by universal institutions despite its remarkable sophistication as a global industry—need to be rethought. As much as Fernando makes off-the-cuff remarks about the fault of Colombia's impoverished subjectivities, both the market's and the government's failure to assign their citizens any value confound him. Fernando comes to the conclusion along with the reader that if the urban subject is not a consumer (economic citizen) or a lettered, productive subject (political citizen), then, according to the dominating symbolic orders of urban Colombia, they are as valuable as cadavers as they are as living humans. For all of his superficial anger, Fernando is just as shocked about this as anyone.

While Fernando's relationship to the *sicario* places him in a position of privilege, he never gains a sense of stability or social potency through time spent with Alexis and Wilmar. On the contrary, every time he attempts to assert his authority or control over the *sicarios*, he is surprised by either the way that they culturally slip out of his control or the extremes of their alternative social order. Beyond the allusions to the pederastic issues that have haunted the Catholic Church, Fernando's amorous connection to the *sicarios* is more complex than the visceral reaction it evokes. For Hermann Herlinghaus, Fernando's relation to the *sicario* has five facets, and only one of them shows signs of any erotic tendencies. For Herlinghaus, in Fernando we read resonances of the paternal figure, of the agent who marks the tension between the global and the local, of Fernando as a witness to the violence that surrounds the *sicario*, of the grammatical standard that clashes with colloquial, mediated culture, and of the contrast between stable male and female gender roles.[49] But only when Fernando stands in as the paternal figure of the *sicario* do we read any erotic tension, in the vein of Fernando as simultaneous totem and taboo. Fernando attempts to assert his authority as the new order, that which replaces the absence of state and market, and he draws the *sicario*'s libidinal drive, which at once adheres to Fernando's order and constantly challenges it. This paternal eros has religious undercurrents that play off the double of *padre* as "father"—any stabilizing *padres* are noticeably absent from the *sicarios'* lives in the novel, with Fernando even going so far as to try to track down Alexis's father after Alexis is killed, with no success: a moment that accentuates the absence of other citizen-evoking institutional frameworks—and *padre* as "priest." For Herlinghaus, there is something eerily shepherd-like and self-affirming in Fernando's preoccupation with giving form to the social relations of Alexis and Wilmar: "Mientras Vallejo esconde la historia de vida del sujeto autobiográfico, releva la autoría autoconsciente, capaz de conocer y, por lo tanto, de dar forma en el discurso, al más alto resultado del sí mismo. Una misión superior es más importante que una memoria imperfecta. Fernando ha decidido actuar como un misionero." (While Vallejo hides his autobiographical subject, he reveals a sort of stream-of-conscious self, capable of laying out in discursive form his best self. A higher mission is more important than an imperfect memory. Fernando has decided here to act as a missionary.)[50] Fernando is the only paternal entity that assigns the *sicario* anything more than temporary value; yet he does so under the terms of perversion. He attempts to stabilize memory and to act as a witness, a meaningful listener, yet he cannot show the necessary dispassion to be an external bearer of justice. He attempts to give order to the *sicarios'* shifting symbolic world but only realizes that the *logos* that he represents does not gain traction in the *sicarios'* cosmology.

Fernando brings to the surface the until then difficulty of the Colombian market, state, and church to evoke a functioning urban citizenry. As he stands in for the regime of letters, ramping up globalization, and a shepherding yet pederastic *padre*, he turns the critique in on himself. He is not so much a fascist, postglobalized *costumbrista* as he is a failed shepherd in need of a change of tack. *La virgen de los sicarios* shifts away from the tendency in the urban novel to use the somatic metaphor of an already mutilated body, and in Vallejo's rendering, we actually watch the body atrophy before our eyes. If there is a shocking cadaver at the start of the novel, it comes in the form of the scar tissue of failed institutions. The metaphor of society as body is complicated when the body acts out the crime scene that leads to Fernando's social surroundings. When he is shocked by the state of his home city after a sojourn abroad, Fernando takes on all of the characteristics of Colombia's governing bodies and reenacts their social relations with the *sicario*, a transmodern subjectivity born out of the overlapping and largely conflicting sociopolitical discourses in twentieth-century Colombia. Fernando's attempt to assign the *sicario* value, to socially save him, to use the religious terminology that acts as an undercurrent throughout the novel, or to meaningfully letter his body, unsurprisingly fails. Fernando as much as anyone realizes by the end of the novel that the *sicario* is a subject that only resonates temporarily, that he is only of value when he is assigned a place in the political economy of narco-cartel urban Colombia. As in Salazar's *No nacimos pa' semilla*, *La virgen de los sicarios* does not lead the reader to question why the young boys have turned to the *sicariato* in the first place; that, if anything, is clear. We realize that they are institutionally orphaned. They are unlettered and disposable according to the discourses of market and state and only find temporary stability and meaningful intersocial relations through the anomic culture that they find in an appendage of the drug trade. As Fernando acts out the double movements of the social bodies that have historically excluded them as much as embraced them, we look on as the soma of both *sicario* and citizen tragically come apart.

Always playing on the tension between global and local epistemologies, Vallejo uses the at once nationally resonant and universally poignant philosophies to frame *La virgen de los sicarios*. He uses a double time to compare ideas of progress and cyclical stagnation. When Fernando unknowingly replaces Alexis with his killer, Wilmar, we read an obvious metaphor of cyclical violence that, whether Vallejo would admit it or not, resonates in the key of Buendía. Yet the cyclical nature of two competing bodies is stripped of its ideological pretense and is depicted simply as two young subjects who act out of basic survival. When Wilmar kills Alexis and is eventually killed himself, Vallejo carries the subject of the *sicario*, and Colombia in microform, to its logical end. But Vallejo also alludes to a linear time. He uses the metaphor of the river to both undergird the theme of Heraclitus's *logos* and to allude to the importance of the river in the Colombian archive. The river, through which time flows, in which cadavers memorialize the extremities of the Violence, where Eustasio Rivera's party travels before being swallowed by wilderness, returns to the polis in *La virgen de los sicarios*, where it overflows and reminds us of the failure of the lettered city to conquer the feral wilderness used as the barbaric negative in the evocation of the lettered city. The river of time and the progressive path of a singular stream do not flow from the European *huerta* into Colombia, nor do they represent a path of development. On the contrary, Vallejo's treatment of this very Colombian theme approaches the river as a poetic symbol of abandonment. In Vallejo's Medellín, aesthetic, religious, and market flows do not end in a rational, ideal tributary but overflow into excess, unquiet, and violence, as the river of time is replaced by a vexed Fernando pleading with an unknown interlocutor to stem the flow of Colombian violence: "Mientras en las comunas seguía lloviendo y sus calles, ríos de sangre, seguían bajando con sus aguas de diluvio a teñir de rojo el resumidero de todo nuestros males, la laguna azul, en mi desierto apartamento sin muebles y sin alma, solo me estaba muriendo, rogándoles a los de la policlínica que le cosieran, como pudieran, aunque fuera con hilo corriente, a mi pobre Colombia el corazón." (While in the poor neighborhoods it kept raining, and in their streets, rivers of blood kept flowing and tainting with red a reminder of all of our collective misdeeds, in the blue lagoon, my empty apartment without furniture and without soul, I was dying, begging the doctors at the clinic to suture, even if just with common thread, my poor Colombia's heart.)[51]

The Colombian iteration of the aesthetic border was not born out of a vacuum. When the Colombian state of exception based in an aesthetic modernism that is rooted in European affective registers at the end of the nineteenth century evolves into a mediated polis where new literary tendencies challenge the primacy of lettered idyll, the lettered city begins to reveal its inherent theoretical flaws. In the roughly sixty years that separate the Colombian regime of letters, in its most potent form under the presidency of Antonio Caro, and the birth of the *novela de la Violencia* as a genre, we observe a shift away from a literary aesthetics that bolsters the authority of a privileged Colombian class into a form that at once gives archival representation to the new subjectivities that follow mass migration to the city during the first half of the twentieth century and works through the collective trauma that failing urban, political, and physical infrastructure cause during the same period. As the "barbarian" other, used to prop up civilization and barbarism paradigms, moves to the city, urban aesthetic systems have to come to terms with a morphing urban visual economy that undoes the fabric of an aesthetics of privileged distancing.

The *novela de la Violencia* evolves into the multiple resonances of the contemporary Colombian urban novel (the *novela urbana*), with subcategories in the Colombian noir novel, the *narco-novela*, and a new gritty urban realism that comes in the form of both cinema and prose. As aesthetic registers shift and the lettered city matures into what I have referred to as the *mediated city*, governmental discourses move away from a semantics of the "lettered" and "unlettered" citizen to that of the "meaningful" and "disposable" body. The change in dominant discourses signals a movement from an idyll based in an aesthetic state to that of the global economy, displacing subjects who do not fit into either schema at first as "unlettered," nonaesthetic citizens and then as "useless," non-consuming citizens. While the *novela de la Violencia* works through the socio-political issues surrounding the crises of the urban and unlettered body, the *novela urbana* works toward a representation of the "cuerpo desechable."

The most interesting subjectivity born out of the political economy of con-temporary Colombia is the *sicario*, a telling icon that, as Salazar argues, is a concise representative of the conflicting social political discourses of the Colom-bian state, the Catholic Church, and global economics. Yet the *sicario* has also proved to be a difficult and highly controversial subject to represent in literary terms, with the two most ambitious attempts coming in Salazar's *No nacimos pa' semilla* and Vallejo's *La virgen de los sicarios*. While both texts come together in many ways, the varying treatments of the *sicario* pull from widely differing approaches, one based in a documentary-style realism and the other in a hyper-realist poetics that almost fantastically attempts to collapse Colombia's entire history into the relationship between its narrator, Fernando, and his two *sicario* lovers, Alexis and Wilmar. The intertextual resonances and the specters of Colombia's aesthetic past that come together in Fernando's relationship with the *sicario* and the late twentieth-century Medellín that acts as their stage make *La virgen de los sicarios* the most nimble representation of the crises of the aes-thetic and economic Colombian state and their relationship to the unlettered and disposable body. Through the relationship between Fernando and the *sicario*, together representatives of the failure of the civilized polis to conquer the feral Latin American landscape, civilization and barbarism standing face-to-face, Vallejo invites us to watch on, as the lettered city comes apart before our eyes.

4

Recasting the Colombian National Story after the Inrush of the World

The life and work of Juan Gabriel Vásquez sits at the crossroads of innovation and cliché. As a writer who has been deemed the new Colombian literary star, this is a bold space to occupy. Colombia, more so even than Latin America in the broader sense, is a country whose relationship with both cliché and innovation is both quotidian and never-ending. Vásquez stands out within his life and times because he took what, in another era, would have been considered a well-worn path to becoming a novelist. It was not until Vásquez was in the final phases of law school, on the brink of entering into a lucrative and stable profession, that he opted to become a writer. While out of step with the more notable path of teenage prizes to the study of literature at the undergraduate level to an MFA, usually in the United States, and festivals put together by Latin American embassies for their young literati, there is something familiar, if not decidedly old school, about Vásquez's path to the letters. His law-to-literature transition puts Vásquez in the world literary company of Goethe, Kafka, and Tolstoy, while more locally it is part of his nation's charter that all participants of government will be well versed in both law and letters. That he finds innovation by embodying the national charter is metonymic to the paradoxes that drive Vásquez's work.

Among these paradoxes is Vásquez's desire to write national novels from outside of Colombia. Perhaps there is no more prominent act in the Latin American literary canon than to write national literature from elsewhere. One need not strain too hard to rifle through the most prominent literary movements to come out of Latin America, such as *modernismo* and the Boom, whose writers wrote largely from Europe. By equal measure, foundational intellectuals such as Domingo Faustino Sarmiento and Simón Bolívar wrote some of the region's most important philosophical and political treatises while abroad. Yet Vásquez, who was born in 1973, does not adhere to the more common experience of "staying home" within his Gen X, post-McOndo and post-Crack, cohort. With regard to image, the contrast struck between Vásquez and these other groups is stark. While the Gen X projects an aesthetics of cosmopolitanism-from-home, be it through television shows such as the *Jaime Bayly Show*, New Wave–inspired cinema such as the films of Alberto Fuguet, or among the editorial boards of *Etiqueta Negra* or *El Malpensante*, Vásquez is like a relic.

Somewhere between what Mariano Siskind calls the Latin American writer's "desire for the world" and the fresh excitement of being able to write from one's home city as if one were writing from Paris is the crux of Vásquez's writerly existence; and it is a telling indicator of his wider oeuvre. Indeed, with Vásquez, we are more in an in-between space that is neither the Latin American writer who craves Paris nor, to paraphrase how the young Peruvian writer Alonso Cueto recently put it, someone who realized that great novels could take place in Latin America, not just London, Paris, or St. Petersburg. Vásquez is a writer who writes about Medellín and Bogotá as if they were Hugo's Paris or Dickens's London, but what complicates the matter is that he does so *from abroad*. He is not the sort of writer who desires elsewhere and wants to shrug off home spaces.[1] This is a canonical calculation that is not lost on Vásquez, who himself describes the Boom when he says:

> Yes, they were all expatriates and they were all obsessed with reinventing their countries in literature. Take Mario Vargas Llosa, Carlos Fuentes. The great novels about Peru were written in London and Paris. The great novels about Mexico were written in Paris and New York. *One Hundred Years of Solitude* was written in Mexico. It's a Latin American cliché. Obviously, the Boom writers didn't invent this: in the 19th century Rubén Darío was the first to believe that being in Paris would make him a poet. He more or less found the same thing that I found, that the literary world in Paris didn't want him to write about modern life, about life in the boulevards. They wanted Darío to write about the Latin American landscapes.[2]

In Vásquez's paradoxically well-established place as a writer and intellectual who is an outsider among his generation, he is a strange candidate to write the new Colombian national novel. This is an undertaking that itself is rife with paradoxes. Is a time when we are roundly, from theory to economic practice, venturing into the postnational really the time to write national literature? Is the national novel not something already covered in the nineteenth through mid-twentieth century by Colombian figures ranging from Jorge Isaacs to José Eustasio Rivera and Gabriel García Márquez? The critic would be, and has been, inclined to agree with these points: that the twenty-first century, when free-trade agreements blur borders and the problems that plague nationhood, especially concerning the Colombian narco-industry, is emphatically postnational. This is what makes Vásquez's undertaking so audacious. It is a bold choice to write national literature in times of global interface, placing a wager on oneself as a writer to have the deft skill to reconstitute the national story, when it was long ago diasporically scattered across the globe.

There is a calculated resistance to romance in the refiguring of the national story in Vásquez's work, which otherwise addresses timeless themes of violence, rebirth, the dense past, and a hopeful future. To do so in a way that does not fall into generational squabbling over form or the triumphant return of an intellectual from abroad who is ready to revisit and reconfigure their homeland in itself is innovative within the contemporary Colombian canon. What makes *The Sound of Things Falling* and *The Informers* stand out is that the novels turn on the most iconographic and emotionally charged moments in Colombia's modern history—the Bogotazo, the bombing of Avianca Flight 203 by Pablo Escobar's Medellín Cartel in 1989, and the dissident countryside that spills into paramilitary and guerrilla wars, as well as the narco-industry—that is touching but not maudlin or gushing. In these novels, Vásquez addresses Colombia's traumatic history frontally, neither flinching nor romanticizing. When the setting is rural, time and space adhere to the same principles as they would in the city. When the theme is violence, each bullet wound or piece of shrapnel cuts equally. When the frame is historical, the same rules that govern the universe guide Antioquia and Cundinamarca.

Vásquez's booming climaxes are born out of his remarkable subtlety. *The Sound of Things Falling* and *The Informers* are studies in pace and tone. Given the media speed of the author's surroundings and the dynamism of his subject matter, the choice to allow themes and emotions to build slowly in both works is a bold one. It is, also, a craft that requires a great deal of talent and study. In the era of limited-character-per-post social media, *longue durée* and deep works on a theme that is felt in the beating hearts of millions of people on a daily basis is a daring undertaking, not dissimilar in boldness to García Márquez's tonal and formal choice of sweeping romanticism. In parabolic contrast, one could go so far as to claim that while García Márquez's maximalism is only held together by the bounding glue of a foundational mythology and nostalgic nods to the past, Vásquez presents a strict realism, whose sober tone does not buck until it explodes. García Márquez's work is an explosion seeking its former, singular composition. Vázquez's is a latent detonation hoping to better understand its very composition and place in the world.

Part of Vásquez's mastery comes from his insistent study of word literary contemporary authors. In keeping with the post–Generation of '72 break with a Latin American literary tone that steeps itself in its own canon, Vásquez is as much at home with the currents of Ian McEwan or Jonathan Franzen (with whom he is often compared) as he is with Carlos Fuentes or Laura Restrepo. This is nothing that the Crack or McOndo generations have not asserted themselves, but there is something to the comfort in style that is both emphatically Colombian in subject and world literary in form. Vásquez may feel liberated by his peers' previous declarations that they are as much a part of the global canon as heirs to the Boom, but the mere fact that he is not known for saying that he is not strictly a Latin American writer but is an author whose works simply bear that out puts him at the head of a curve of post–Gen X and after-Bolaño writers who are doing the same.

At every cross-section of form, life, and literary project, there is, in Vásquez's work, an outsider's insiderness, one that acts as a poetics born out of the aesthetic border. He is old-fashioned for his cohort, yet his work is exemplary of his generation. His path to a literary career traveled the well-established route to world letters of the law degree first and literary studies in Paris second, yet he is at odds with the times. He writes national novels at a time when the nation is, theoretically and stylistically, considered to be a footnote to history. The critic must wonder if this is the secret to Vásquez's reception: if to be out of fashion and high register in a culture steeped in the popular, to write slow-building novels in a time of cinematic pace and speed, and to incorporate known elements of previous Latin American generations in a time of socioeconomic and experiential novelty is a nod to the deeper flows of time that surround Colombia's slow unfolding as a country. Not dissimilar to Gabriel García Márquez's or Fernando Vallejo's placement of the frenetic cultural and political present in relief against the eternally flowing river of time, there is a broad view in the work of Vásquez that gestures toward the larger scope of humanity; and, as is the case in García Márquez's and Vallejo's work, it is both comforting and dizzying.

In what follows, I analyze two of Vásquez's works that I consider to be his "national novels," *The Sound of Things Falling* and *The Informers*. As telling as they are untimely, these works offer alternatives to the literary responses to globalization, a violent national history, and the narco-industry in the works explored in previous chapters. In contrast to urban, Violence-era, and narco-novels, these national novels take a wider view of the nation, its tropes, and unfulfilled promises from the long view. There are fewer attention-grabbing corpses in the opening sequence and more case studies in national promises rooted in mythology older than the 1886 constitution: a reexamination of nationhood from the pushing and pulling at the aesthetic border.

The theoretical approach to this chapter revisits the now readily explored "Foundational Fictions" framework put forward by Doris Sommer in 1984.

This may feel out of fashion, but given Vásquez's own insistent anachronism to refigure the nation, I consider Sommer's argument, when complemented by more recent approaches to literary theory, to be a beneficial guide. When Sommer argued in *Foundational Fictions* that the nineteenth-century literary archive did as much as any other cultural or institutional apparatus to help invoke a citizenry in bourgeoning nation-states, she was on the theoretical precipice of the postnation. Her work is not so much a celebration of the Latin American nation as it is a postmortem. As national economic and cultural borders buckled, and theorists began to question what purpose the nation-state actually served in an era of free-trade agreements and cultural globalization, Sommer examined the cultural building blocks on which Latin American nations were formed. Romances, and particularly works that turned on "will they, won't they?" courtships that spanned divisions in class, race, and cosmology were supposed to, symbolically at least, help guide young nation-states to a brighter collective future. In retrospect, and in the light of the fractious present, this theory is not without its critics. The foundational relationships, in their amorous shrugging off of old symbolic hierarchies, do not, in fact, recharter the populace. True love, in short, does not always conquer all.

The innovation in my approach comes in the analysis of Vásquez's "national narrative," which stands in contrast to his gestures toward a more profound envisioning of what it means to be Colombian that lurks at the edges of the framed nation. There is something insistently post-postnational in Vásquez's encircling of nationhood after the storm, something that rounds up all the clichés and the inhabitants of diasporic nationhood and tries to draw a boundary around them. There is on Vásquez's behalf, in other words, an attempt to reconstitute the nation in his own right. This places Vásquez in the interesting terrain between nineteenth-century realist writer and postglobalization Gen Xer. He addresses what Ericka Beckman has referred to as the "export reverie" of the incipient period of Latin American globalization and the constitutive aesthetic force that attempted to define nationhood a priori to, if not beyond the scope of, the economic world. Vásquez picks up the pieces of the nation and asks if we are trapped in a cyclical history or if Colombia's national promises are coming true. Does the economic present augur an emergence, as allusions to an Andean Silicon Valley might indicate, or are we in a rebooted moment of export reverie whose structural makeup is composed more of code than rubber?[3] In *The Sound of Things Falling* and *The Informers* Vásquez perhaps writes a national story that, while heeding the warnings of the booms and busts of the past, considers Colombia ready to emerge. This is a milieu that Beckman describes when she claims, "Although Latin America has frequently played the sleepy backwater to the dynamic centers of industrial Europe, the time has come, I think, to reposition this region's cultural production at the vanguard, and not the rear guard, of the history of global capital" (xviii)[4] One must wonder if Vásquez goes beyond the nineteenth-century Latin American novel or if he simply writes peripheral national literature by revealing to the global literati what the national novel might look like in the twenty-first century.

Bombs Bursting in the Bright Night Sky: Juan Gabriel Vásquez's Post-Escobar Novel

Like *One Hundred Years of Solitude*, the novel that all contemporary Colombian writers push against, *The Sound of Things Falling* is a tale about a family whose life is intertwined with the national story. This is not the facile sort of family-for-nation, nation-for-continent synecdoche that is well trod both in South and North America, however. On the contrary, *The Sound of Things Falling* gestures toward the family novel, only to show that when things fall apart, they do so in a way that resists the sweeping romanticism of hundred-year intervals, distant battlefields, and glossy tones that pull one's attention away from the materiality and matter-of-factness of violence. Vásquez assures his readers as much, when he begins the novel with allusions to a Macondean world in which hippopotamuses run rampant in the wild, playing with a semantics that would conjure images of an overflowing menagerie that would feel familiar to readers with a background in magical realism. As remote as this opening narration feels, however, Vásquez lets material historicism do the narrating when showing that this particular hippo happened to belong to Pablo Escobar and was killed by a sniper with a .375-caliber rifle after Escobar's death. Historical detail immediately, within the opening paragraph, supplants fantastical notions of the jungle, and Vásquez sets a tone that is going to both parallel García Márquez's claim that, in his gravity-defying magical realism, he never wrote anything that was not part of a real Colombian archive and show us that this novel is going to pierce that fantasy, just as the rifle's bullet does the "thick skin" of a hippopotamus that has run wild in the national imaginary.[5]

Vásquez drags the tropes of the hyperbolic national story into the twenty-first century with a nineteenth-century verve. The description of the hippo run amok is recounted by the Bogotá-based narrator, Antonio Yammara, who watches the sequence on television with the same distance as other viewers all over the world. He may be entangled in the event emotionally, but he maintains the same physical distance, as he would if he were watching the scene unfold from another country. Vásquez lets the reader know as early as the opening sequence that this is a realist novel. Borrowing from a stylized literary national experiment that would resonate within the Hispanic canon with the likes of Benito Pérez Galdos, Vásquez sets a scene filled with intriguing yet plausible characters and lets the laws of existential and experiential physics take over. Underscored in a bar in which the narrator meets the mythology-infused historical figure around whom the novel revolves, Ricardo Laverde, this is a story of people and objects bumping into one another. As the narrator and Laverde play billiards in the folkloric and densely urban Candelaria neighborhood of Bogotá at the beginning of the novel, the narration alludes to as much: "El billar no era para él un pasatiempo, ni una competencia, sino la única forma que Laverde tenía en ese momento de estar en sociedad: el ruido de las bolas al chocar" (Billiards wasn't a pastime, nor a competition, but the only way Laverde had at that time to be in society: the sound of the balls crashing).[6] Amid neon lights, televisions humming in the background, and urban billiards parlors, cut by the hallmark events of the life and death of Pablo Escobar circulating in the historical imaginary of the narrator, Vásquez makes sure that the reader knows that this is going to be a novel not about levitating but about falling: the weight of history falling through the safety net of romanticism; commercial airplanes falling through the night sky; bodies falling to the sidewalk in Colombian cityscapes; and families falling apart.

The intrigue in *The Sound of Things Falling* turns on the narrator's attempt to decipher the enigmatic figure that is Laverde. With the novel having one foot in the Colombian noir aesthetic described in chapter 3, there are hooks in *The Sound of Things Falling* not dissimilar to those found in crime fiction. This narrative vehicle is populated with the tropes and traumas, hallmarks and hallowed ground, of the Colombian '80s and '90s, which are used to work through, in a remarkably careful way given the entertainment value of the novel, the knots in the sinew of the national body. From the time that the narrator meets Laverde, there is a weight of unknowing that burdens the narrator and reader: Does Laverde hold a truth that will unlock the understanding of traumatic events, namely, the Avianca Flight 203? Does he have connection to the narco-trade or perhaps to the narrator? Is he a spy, set to infiltrate popular spaces and disrupt collective memory? This mystery is redoubled by the fact that we find out in the first chapter, and through the retrospective first-person narration, that Laverde was killed in 1996. In a shared tendency with writers of Colombian noir, there is an appearance of a dead body early on, and the schematics of the somatic metaphor hold true. This is, in other words, not an attempt to breach a divide through romance or befriending but a post facto analysis of a crime scene that has deep roots.

What sets *The Sound of Things Falling* apart is that it is not a mere crime novel. The work's innovation is that it combines the noir novel with the family novel. The formal tension born out of trying to square the two otherwise differing tones and plots is where *The Sound of Things Falling* finds its energy. Throughout the novel, the narrator attempts to trace the cause of Laverde's death while coming to grips with the fact that he will soon become a father. Antonio finds out soon after Laverde's death that his wife, Aura, is expecting a baby, leading to a double grasping, toward the past in one direction and toward the future in the other. The narrator could be describing either when he says about his unborn child, "Sentía que estaba a punto de transformarse en una criatura nueva y desconocida cuyo rostro no alcanzaba a ver, cuyos poderes no podía medir, y sentía también que después de la metamorfosis no habría vuelta atrás. Para decirlo de otro modo y sin tanta mitología: sentía que algo muy importante y también muy frágil había caído bajo mi responsabilidad, y sentía, improbablemente, que mis capacidades estaban a la altura del reto." (I felt as though he were about to transform into a new and unknown being whose face I could not quite see, whose abilities I could not quite measure, and I felt that after the metamorphosis there would be no going back. To put it another way and without so much mythology: I felt that something very important and at the same time very fragile had fallen under my responsibility, and I felt that, improbably, I was up to the challenge.)[7] What this double framing does is allows for a post-Escobar narrative at a time when the nation is attempting to come to grips with the immediate past while beginning to envision a new national future. It is a narrative that captures the task of simultaneously naming both the rear view and the horizon. The metaphor of a young professional, an academic, who is called on to decipher the enigmatic past while awaiting a child born from an aptly named and equally mystical Aura is a clever plotline, one that arguably best typifies the novel of the post-Escobar era. It is, to put it most acutely, both postmortem and prenatal.

Vásquez uses his narrator to acknowledge the terms of the post-Escobar novel. It is a medium that addresses what everyone feels the visceral and intellectual impulse to discuss but that everyone is also tired of hearing. Here, perhaps, we are at a crossroads opposite to those of "national romances," though equally in a moment of national constitution. The use of a narrator who is a professor of jurisprudence supports this point. He attempts to teach justice to future generations but often feels that he does not have the vocabulary, or indeed energy, to do so, while he himself attempts to come to terms with the paradoxes of justice in the immediate aftermath of the narco-state. Aura claims to the narrator, "Con el tiempo la gente, mi gente, se acostumbró a esos llantos momentáneos, y cesaron las palabras de consuelo, y los abrazos desaparecieron, y la vergüenza fue mayor entonces, porque era evidente que yo, más que producirles lástima, les resultaba ridículo" (With time, people, my people, got used to these occasional moments of weeping, and consoling words began to fall by the wayside, and the hugs dried up, and shame felt larger then, because it was evident that I, more than making them cry, was beginning to seem ridiculous).[8]

These scenes of giving up and boundless trauma would make *The Sound of Things Falling* appear to be a hyperbolic novel, a perception out of sorts with the novel's overall measure and poise. It is the allusion to the extremity of experience beyond the frame of the novel that gives the work its inner quiet. Even among the gunfire, the bullets, the things falling, there is a slow-paced resolve to make sense of it all. Part of this structural calm is the calculated resistance

to melodrama in the work. Given that few novels so roundly address the iconography of the Escobar era, it would be easy to produce a work that moved
quickly through an almost nostalgic trip of the '80 and '90s or that worked
toward a disingenuous or superficial catharsis. The proliferation of popular
telenovelas that play on similar tropes clumsily but enjoy wide viewerships
speaks to as much. There are two scenes in *The Sound of Things Falling* that act
as practical case studies in how to write a gripping sequence that treats a charged
moment of national history carefully and cautiously without losing anything
in the formal, or indeed entertainment, sense. The first of these scenes consists
of an imaginative rendering of the inside of a plane during a crash that has clear
allusions to Avianca Flight 203. One of the defter maneuvers in Vásquez's
handling of the scene is to focus on a single passenger on the plane, Laverde's
wife, Elena Fritts. In a treatment that is not out of step with the Colombian
noir's use of the somatic metaphor in order to resist the banalization of violence,
Vásquez allows a single story to stand in for the more widely affected group. It
is easier to understand from and to where Elena Fritts is traveling, who is wait-
ing for her, and whom she is leaving behind. It is easier to view not only the
presumptive tragedy comprising names flashing across screens across the world,
or a mass of bodies, but a human being with a past and notional future. It is
easier to come to terms, in the singular sense, with what is at stake when things
eventually fall.

The scene opens mundanely. The captain greets his passengers routinely, and
it is the precise mundane tone of the tableau that gives the scene its force. Violence, in this case, does not happen in a remote and difficult-to-sympathize-
with part of the Andes but literally and metaphorically erupts, like the fireworks
that explode in the dark night sky throughout the novel, against the backdrop
of the quotidian experience:

> "Quiero desear a todos unas vacaciones muy felices, y un 1996 lleno de salud y
> prosperidad," dice el capitán. "Gracias por haber volado con nosotros." Elena
> Fritts piensa en Ricardo Laverde. Piensa que ahora podrán retomar la vida
> donde la dejaron. Mientras tanto, en la cabina, el capitán le ofrece maní al
> copiloto. "No, gracias," dice el copiloto. El capitán dice: "Qué bonita noche,
> ¿no?." Y el copiloto: "Sí. Está muy agradable por estos lados." Luego se dirigen a
> la torre de control, piden permiso para descender a una menor altitud, la torre
> les dice que bajen al nivel dos cero cero, y luego el capitán dice, en español y con
> acento pesado: "Feliz Navidad, señorita." ("I want to wish everyone happy
> holidays, and a 1996 filled with happiness and prosperity," the captain says.
> "Thanks for flying with us." Elena Fritts thinks about Ricardo Laverde. She
> thinks that now they will be able to pick up life where they left off. In the
> meantime, in the cabin, the captain offers nuts to the copilot. "No, thanks," the
> copilot says. The captain says: "What a nice night, isn't it?" And the copilot:

"Yes, it's really nice around here." Then they steer toward the control tower, ask for permission to begin descent, and the tower tells them to go the level of two zero zero and the captain says in Spanish with a horrible accent: "Feliz Navidad, señorita.")[9]

By this point in the novel, a specter of intrigue and unquiet shadows the mundane. Following Laverde's death, the narrator finds a recording among Laverde's possessions that obliquely alludes to his participation in the bombing of the flight. That his wife was traveling to Colombia in order to rekindle her relationship with Laverde is the sort of heavy-handed narrative turn that could fall into the trappings of the maudlin. In this case, it is the same mundane detail that adds a sense of slow-building unease that roots the scene in the real experience of tragedy. Avoiding the flight of fancy of a scene that could otherwise trivialize a moment of national trauma, Elena Fritts's flight to Colombia is a mixture of slowly-falling-apart relationships and the prosaic routine of flight:

La mesa auxiliar está abierta; Elena Fritts ha querido cerrarla cuando el capitán ha anunciado el descenso, pero todavía nadie ha pasado a recoger su vasito de plástico. Elena Fritts mira por la ventanilla y ve un cielo limpio; no sabe que su avión está bajando a veinte mil pies de altura; no le importa no saberlo. Tiene sueño: son más de las nueve de la noche, y Elena Fritts ha comenzado a viajar desde muy temprano, porque la casa de su madre no queda en Miami propiamente, sino en un suburbio. O incluso en otro lugar completamente distinto, Fort Lauderdale, digamos, o Coral Springs, alguna de esas pequeñas ciudades de la Florida que son más bien gigantescos hogares geriátricos, adonde llegan los viejos del país entero a pasar sus últimos años lejos del frio y del estrés y de la mirada resentida de sus hijos. (The tray table was down; Elena Fritts wanted to close it when the captain announced their descent, but no one had come by to clear her plastic cup. Elana Fritts looks out the window and sees a clean sky; she doesn't know that her plane is descending from twenty thousand feet; she doesn't care. She is tired: it is after nine o'clock at night, and Elena Fritts began traveling very early, because her mom's house isn't in Miami exactly, but a suburb. Or actually in a completely different place, Fort Lauderdale, let's say, or Coral Springs, one of those little cities in Florida that are more gigantic retirement homes, where old people from all over the country go for the final years of their lives, far away from the cold, stress, and resentment of their children.)[10]

Foregrounding the life that extends beyond the pending tragedy, the description of Fritts's trajectory and the mother she left hours earlier is a detail in the careful setting of a tone that resists gloss. Fritts travels from visiting her mother not in Miami but in a geriatric suburb where there are not sleek nightlife or chiseled physiques populating beaches but an exterior that orbits distantly around a more glamorous existence. The age of Fritts's mother both puts in context what is at stake in the plane's bombing, a life long lived versus an untimely death, and goes to great lengths to present a scene of violence that is tonally and thematically very different from the party atmosphere of narco-tragedies that, one might posit, always struggles to resist a romance and joie de vivre rendering of the drug trade. These are not *sicarios* living fast in Medellín or traffickers partying with ocean views. The life at stake here is a young woman who has been visiting her aging mother in the quiet suburbs.

Vásquez's treatment of the plane crash posits that the extremity of a tremendous experience is best narrated by its contrast to the slow-paced tenor of day-to-day life. The perceived glamor that many times follows the recounting of tragedy, especially within narco-genres, tends to gloss over what is really at stake: actual bodies with mothers and daughters, basic routines and jobs that keep the world moving, and flights flown in economy class. The bomb that explodes on the plane is seen best when set against a serene and cloudless black sky: "El Boeing 757 ha bajado a trece mil pies dando giros a derecha primero y a izquierda después, pero Elena Fritts no se da cuenta. Es de noche, una noche oscura aunque limpia, y abajo ya se ven los contornos de las montañas." (The Boeing 757 has descended to thirteen thousand feet circling first to the right and then to the left, but Elena Fritts doesn't notice. It is a dark but clear night, and below she can already begin to see the outlines of the mountains.)[11] This is tragedy writ small. It is presented as a disruption of existence and balance. Its scale is personal. And embedded in the scene is a blueprint for how to treat mass tragedy at the beginning of the twenty-first century.

When the bomb does detonate, Vásquez neither attempts to embody the overwhelming and largely unrelatable experience nor offers visual or cinematic renderings of what could be a climactic moment. Taking a different tack altogether, the narration turns its gaze away and acknowledges the unseemliness of prying voyeuristically into the highly personal moment of death, even if the death does affect a wider political and national body:

> No hay nada tan obsceno como espiar los últimos segundos de un hombre: deberían ser secretos, inviolables, deberían morir con quien muere, y sin embargo allí, en esa cocina de esa casa vieja de La Candelaria, las palabras finales de los pilotos muertos pasaron a formar parte de mi experiencia, a pesar de que yo no sabía y todavía no sé quiénes fueron esos hombres desventurados, cómo se llamaban, qué veían cuando se miraban al espejo; esos hombres, por su parte, nunca habían sabido de mí, y sin embargo sus últimos instantes ahora me pertenecían y me seguirían perteneciendo. (There is nothing as obscene as spying on the last few seconds of someone's life; they should be secret, impenetrable, and should die with the dying, and yet there in the kitchen of that old

house in La Candelaria, the final words of the dead pilots became part of my experience, although I didn't, and still don't, know who those unfortunate men were; they also never knew about me, and yet their final moments now belonged to me and they will always belong to me.)[12]

The scene averts its gaze, and the visual sense fails altogether. It is the titular "sound of things falling" that the narrator adheres to: "Es el ruido de las cosas al caer desde la altura, un ruido interrumpido y por lo mismo eterno, un ruido que no termina nunca" (It is the sound of things falling from great heights, an uninterrupted and in itself eternal noise, a noise that never stops).[13] This sound encircles an experience of tragedy by refusing to dramatize it with a frontal yet distant gaze. In an attempt to refute the tragedy as is filtered through mass visual media, as is referenced as early as the opening bar scene and redoubled by the fact that the narrator himself recounts the experience on the basis of the black-box video of the crash that he found in Laverde's possessions, the narrator wonders if the obliqueness of sound compared to the visual is perhaps a more apt approach to conveying tragedy. Running in tandem with the already subtly posited notion that the Andes are best viewed in their silhouetted darkness, the narrator wonders if the averted gaze is not only the more tactful but also the most functional approach to understanding as practically and symbolically large a moment as a plane exploding in the sky. Even the averted gaze records an indelible message: "Desde que la cinta cayó en el silencio, desde que los sonidos de la tragedia cedieron el lugar a la estática, supe que habría preferido no escucharla, y supe al mismo tiempo que mi memoria seguiría escuchándola para siempre" (From the moment the tape fell silent, from the moment the tragic sounds gave way to static, I knew I would have preferred to never hear them, and I knew at the same time that my memory would hear them forever).[14]

A scene that complements the plane crash is a tableau of national celebration. In a sequence that captures an award ceremony for a lauded air force pilot, it is not surprising that the scene will defy expectations, beyond the tone already set in previous sections, and that it comes in a chapter titled "La mirada de los ausentes" (The gaze of those absent). Even the ocular sense of viewing is framed as "absent," and the scene's foregrounding emphasizes the sounds and smells, in keeping with the opaque national: "Y tal vez fue el ruido que hacía la gente, sus saludos entusiastas, sus conversaciones a gritos, o tal vez los olores mezclados que despedían sus alientos y sus ropas, el caso es que Julio se sintió de repente metido en un carrusel que giraba demasiado rápido, sintió que los colores sabían a algo amargo y que tenía pasto en la lengua" (Maybe it was the noise the people made, their enthusiastic greetings, their yelling of conversations, or maybe it was the mixed smells that their clothes and breath gave off, but all of a sudden Julio felt as though he were on a carousel that was spinning too fast; he felt as though colors had a bitter taste to them and that he had paste on his tongue).[15] This is not an edifying moment of national consolidation of a heroic figure filled with regalia and pomp. It is, according to the telling, a dizzying carousel that threatens to jettison even its eager attendees.

The unfolding scene consists of an air display, in which the national pilot will display his deft acrobatics. Paralleling the previous chapter, in which a plane is bombed and falls from the sky, the scene is structurally there to remind the reader of a time, presumably at least, when the Colombian government was symbolically strong. Within the novel, it is an attempt to reclaim the imaginary of the sky. The narco-industry may have created a milieu of chaos, but the sky is a place of order, and it is run by a Colombian government that not only has military might but can flaunt its skill as a form of dressage. Bogotá's elite attends the event, alongside the president and members of every governmental institution. This is a place to be seen, an event to have attended, as much for one's own reassurance. The event is narrated in the third person but follows the perspective of Laverde's grandfather Julio. In a tangle of national symbolism and mythology, it is implied that this is the moment, as recounted through endless family dinners that would follow, that encouraged Laverde to become a pilot, the ironic undercurrent being that it is heavily implied, at this point, that Laverde is entangled in the drug trade himself.

The scene is filled with charged imagery. There are eight pilots pirouetting in the sky above the presidential palace. The pilots disappear into the clouds and then reemerge acrobatically, slipping between one another. There is an undercurrent of unease that fills the scene that is not out of step with similarly resonant moments in Ian McEwan's *Enduring Love* or Roberto Bolaño's *Distant Star*, two contemporary authors to whom Vásquez has some formal indebtedness. The scene in relation to national celebration would be run of the mill, another humdrum celebratory exercise, if it were not that one pilot, named Abadía, did not break with the pack and aim at nadirs progressively closer to the onlooking crowd. As it is narrated: "—¿Qué está haciendo?—dijo alguien. El Hawk de Abadía venía en línea recta hacia donde estaban los asistentes.—Pero qué hace ese loco—dijo alguien más" ("What is he doing?" someone asked. Abadía's Hawk plane was aiming right for the crowd. "Is that guy crazy?" someone seconded).[16] Abadía's flight trajectory comes closer and closer to the crowd and the buildings surrounding it, until it occurs to Julio, who says out loud, though to no one in particular, in reference to the flag waving above the presidential palace: "Caray. Quiere coger la bandera" (My God. He is trying to touch the flag).[17] The plane swoops increasingly near the presidential palace, setting the audience, including the president, who are not sure if they are witnessing one of the most fluid commands of an aircraft in their nation's history or an act of terrorism, decidedly on edge. Abadía finally gets close enough to the palace to reach out and graze the Colombian flag before crashing into the diplomats' quarters of the presidential compound.

The weight of the moment is profound. It escapes the frame of typical lived experience by multiples. As is the case in the previous flight scene, Vásquez uses the moment to show that the author can encircle such moments of unquantifiable measure aesthetically. In what would feel like a highly visual display of acrobatics and tragedy, Vásquez minimizes the visual, opting instead to present the scene through the perspective of the crowd in a frenetic synesthesia:

> Las bocas abiertas como si gritaran. Pero no había gritos: el mundo se había callado. En un instante Julio comprendió que su padre tenía razón: el capitán Abadía había buscado terminar sus dos rollos pasando tan cerca de la bandera ondeante que pudiera coger la tela con la mano, una pirueta imposible dedicada al presidente López como un torero dedica un toro. Todo eso lo comprendió, y tuvo tiempo aun de preguntarse si los demás lo habían comprendido también. Y entonces sintió en los ojos la sombra del avión, cosa imposible porque no había sol, y sintió un soplo que olía a algo quemado, y tuvo la presencia de espíritu para ver cómo el caza de Abadía daba un salto extraño en el aire, se doblaba como si fuera de caucho y se precipitaba a tierra, destrozando al caer las tejas de madera de la tribuna diplomática, llevándose por delante la escalera de la tribuna presidencial y reventando en pedazos al chocar contra el prado."
> (Mouths opened as if screaming. But there were not screams: the world had fallen silent. In an instant Julio understood that his father was right: Captain Abadía had tried to finish his double roll so close to the waving flag that he could touch it with his hand, an impossible pirouette dedicated to President López, just as a bullfighter squares to a bull. He understood all of this, and yet he still wondered if everyone else understood too. And then he felt the plane's shadow fall across his eyes, which was impossible because the sun wasn't out, and he felt a gust of wind that carried the smell of burning, and he had the presence of spirit to observe how Abadía's trajectory gave a strange jump in the air, and turned sharply as if blowing a tire and fell to the earth, destroying the wood tiles of the diplomatic headquarters, continuing onto the staircase leading into the presidential palace, and exploding to pieces against the front lawn.)[18]

The scene is filled with not quite quantifiable and nameable measure. The screams that would help readers feel that they might begin to come to terms with the experience of the event never arrive. Members of the crowd open their mouths, but the screams do not come out. Even the sound of destruction is muted, and the visual detail of the plane comes through its shadow. Vásquez underscores this narrative encircling with the allusion to a bullfighter. The author attempts to come as close as possible to the actual violent act with an artistry of proximity. As Abadía lightly grazes the Colombian flag, so too would the bullfighter allow the bull to caress his cape, as Vásquez himself plays a cloak-and-dagger game with his reader. He wants us to come as close as possible to the climax of a scene that he knowingly cannot deliver as we expect it. The bull is not intended to reach the matador, but the event itself is in its close encounter. Vásquez leads us to think we are going to witness a larger-than-life experience through narrative, only to show that nearly, but not quite, reaching it is all the more profound. The plane's shadow, as Plato argued in frustration fifteen hundred years prior in *The Republic*, is the closest the artist can come to depicting the experience of the world. This is not an aesthetic principle from which Vásquez flees. This is something he celebrates.

The ironies at play in both airplane scenes, that of the flight bombing and that of the national celebration, add a tangled sense of moral ambiguity to the already complicated renderings of national hallmarks. It is Abadía's piloted acrobatics, as is recounted through generations of mythology at family dinners, that leads Laverde to become a pilot. This young boy, we realize at this point in the novel, will go on to use his piloting skills to become a drug runner. Similarly, the plane bombing that occurs as part of the narco-trade kills Laverde's wife. The calculated resistance of melodrama and structural irony in the story goes a great distance to show that within the teleological give-and-take of a nation, with micro industries entirely predicated on the narco-trade, every give implies a take, every winner begets a loser, and every celebration predicates mourning. This is not a socioeconomic milieu in which compounding capitalism opens avenues of upward mobility; it is more a pact with the world that implies the exportation of a chemical experience in exchange for capital and instability. Depicting the local ecosystem for the same world that consumes its product is not an easy one. Vásquez does so in the novel in a way that shows both that it can be done and how to do it. The scenes depict the national attempt to defy gravity. They show an attempt to pirouette with the world while caressing the nation. Yet the rules of physics take hold, and things fall.

Reforming the Clichés of Colombian Narrative

More than a blueprint for how to write scenes of national trauma, *The Sound of Things Falling* addresses the themes of memory and redemption that have been previously written to the extent of cliché within the Latin American canon, notably from dictatorial literature to the present. There is an evident working through in the novel that, similar to the scenes previously discussed, attempts to reform these regional and national tropes, without falling into the trappings of cliché. It nods toward convention without falling into it. The theme of memory is a prevalent one in the Colombian canon. With a society whose school-aged children are the first in generations to come of age during a time of relative peace and outside the prevalence of the narco-trade (relatively speaking), the question of how to preserve a memory while pivoting into a more hopeful future is a salient one. *The Sound of Things Falling*, written amid this transition period and within the existential questioning of the post-Escobar era, does so by using a family structure that includes the injured narrator, himself harmed by a narco-related bombing, and the birth of his daughter, Leticia.

Tied together by the "sound" and "falling" motif, the otherwise expansive accumulation of narrative exercises builds toward a new post-Escobar national novel. Here, it is not the sound of planes or bodies falling but of a family relationship. The strain on the narrator's relationship after he is injured is presented as one of silences and tones. Resisting the melodrama of torrid affairs and slamming doors, this is a relational entropy, as affected by violence, that occurs by degrees of subtlety. The narrator describes his relationship with Aura as one of shifts in tone:

> "No, espera," traté de decirle, pero ya era tarde, ya se había desembarazado del auricular y me había dejado en manos de Aura, mi voz en manos de Aura, y mi nostalgia colgando del aire cálido: la nostalgia de las cosas que aún no se han perdido. "Bueno, ve a jugar," oí que le decía Aura con su tono más dulce, hablándole casi en susurros, una canción de cuna en cinco sílabas. Entonces me habló a mí, y el contraste fue violento: había tristeza en su voz, por más próxima que me sonara; había desencanto y también un velado reproche. ("No, wait," I tried to tell her, but it was too late; she had already pulled away from the earphone and had left me in the hands of Aura, my voice in the hands of Aura, and my nostalgia hanging in the hot air: nostalgia for things that still haven't been lost. "Okay, go play," I heard her say to Aura with a sweeter tone, speaking almost in whispers a five-syllable lullaby. Then she spoke to me, and the contrast was violent: there was sadness in her voice, intimate though it may have sounded, that brought with it a disenchantment and veiled reproach.)[19]

The ineffable quality of tonal distancing, of Aura's way of addressing their daughter as compared to the way she addresses him on the phone, frames the failing of the relationship in a measured and mature way. It is the sonic and oblique absence of the scene that motions toward a negative externality of life affected by violence. It is the sound, in this instance, of a relationship falling.

The family structure also presents an attempt to reconstitute the nation. The narrator and Aura's daughter, Leticia, give their actions a scene-setting quality. Antonio's attempt to retrace Laverde's life and to trace the thread of violence that ended in his own injury are an attempt to structure a new reality that will be inhabited by their daughter. This intergenerational thrust is a vehicle that gives what would otherwise be a crime novel a weightier feel. There is a multilayered attempt to reconcile with the past, to reform the individual and social body, and to reconstitute a nation for future generations. These upward thrusts are all undercut by entropic inevitability. As hopeful as the novel is, we are always aware as readers that this is a novel ultimately governed by the law of physics, and remembering and reforming are always acts of fighting gravity.

In the fifth chapter of the novel, "What's There to Live For?," the narrative turns to and Elena's relationship, and it is revealed that they too have a daughter. The narration focuses on Elaine's pregnancy and their experience trying to counterbalance the fast-paced life of the drug trade with the reality of expecting a child. This narrative tactic adds layers to the family-structured novel. It shows that future generations will be a tributary born out of varied memory flows. Children who will come of age in a post-Escobar era will hail from families with their own recountings and experiences of the '80s and '90s that will resist a singular memory. The narrative tactic also implicates Laverde in the hollowing out of a state that his daughter will inherit through the drug trade. Laverde attempts to rationalize his place within the socioeconomic structure of the narco-industry: "La voz de Ricardo cambió, hubo en ella un falsetto, algo impostado. 'La gente quiere un producto,' dijo. 'Hay gente que cultiva ese producto. Mike me lo da, yo lo llevo en un avión, alguien lo recibe y eso es todo. Le damos a la gente lo que la gente quiere.' Se quedó en silencio un segundo y añadió: 'Además, la cosa va a ser legal tarde o temprano.'" (Ricardo's voice changed and took on a projected falsetto. "People want a product," he said. "There are people who cultivate this product. Mike gives it to me. I take it in a plane. Someone receives it, and that's that. We give people what they want." He was quiet for a second and then added: "It's all going to be legal sooner or later, anyway.")[20] But Laverde himself realizes in a deeper way that he is momentarily pushing against the reality of things to come. At a luxury hotel, while he is on a drug run, he sits in a pool attempting weightlessness, yet he and Elaine are weighted down by the reality of physics:

> Elaine odió la presión que su propio peso ejercía sobre sus pantorrillas, odió la tensión que aparecía en sus muslos cada vez que subía cuatro escaloncitos de nada, odió que sus areolas pequeñas, que siempre le habían gustado, se agrandaran y se oscurecieran de repente. Avergonzada, culpable, comenzó a ausentarse de las reuniones diciendo que no se sentía muy bien, y se iba al hotel de los ricos para pasar la tarde en la piscina por el solo placer de engañar a la gravedad durante unas horas, de sentir, flotando en el agua fresca, que su cuerpo volvía a ser la cosa liviana que había sido toda la vida. (Elaine hated the pressure her own weight exercised against her calf muscles, hated the tension she felt in her thighs while walking up four simple floors, hated that her small areolas, which she had always liked, had gotten bigger and darker all of a sudden. Ashamed,

guilty, she began to skip meetings, saying she wasn't feeling well. She would go to a luxury hotel to spend the afternoon in the pool for the simple pleasure of fighting gravity for a few hours, to feel, floating in the fresh water, that her body was the light thing it had been all her life.)[21]

Elaine's pregnancy weighs down her and Laverde's experience. According to more glamorous renderings, they should be leading a fast-paced and luxury-filled life. Yet the physical demands of pregnancy have slowed them down, and psychologically, the weight of their child being heir to a nation whose infra-structure has built up around the narco-industry, no matter how matter-of-fact Laverde's understanding of the economics of the situation may be, begins to dawn on them. This metaphor of institutions that give and take is redoubled by the fact that Elaine and Ricardo begin to work with the Peace Corps as a way of running drugs. The two-way flow of institutions that are in the eyes of their practitioners supposed to bolster humanity but cave into the gravity of the drug trade shows the complexities of the geopolitics at stake; and the per-sonalized psychology begins to take hold when future generations are taken into consideration, be they the children of the narrator, who is trying to retrace vio-lence, or of Laverde, who attempts to successfully play the narco-industry to his advantage. The children add a new temporal dimension to the novel. What was once about remembering in the face of erasure is now just as much about reconstituting in the name of the future.

The setting of a coming-of-age structure for future generations takes on paternal airs when the narrator tracks down Laverde and Elaine's daughter, Maya, in order to inform her of her parents' past. That the chapter is titled "Arriba, Arriba, Arriba" (Up, Up, Up) implies that there will be a triumphant ending to a novel about the personalized trials and tribulations of the high narco era. The chapter's atmosphere and poetics belie this point, however. The opening lines of the chapter discuss the deception of maturity, the erosion of idealism in the world that parallels the natural decadence of the body. The nar-rator at this point has left his house after a fight with Aura and decides to track down Maya in her countryside home. The narrator's insistence on mak-ing contact with Maya, in order to fill in missing details about Laverde and Elaine's past, is the stabilizing force in an otherwise tumultuous trajectory. The only thing lending him any real sense of grounding is this project that works to build an architecture of the future.

The scene surrounding the narrator is at odds with this project. Everywhere he looks he is reminded of the decadence of real and institutional bodies, of memory, and of place. This entropy has a double edge, however. At times, it reminds the reader of the constant tending needed to keep memory alive. At others, it shows that there is a natural working through traumatic moments implied in the passage of time: that it takes active work to create a more hopeful future but that sites of trauma themselves erode. On a lark, Maya and the narrator visit Escobar's compound in the hills outside of Medellín. One of the most visible icons of the narco era, the former house is a site of charged memories and is a veritable symbol of Escobar's onetime eclipse of the Colombian nation. Yet it is also cathartic when they find Escobar's old house in ruins: "Desde 1993, cuando Escobar fue muerto a tiros sobre un tejado de Medellín, la propiedad había entrado en una decadencia vertiginosa, y eso, sobre todo, fue lo que vimos Maya y yo mientras el Nissan avanzaba por el sendero pavimentado entre campos sembrados con limoneros. No había ganado pastando en esos prados, lo cual, entre otras cosas, explicaba que el pasto estuviera tan crecido. La maleza devoraba las estacas de madera. En eso me estaba fijando, en las estacas de madera, cuando vi los primeros dinosaurios." (Since 1993, when Pablo Escobar was shot down on a roof in Medellín, the property had entered into vertiginous decline, and that, more than anything, was what Maya and I noticed while the Nissan advanced over the paved pathway between fields planted with lemon trees. He had not earned anything from plowing these meadows, which, among other things, explained why the pasture was so overgrown. Weeds devoured the wooden posts. I was fixing my gaze on the wooden posts, when I saw the first dinosaurs.)[22] The once symbols of dominance over the state, of the ability to have anything, and the Macondean nature of his personal menagerie have given way to natural decay or, as it is implied in the symbolism of the passage, gone the way of the dinosaurs. The interesting aspect is the cathartic nature of this decline. Witnessing Escobar, retrospectively, as a figure on the precipice of decline has a quality of memorializing and working through. Here, it acts as a visual eulogy that helps to bury the traumatic past: "Pero tal vez no fue nuestra decepción lo que nos sorprendió, sino la manera en que la vivimos juntos, la solidaridad impredecible y sobre todo injustificada que de repente nos unió: los dos habíamos venido a este lugar por la misma época, este lugar había sido para los dos el símbolo de las mismas cosas" (But maybe it wasn't our disappointment that surprised us so much as the way in which we experienced it together, the unpredictable and unjustified solidarity that above all unified us: we had both come to this place at the same time; this place had been for both of us a symbol of the same things.)[23] Shared trauma, it is implied, needs to be worked through collectively, and it needs to be worked through in order to set the stage for future generations. The only issue with this idea is that, as the narrator puts matter-of-factly as they explore the ruins of a narco past, "recordar cansa" (remembering is exhausting).[24]

This memorializing sets the scene for the novel's climax: the moment when the narrator replays the black-box recording for Maya. With the overt expressions of a generational and collective working through in the previous pages, the moment feels weighty, like a victim confronting their attacker. In keeping with the novel's tone, Vásquez focuses on the mundane serenity of the moments right before the bombing. Pilots navigate routinely; passengers think idly about their approach. When the bomb does explode, it is a sound that is not isolated to a plane in the sky but is a larger roar of history:

> La madrugada fresca se llenó con el llanto de Maya, suave y fino, y también con el canto de los primeros pájaros, y también con el ruido que era la madre de todos los ruidos, el ruido de las vidas que desaparecen al precipitarse al vacío, el ruido que hicieron al caer sobre los Andes las cosas del vuelo 965 y que de alguna manera absurda era también el ruido de la vida de Laverde, atada sin remedio a la de Elena Fritts. ¿Y mi vida? ¿No comenzó mi propia vida a precipitarse a tierra en ese mismo instante, no era aquel ruido el ruido de mi propia caída, que allí comenzó sin que yo lo supiera? "¿Cómo, también tú has caído del cielo?," le pregunta el Principito al piloto que cuenta su historia, y pensé que sí, también yo había caído del cielo, pero de mi caída no había testimonio posible, no había caja negra que nadie pudiera consultar, ni había caja negra de la caída de Ricardo Laverde, las vidas humanas no cuentan con esos lujos tecnológicos. (The fresh morning filled with Maya's crying, soft and fine, and also with the singing of the first morning birds; it also filled with the mother of all noises, the noise of lives disappearing into emptiness, the noise that the fragments of flight 965 made as they fell over the Andes that in some absurd way was also the noise of Laverde's life tied without remedy to that of Elena Fritts. And my life? My life did not start to fall to the earth in that exact moment. Was that not the sound of my own falling, that it all began there without my realizing it? "What, you also feel from the sky?" the Little Prince asks the pilot who tells his story; and I thought that yes, I also had fallen from the sky, but there was no way to witness my fall. There was no black box to be consulted, and by the same token there was no black box for Ricardo Laverde's fall. Human lives do not have such luxuries.)[25]

Somehow, set against the backdrop of eternal misdeeds, the narrator's own struggles are put into perspective. Formally, this turn toward the wider scope of the cosmos is impacting. After all of the small details and measured focus in times of otherwise-immense trauma, the narrator's realization that he is a largely powerless figure within the wide scope of the world, that he is a particle ricocheting physically off other particles, as implied in the billiards match of the opening pages, is oddly empowering. It is this realization that allows him to turn toward the future. It allows him to symbolically and literally, in this case, go home and begin to rebuild.

The Sound of Things Falling is the post-Escobar novel par excellence. It marks a moment of national reconciliation at a time when the theoretical world is conceived of as postnational. It rounds up all the clichés of Colombian testimonial and narco-literature and shows how to present them with a governing poetics. Formally, the novel plays a multilayered game that turns on the trope of gravity and entropy. Vásquez fights both, while acknowledging the inevitability of falling and failing. As the narrator's body slowly heals and he works through both psychological and physical wounding toward a sounder body, the overcoming brings with it the presence of the past. Always avoiding the pitfalls of the maudlin, Vásquez reminds us to the very end that, as the visual aspect of falling is best captured through sound, the reconstitution of actual and symbolic bodies is best presented alongside its vulnerability.

Colombia Meets the World

At the heart of Juan Gabriel Vásquez's *The Informers* (2009) is a set of calculated meditations on Colombia and its place in the cultural world. On the surface, *The Informers* is a World War II novel. As has been established by the Crack generation that directly precedes Vásquez, to write a novel about World War II, as did Jorge Volpi in *En busca de Klingsor* in 2008, as a Latin American is itself an act of provocation. Volpi's own stance, for instance, lies in the implication that the wider world expects Latin American writers to write Latin American novels, be they the magical or existential realism of the Boom or the dictatorial and exilic literature of the Generation of '72. Volpi's decision to write a novel set in World War II Paris, in other words, defies the expectation of a young Latin American author who tries to write the new great Latin American novel. Volpi's argument is that Europeans and North Americans can write novels set outside their natural habitat, so why can a Mexican not take up a European theme and setting without it speaking deeper truths about his home space?

One might argue that Volpi's rush to the world displays some continued dependence on cosmopolitan expectations, given its negative dialectical stance. If the world wants Mexican literature from a Mexican author, to defy that expectation outright remains entangled in cosmopolitan taste. Yet the provocation marks an inflection point in the way that Latin American writers view their relationship to the world of letters. The interesting moment, however, comes when the writer is not so concerned with negating global expectation but allows oneself to be sublated, or perhaps stranded between, the nation and the world. What happens when the writer either takes Latin American themes to Europe and North America or writes a global novel in the Latin American space? Here I argue that there is much more to be learned from the entanglement between Colombia and the world than by simply affirming or negating Latin America's place in the geocultural sphere. The subtler teasing out of Colombia's place in the world plays out in *The Informers*, as Vásquez sets a World War II novel in Colombia and retraces history from the local perspective, presenting the more productive literary vessel to reflect reality as it is lived and imagined. If Latin American literature is hung up on bouncing between orbital fields of the "core" and "periphery," then *The Informers* focuses on the gaps between the two constellatory pulls.

In a trope that is commonplace among Colombian realist writers after García Márquez, novels written from the late '80s to the present at least gesture toward the overflowing abundance of magical realism. The tendency is to set the romantic scene and then slash through it with an unexpectedly blunt realism. Perhaps as a means to hook cosmopolitan readers by playing to their expectations or perhaps reflective of jocular canonical play, the Colombian realist novel alludes to romance only to quickly reply with the tonic note of more real and more representative stories. This is the case in the urban novels discussed at length in chapter 3. It is the case in *The Sound of Things Falling*, analyzed earlier in this chapter. And it is the case in Vásquez's *The Informers*, a novel that could be described as Vásquez's diasporic novel.

The work begins with a familiar lack of measure that we might refer to as a Vásquez-styled reality check: "En la mañana del siete de abril de 1991, cuando mi padre me llamó para invitarme por primera vez a su apartamento de Chapinero, había caído sobre Bogotá un aguacero tal que las quebradas de los Cerros Orientales se desbordaron, y el agua bajó en tropel arrastrando ramas y tierra, tapando las alcantarillas, inundando las calles más angostas y levantando carros pequeños con la fuerza de la corriente, y llegó incluso a matar a una taxista desprevenida que se quedó atrapada, en circunstancias confusas, bajo el chasis de su propio taxi." (On the morning of April 7, 1991, when my dad called to invite me for the first time to his apartment in Chapinero, Bogotá had experienced such a torrential downpour that the ravines in Cerros Orientales flooded, and the water spewed over, sweeping branches and mud down the mountains, blocking drains in the city, and flooding the wide streets, carrying away small cars, and even going so far as to kill an unprepared taxi driver who got caught, in confusing circumstances, under the chassis of his own taxi.)[26]

The opening line is carefully constructed. It sets the scene: Who is the narrator's father, and why has the narrator never been to his father's apartment? It overflows both literally and metaphorically with nature: the streets are flooded, with a presumably unending rain. And it marks the weight of material reality: this flooding does not wash down unoccupied valleys but rushes through wide boulevards and upends cars. The human cost is not measured in hundreds of unknown characters but in taxi drivers, easily identifiable to an urban audience. Vásquez's innovation is that this expected flooding is not remote and provincial. It happens in the capital city. If part of the project of the contemporary Colombian novel is to reimagine nationhood in the twenty-first century, the blending of the two imaginaries, that of town and that of country, is a deft one. What is supposed to be so provincial as to be romantic, even to urban

Colombians, the natural overflowing of magical realism comes to the city and decorates the local experience. If magical realism is the prevailing aesthetic of rural Colombia, and the narco-novel is the prevailing aesthetic of urban Colombia, then Vásquez's post-Escobar novels are attempts to successfully wed the two.

If, as I argue earlier in this chapter, much of *The Sound of Things Falling* works to reimagine the Colombian national novel as the dust settles on a post-narco Colombia, then *The Informers* works in complementary fashion. In an effort reminiscent of Vásquez's previous works, the novel is an attempt to revisit and address all the major themes of Colombian culture and to weigh their value at the end of a violent and tumultuous twentieth century. Is violence still too fresh in the public's memory to address historical hallmarks ranging from the Medellín in the '90s to the Bogotazo of 1948? Does the Colombian intellectual's rite of passage to Europe bear weight in a moment when Colombian bodies travel more massively to seek refuge and to seek political exile than out of an act of lettering? These questions are the bedrock of the most salient contemporary literary works that attempt to reconstitute the nation in Colombian literature, and *The Informers* is at the heart of that project.

Given Vásquez's concern with approaching Colombian tropes after the nation's tumultuous entrance into globalization, it is no surprise that *The Informers* also borrows from the poetics and themes of the Colombian urban novel. Similar to the somatic metaphor that I describe in chapter 3, *The Informers* plays off the theme of entropy and decay of real and institutional bodies. Here, we witness the atrophy of memory that parallels the decline of a physical body, not in the immediate and abrupt way that we witness throughout the contemporary Colombian urban novel but as a matter of natural aging. An inversion of a coming-of-age tale, *The Informers* is about working through challenges while in the act of decline. In short, it is a somatic novel in slow motion. The novel is riddled with allusions to the aging of bodies, and again, as in *The Sound of Things Falling*, there is an attempt to fight the gravity of the world. Here, however, planes do not fall from the sky and relationships do not decay, but it is the more visceral stuff of body and memory that fade.

There is a race in the novel between fading memory and reconstitution, a philosophical problem that runs through Vásquez's work. If one can retrace memory, through what avenue? If one can conceive of nationhood, after one of the most violent periods in the history of the Americas, what do peace and justice look like? The literary maneuver used to address such weighty and expansive problems is to put them in the context of the individual. If, as is the case in the somatic metaphor, violence does not occur to thousands but to individuals whose psychology can be grappled with, then experiential and existential problems of a nation attempting to deal with trauma productively are more resonant. Or, as Gabriel Santoro, the protagonist of *The Informers* and arguably a voice for Vásquez, puts it,

> Que ciertas zonas de mi experiencia (en mi país, con mi gente, en este tiempo
> que me tocó en suerte) se me habían escapado, generalmente por estar mi
> atención ocupada en otras más banales, y quería evitar que eso siguiera
> sucediendo. Darme cuenta: ésa era mi intención, sencilla y pretenciosa al mismo
> tiempo; y pensar en el pasado, obligar a alguien a recordarlo, era una manera de
> hacerlo, un pulso librado contra la entropía, un intento de que el desorden del
> mundo, cuyo único destino es siempre un desorden más intenso, fuera
> detenido, puesto en grilletes, por una vez derrotado. (That certain parts of my
> experience (in my country, with my people, in this moment where fate landed
> me) had escaped me, generally because my attention had been occupied by
> other more banal things, and I wanted to prevent that from continuing to
> happen. To realize: this was my intention, simple and pretentious at the same
> time; and to think about the past, to force someone to remember it, was a way
> of achieving just that, a liberating pulse against entropy, an attempt to show
> that the disorder of the world, whose endgame was always an even more intense
> disorder, could be detained, shackled, and defeated once and for all.)[27]

Like *The Sound of Things Falling*, *The Informers* is a family novel in miniature. In this instance, the protagonist set is dominated by a pared-down cast of characters, largely the narrator, Gabriel; his wife, Sara Guterman; and the narrator's father, an old academic whose critical approval Gabriel, a writer and budding intellectual, passionately seeks. The larger cast of characters looms in the background, as Gabriel and Sara try to retrace her family lineage to the Holocaust. Sara is of Jewish decent and knows that her family fled to Colombia during World War II but is not sure of much beyond this fact. The attempt to reconcile her present life, and to do so through literary-styled investigation, marks the novel's most prominent theme: to retrace and understands one's routes. The attempt for Sara to understand her family's trajectory and arrival in Colombia parallels the notional attempt to retrace and understand the national story following a period of tumult and to do so in a way that brings multiple global threads together. In reconstituting the national story, it seems odd to focus on a Swiss-Jewish immigrant, but this unexpected thread allows Vásquez both to upend literary expectation by writing a novel as much inspired by Phillip Roth as any of his compatriots and to add the level of World War II spy-novel intrigue to a work that is really about investigating diasporic lineage.[28] This brings the world and nation together and lets Colombians understand their collective and personal life against one of the largest of historical backdrops. Or, as Vásquez himself puts it, "una novela de individuos, de cómo los grandes movimientos históricos entran dentro de la vida de los individuos" (a novel about individuals and how big historical movements enter into their lives).[29]

The novel pivots on the multilayered tension of World War II intrigue, Sara's hope to reconcile her present with her past, and Gabriel's desire to meet his father's approval. Simple as it may be, the story line is rich with metaphor. Sara's looking back presents a story written by Vásquez in a moment when, after Escobar and in a moment of high globalization, the country wonders if anything unites it at all, beyond a shared trauma. In parallel, Gabriel's use of journalism addresses the popular register's influence in this national soul searching, while his attempt to meet the approval of his high-literary father—literal in this sense, but one could easily read his relationship to his biological father as one filled with generational and stylistic anxiety—cuts the story line with the worry of reimagining a nation that will hold up to the one envisioned by its forebears. This task, as the second chapter of the novel, "La segunda vida" (Second life) puts it, is a weighty one. To have the chance to refashion the nation for a future generation is both inspiring and daunting. Vásquez uses the immigrant who re-creates themselves in the New World as the story line to capture this tension.

The novel's hook plays off the intrigue created as Sara and Gabriel unearth facts about German and Swiss immigrants who arrived in Colombia in the 1940s. One of their interlocutors, Konrad, it turns out, ended up on the Colombian blacklist, and they are not sure why. Konrad's presence in the novel offers insight into the immigrant's experience, though it is reframed outside the popular imaginary. When one conjures up notions of Colombian immigration, it is an outward exilic force that projects Colombians onto the world, taking with them their rituals, foods, and customs (most popularly associated with coastal Colombia). So it is innovative to explore a European arriving to Colombia with his cultural baggage in tow. As the narrator describes Konrad, "Todavía con el aperitivo en la mano, Bethke empezó a contarle a Konrad de las cosas que había traído de su viaje. Discos, libros, hasta dos dibujos al carbón de nombres que a mí no me decían nada. Yo dije que me gustaba mucho Chagall. Por participar en la conversación, nada más. Y Bethke me miró como si ya fuera mi hora del tetero. Como si tuviera que ir a cepillarme los dientes y directo a la cama." (With his aperitif in hand, Bethke began to tell Konrad the things he had brought with him on the trip. Records, books, even charcoal etchings by names that didn't mean much to me. I told him that I really liked Chagall, really just to participate in the conversation. And Bethke looked at me as if I were in diapers; like it was time for me to brush my teeth and go to bed.)[30] The things that Bethke carried across the Atlantic to a place where he would try to reinvent himself run parallel to his attempt to find a Colombian self in culture. It is telling of Vásquez's literary project that Konrad does this through literature: he listens to a recorded version of *La vorágine* by José Eustasio Rivera. The inclusion of the Colombian classic in the cultural mélange both marks Konrad's attempt to reinvent himself in an imagined wilderness and adds to the level of intrigue. Will the jungle swallow him as it does the characters of *La vorágine*, and are his motives trustworthy in the first instance?

At this point in the novel, the narrative feeds off the notion that Konrad's trip to Colombia may not have been to flee the Nazis so much as to attempt to found a Colombian Nazi party. Gabriel and Sara's detective work begins to resemble as much an investigation into a nefarious past as a study of tracing one's roots. Here we see the give-and-take, if not better described as plight, of immigration, though framed in an innovative context. The assumption that Konrad and other German immigrants are all Nazis leads Colombians to mistreat them socially. They ban the German language. They loot German schools. And they burn German books in the street. To this end, Gabriel and Sara's analysis of the past becomes complex and nebulous. In what started as an effective tracing of a family tree has spilled over into German and Swiss exile to Colombia in the 1940s. This presents the bigger problem of a moving target of justice. Were Konrad and his friends Nazis, or were they mistreated by Colombians who judged them to be Nazis simply because they spoke German and listened to Wagner? This double thrust anchors the realism of the story. As readers, we may have thought that this study into Colombian immigration was going to offer clear answers. But the reality is that in moments of historical tumult and forced exile, answers are rarely that clear cut. As World War II ends, some Germans return to Europe, and others leave for other spaces of reinvention. With a studied lack of melodrama that is characteristic of Vásquez, Konrad's story ends in a fade-out that resists a clean catharsis. The narrator claims,

Unos se devolvieron a Alemania, otros se fueron a Venezuela o a Ecuador para hacer lo mismo que habían estado haciendo en Colombia, sólo que empezando de ceros, y eso hacía la diferencia. Volver a empezar, ¿no? Eso es lo que rompe a la gente, la obligación de volver a empezar una vez más. Konrad, por ejemplo, no pudo. Se dedicó a morirse despacito durante un año y medio. . . . Me lo imagino perfecto, acostado con Josefina como si esta mujer fuera una balsa de náufrago, dividiendo el día entre sus discos de ópera y los carajillos de un cafetín cualquiera. (Some returned to Germany, others went to Venezuela or to Ecuador to do the same thing that they had been doing in Colombia, but starting from scratch, and that made all the difference. Start again, right? That is what breaks people, being forced to start over one more time. Konrad, for example, didn't have it in him. So he spent his days slowly and quietly dying over the course of a year and half. . . . I can imagine it perfectly, sleeping next to Josefina as if she were a life raft, dividing his days between his opera records and espresso cocktails in run-of-the-mill coffee shops.)[31]

One might argue that by filtering his assimilation to Colombian culture through *La vorágine*, he was preparing himself for what he knew was coming all along: that this new and open country that at once presented the opportunity for reinvention and the trappings of the unknown would eventually devour him.

The final two sections of the novel take a decidedly diasporic turn. What was a novel about a journalist and child of immigrants with an intellectual project becomes more bluntly about retracing one's past in an era of globalization and what national collectivity looks like when everyone is making attempts to understand their own personal histories. These questions play out for Sara, whose self-searching, at this point in the novel, has brought up questions of pasts more nebulous than she had imagined. Personal and national identity are less clear cut than she had hoped, yet as Sara herself puts it, this could be the mark of a nation whose prevailing national trope is perhaps that of the migrant. As Sara puts it,

> Uno es de donde mejor se siente, y las raíces son para las matas. Todo el mundo lo sabe, ¿no es cierto? Ubi bene ibi patria, todas esas frases de cajón. (De cajón romano, eso sí. Por lo menos califica como antigualla.) Yo, por mi parte, no he salido nunca de este país, y a veces se me ocurre que nunca lo haré. Y no me haría falta, ¿sabes? Aquí están pasando muchas cosas; es más, aquí es donde pasan cosas; y, aunque a veces me tropiezo con los provincianismos de la apenas suramericana, suelo pensar que aquí la experiencia humana tiene un peso especial, es como una densidad química. (You are from where you feel best, and roots are best left to plants. Everyone knows it, right? Ubi bene ubi patria, and all of those stock phrases. (Of roman stock, yes, which at least gives it an air of antiquity.) As for me, I've never left the country, and sometimes I think I never will. It wouldn't bother me, you know? There is so much going on here; I would even wager that this is where things are happening; and even though I stumble through the provincialisms of those who have not looked beyond South America, I also tend to think that the human experience here has a special weight, like a unique chemical density.)[32]

There is an odd cosmopolitanism that finds its basis in a simple getting-by Heimlich of the here and now. Sara realizes that perhaps the weight of, to use the name of the chapter, her "vida heredada" (inherited life) is perhaps not as salient as the experiences she shares in Colombia with her fellow citizens. This turn is doubly charged: on the one hand, it puts forward the argument that cultural fluxes and the decontextualizing movement of bodies are perhaps the most shared Colombian experience; and on the other, it presents the notion that this collective Colombian experience is larger in and of itself than the sources of origin for the moving bodies. Sara refuses to be devoured by the land. She can adapt to her surroundings.

The Informers begins as an urban realist novel, becomes a World War II novel, and by the end is a diasporic novel with a twist. The last section, as a literary play titled "Postdata de 1995" (Postscript from 1995), revisits the relationship between the narrator and his father. If the work's central theme is national identity after migratory flux, then it is framed by the notion of generational approval. Gabriel's father has been looking over the reader's shoulder throughout the work and comes back to close the novel. The section takes the abrupt perspective of the author looking back on what is presupposed as a work of journalistic realism. Both Gabriel's father and Sara have died at this point, and Gabriel feels free to look at his work and its reception more objectively. Yet the reproach continues. One of Gabriel's friends, who was included in his work, makes similar claims that he never should have pried into and published material (the work he refers to in the novel is *The Informers*) on the personal past of others. To that end, it comes as an unnerving surprise when the narrative-propelling German emigrant Dresser requests to see Gabriel, following the publication of his novel.

One might make the argument that this section of the novel is less a postscript than the rest of the novel is a preamble. While in formal terms, it may seem heavy-handed in the postmodern sense of breaking down the relationship between the author and the reader, the literary device of allowing a fake author to address his readers regarding the first two-thirds of the novel does not feel forced. When Gabriel visits Dresser, the two generations referenced in the novel come face-to-face. This is a chance to sit in front of each other, turn on the tape recorder, and allow the generation that experienced the referenced moment and the generation that attempts to reframe it in their own context to work through a shared reality. It is at this point that a teleology of violent moments resonant in the national imaginary comes up. Dresser describes the themes that dominated day-to-day conversation in Colombia for him: where people were during the "disputa en el parqueadero, y cuánto tiempo había tardado en desangrarse, tras seis balazos de una pistola calibre 38, el futbolista Andrés Escobar. Mucho después alguien me haría esa pregunta: ¿Dónde estaba cuando mataron a Escobar? Antes me habían preguntado: ¿Dónde estaba cuando mataron a Galán, a Pizarro? Pensé que era posible, en efecto, una vida regida por el lugar donde uno está cuando asesinan a otro; sí, esa vida era la mía, y la de varios" (parking lot dispute, and how long had it taken for Andrés Escobar to bleed to death, after being shot by three .38-caliber bullets. Years later someone would ask me, Where were you when they killed Escobar? They may as well have asked me, Where were you when they killed Galán or Pizarro? I thought that it was possible, in effect, to have a life governed by the place you were in when one

person assassinated another; that was my life, and it was the life of many).[33]
The theme runs parallel to Sara's claim that if she has never been out of
Colombia, then what does her own family history reveal that would supersede
her shared experience with her fellow Colombians? What might make one
Colombian, from the perspective of a refugee whose life has been spent, in its
majority, in proximity to violence? This is where the figuration of nationhood
evolves in the novel, and the work's philosophical end bleeds through. Perhaps,
it is posited, both in Sara's claim that shared local experience defines identity
more so than personal history and in Dresser's insistence on spatial proximity
to the violent hallmarks that have shaped the nation, that what defines Colombia is its inability to reconcile as a nation. Arguably, the work ponders if it is
more the cacophony of groups of migrants who abruptly move to urban spaces,
the multiple ethnic groups represented in the country who have individual historical trajectories of their own, and the particular institutions participating
in varying degrees with global or local socioeconomic projects in a single space
that define the nation. Put another way, Vásquez's work proposes that perhaps
what defines Colombian nationhood after an uneasy entrance into globalization is its struggle to define itself outside the terms of shared trauma. What
reconstitutes the Colombian nation is its struggle to do just that. In reconciling generational differences, as Gabriel comes to terms with the tension between
him and his father, while channeling Dresser, he concludes, "Pues a pesar de
que no se lo haya dicho en ese momento, para mí lo de Escobar era un memo-
rando (una tarjeta amarilla, pensé después con algo más de ligereza) que me
enviaba el país y que subrayaba, más que la imposibilidad de entender a Colombia, lo ilusoria, lo ingenua que era cualquier intención de hacerlo escribiendo
libros que muy pocos leen y que no hacen más que traer problemas a quien los
escribe" (Even though I didn't say it in exactly that moment, for me the Escobar incident was a memorandum (a yellow card, I later thought with a bit more
levity) that the country had sent me and that underscored more the impossi-
bility to understand Colombia, and the illusory naivety of any attempt to
understand Colombia by writing books that few people will read and will probably do nothing but bring problems to the person who writes them).[34] Colombia is the people sharing an experience in the day-to-day. The rest is just
literature.

The end of this story of inverted clichés and paradoxes comes in that Juan
Gabriel Vásquez is oddly a loner among his generation, notably because he opted
for the road *more* traveled. While the Colombian urban novelists who run parallel to Vásquez stay in their respective cities and work toward a largely productive local realism, Vásquez set his sights on the world. He follows the age-old
path to Europe and other traditional centers of literary capital in order to look
back on his home nation from a "place of letters." As such, there is meta-arc of

Colombian intellectual history that follows him. To capture the acute experience of Colombian cities from the '90s to the present is inarguably of great sociological and existential necessity. By doing so from elsewhere, Vásquez does the double duty of weaving himself into the cultural tapestry that harks back to Colombia's inception and allows him to write the local with the tonic note of the global in mind. The world, for him, acts as leverage to pry open the local.

Vásquez revisits the tropes, clichés, and real experiences of nationhood at a moment when nationhood itself buffets against the world. In short, he marks an attempt to reconstitute Colombian nationhood from the place of the aesthetic border. One might argue that addressing the Colombian canon of aesthetic themes and national hallmarks in a way that leaves no stone unturned marks an attempt to bring the Colombian story in line with a globalized Latin America. To understand the local, as Vásquez's work show us, it takes the world.

Notes

Introduction

1 Mignolo writes,

   La palabra *aesthesis*, que se origina en el griego antiguo, es aceptada sin modificaciones en las lenguas modernas europeas. Los significados de la palabra giran en torno a vocablos como "sensación," "proceso de percepción," "sensación visual," "sensación gustativa" o "sensación auditiva." De ahí que el vocablo *synaesthesia* se refiera al entrecruzamiento de sentidos y sensaciones, y que fuera aprovechado como figura retórica en el modernism poético/literario. . . . A partir del siglo XVIII, el concepto *aesthesis* se restringe, y de ahí en adelante pasará a significar "sensación de lo bello." Nace así la estética como teoría, y el concepto de arte como práctica. Mucho se ha escrito sobre Immanuel Kant y la importancia fundamental de su pensamiento en la reorientación de la *aesthesis* y su transformación en estética. A partir de ahí, y en retrospectiva, se comenzó a escribir la historia de la estética, y se encontraron sus orígenes no sólo en Grecia, sino en la prehistoria. Esta operación cognitiva constituyó, nada más y nada menos, la colonización de la *aesthesis* por la estética, puesto que si *aesthesis* es un fenómeno común a todos los organismos vivientes con sistema nervioso, la *estética* es una versión o teoría particular de tales sensaciones relacionadas con la belleza.

   Walter Mignolo, "Aiesthesis decolonial," *Calle 14* 4, no. 4 (2010): 13.
2 For more on the predecessor to Kant's aesthetic theory, see Alexander Baumgarten, *Aesthetica* (Frankfurt: Hildesheim, 1961).
3 See Nestor García Canclini, *Hybrid Cultures: Strategies for Entering and Leaving Modernity* (Minneapolis: University of Minnesota Press, 2005) and Mariano Siskind, *Cosmopolitan Desires: Global Modernity and World Literature in Latin America* (Evanston, IL: Northwestern University Press, 2014).
4 See Dierdra Reber, *Coming to Our Senses: Affect and an Order of Things for Global Culture* (New York: Columbia University Press, 2016).
5 See Enrique Dussel, *Philosophy of Liberation* (Maryknoll, NY: Orbis Books, 1985); Antonio Cornejo Polar, *Writing in the Air: Heterogeneity and the Persistence of Oral Tradition in Andean Literatures* (Durham, NC: Duke University Press,

2013); Ignacio Sánchez Prado, *Strategic Occidentalism: On Mexican Fiction, the Neoliberal Book Market, and the Question of World Literature* (Evanston, IL: Northwestern University Press, 2018); and Mariano Siskind, *Cosmopolitan Desires: Global Modernity and World Literature in Latin America* (Evanston, IL: Northwestern University Press, 2014).

6   Rory O'Bryen. *Literature, Testimony and Cinema in Contemporary Colombian Culture: Spectres of La Violencia* (Rochester, NY: Tamesis, 2008), 8.

7   Jean Franco, *The Decline and Fall of the Lettered City: Latin America in the Cold War* (Cambridge, MA: Harvard University Press, 2002), 16.

8   "While the province's number of urban inhabitants grew 77 percent between 1938 and 1951, the number of rural residents increased by only 13 percent during the same period. As Medellín grew, so did the number of potential voters and provincial migrants in search of education and a chance to break into regional politics." Mary Roldan, *Blood and Fire: La Violencia in Antioquia, Colombia, 1946–1953* (Durham, NC: Duke University Press, 2002), 49.

9   Roldan, 20.

10 María Ospina, "Las naturalezas de la guerra: Topografías violentas de selva en la narrative contemporánea colombiana," *Revista de Crítica Literaria Latinoamericana* 40, no. 79 (2014): 243–64.

11 Angel Rama, *La ciudad letrada* (Hanover, NH: Ediciones del Norte, 1984), 38.

12 For more, see Flor Edilma Osorio Perez, "Armed Conflict and Forced Displacement in Colombia: Data, Facts and Tendencies as of the Year 2000," in *Internationally Displaced People in Colombia, Victims in Permanent Transition*, ed. Sandro Jimenez Ocampo (Bogotá: Ediciones Antropos, 2009), 27–55.

13 Osorio Perez, 27.

14 María Guadalupe Pacheco Gutiérrez, *Representación estética de la hiperViolence en "La virgen de los sicarios" de Fernando Vallejo y "Paseo nocturno" de Rubem Fonseca* (Mexico City: Miguel Angel Porrua, 2008), 94.

15 Two texts that deal heavily with the framing of trauma in narrative in the Colombian context are Daniel Pécaut, *Orden y la Violencia: Evolución socio-politica de Colombia entre 1930 y 1953* (Bogotá: Grupo Editorial Norma, 2001); and O'Bryen, *Literature, Testimony and Cinema.*

16 Marco Palacios, *Entre la legitimidad y la Violence: Colombia 1878–1994* (Bogotá: Grupo Editorial Norma, 1995), 310.

17 Jesús Martín Barbero writes about the media in a post-Violence context:

> A su lado accede al poder una élite que difícilmente puede ser asimilada a una 'nueva capa' y que cuenta con miembros que disfrutan en su propio provecho de la fortuna y la influencia, Como Eduardo Santos y su hermano que reinan en *El Tiempo*; con hombres ilustres, como los dos primos Carlos Lleras Restrepo y Alberto Lleras Camargo que, a falta de fortuna, ocupan de manera permanente durante cincuenta años los más altos cargos y asumiendo las más altas responsabilidades; o con integrantes del medio cooptado de la *intelligensia* de Bogotá, como Felipe Lleras Camargo, Gabriel Rubay, José Mar, Jorge Zalamea y Darío Echandía, quien profesaba el socialismo antes de adherirse en 1930 al liberalismo y de vincularse con el poder. Estos últimos no tenían necesariamente vínculos con el mundo de los negocios, no son los representantes 'orgánicos' de una burguesía pero definen el campo cultural e institucional en el cual se afirma el capitalismo colombiano.

Jesús Martín Barbero, "Transformations in the Map: Identities and Culture Studies," *Latin American Perspectives* 27 (2000): 33.

18 Barbero, 33.

19 Jean Franco claims, "In the United States, modernism became institutionalized in the Cold War years, when the focus was on the 'spiritual critique' of literature. In Latin America it was a time of acerbic polemics and debate as writers' hitherto untested claims of commitment were challenged by publics whose imaginations were fired by armed struggle and revolution. All kinds of aesthetic and political projects now appeared possible—the aesthetic utopias of modernism and the historical avant-garde, the notion of pure art and pure literature, participatory theater, liberation from capitalism" (*Decline and Fall*, 10). But this distancing was arguably most poignant during Caro's era through writers such as Jorge Enrique Rodó, José Martí, and Rubén Darío.

20 Franco, 10.

21 Pascale Casanova theorizes the world literary system in *The World Republic of Letters* (Cambridge, MA: Harvard University Press, 2004). See also Héctor Hoyos, *Beyond Bolaño: The Global Latin American Novel* (New York: Columbia University Press, 2016).

22 Aníbal González, "Entrando en materia: Novela, poesía y cultura material en *El ruido de las cosas al caer*," *Cuadernos de Literatura* 20, no. 40 (2016): 481.

Chapter 1   Gabo against the World

1 Fredric Jameson, "Third-World Literature in the Era of Multinational Capitalism," *Social Text* 15 (1986): 65–88; Jameson, "No Magic, No Metaphor: Fredric Jameson on 'One Hundred Years of Solitude,'" *London Review of Books* 39, no. 12 (2017), https://www.lrb.co.uk/the-paper/v39/n12/fredric-jameson/no-magic-no-metaphor.

2 This quote is taken from Mario Vargas Llosa's foreword to the below listed edition of *Cien años de soledad*, by Gabriel García Márquez (Madrid: Real Academia Española, 2007), xxv.

3 García Márquez, *Cien años de soledad*, 9.

4 The "Dutch Disease" is the term used to describe the macroeconomic principle that countries with abundant resources have performed relatively poorly in the global economy in the twentieth century. The *Economist* coined the phrase in 1977. "The Dutch Disease," *Economist*, November 26, 1977, 82–83.

5 See Lucila Inés Mena, "La huelga de la compañía bananera como expresión de lo 'Real Maravilloso' americano en *Cien años de soledad*," *Bulletin Hispanique* 74, nos. 3–4 (1972): 379–405.

6 Charles Bergquist, *Coffee and Conflict in Colombia, 1886–1910* (Durham, NC: Duke University Press, 1986), 23.

7 Marco Palacios, *Entre la legitimidad y la violencia: Colombia 1875–1994* (Bogotá: Grupo Editorial Norma, 1995).

8 John Crow, *The Epic of Latin America* (Berkeley: University of California Press, 1992), 805.

9 Charles Bergquist's chapter, "Waging War and Negotiating Peace: The Contemporary Crisis in Historical Perspective," in *Violence in Colombia, 1990–2000: Waging War and Negotiating Peace*, edited by Charles Bergquist, Ricardo Peñaranda, and Gonzalo Sánchez G. (Wilmington, DE: SR Books, 2001), 205.

10 This is from the introduction of Andrea Fanta Castro, Alejandro Herrero-Olaizola, and Chloe Rutter-Jensen's edited volume, *Territories of Conflict: Traversing Colombia through Cultural Studies*, edited by Andrea Fanta Castro, Alejandro Herrero-Olaizola, and Chloe Rutter-Jensen (Rochester, NY: University of Rochester Press, 2017), 1–20.

11 García Márquez, *Cien años de soledad*, 48.

12 García Márquez, 125.

13 Maria del Carmen Porras, "La familia Buendía en tiempos de globalización: 'Melodrama' de Jorge Franco," *Revista de Crítica Literaria Latinoamericana* 69 (2009): 210.

14 Doris Sommer, *Foundational Fictions: The National Romances of Latin America* (Berkeley: University of California Press, 1991).

15 García Márquez, *Cien años de soledad*, 22.

16 García Márquez, 22.

17 García Márquez, 23.

18 García Márquez, 67.

19 García Márquez, 460.

20 García Márquez, 462.

21 García Márquez, 470.

22 Mario Vargas Llosa, "Vargas Llosa rompe el silencio sobre García Márquez," *El País*, July 7, 2017, https://elpais.com/cultura/2017/07/06/actualidad/1499366796_414985.html.

Chapter 2   Literary Shipwrecks

1 Mario Vargas Llosa, "García Márquez por Vargas Llosa," *El País*, July 10, 2017. https://elpais.com/cultura/2017/07/07/babelia/1499445200_348553.html.

2 See Brantley Nicholson, "Fernando Vallejo: Ciudadanía y la clausura de la literatura mundial." *Revista Calle* 5, no. 14 (June 2011): 69–78.

3 See Annie Mendoza, *Rewriting the Nation: Novels by Women on Violence in Colombia* (Tempe, AZ: Asociación Internacional de Literatura y Cultura Feminina Hispánica (AILCFH), 2015).

4 Later in this chapter, I discuss Christopher Prendergast's tracing of the semantic root of world literature to Goethe's *Weltliteratur*. Here it is also worth noting that James English writes, "It dates back, after all, to Goethe's coinage of 1827 (*Weltliteratur*), and has essentially served, at least since the early decades of the twentieth century, to name the canon of comparative literature—a canon constructed in and for the core Euro-American educational apparatus, but which includes texts drawn from peripheral cultures." James F. English, *The Economy of Prestige: Prizes, Awards, and Circulation of Cultural Value* (Cambridge, MA: Harvard University Press, 2005), 305.

5 See Héctor Hoyos, *Beyond Bolaño: The Global Latin American Novel* (New York: Columbia University Press, 2016); Ignacio Sánchez Prado, *América Latina en la "literatura mundial"* (Pittsburgh: University of Pittsburgh Press, 2006).

6 See Nicholson, "Fernando Vallejo," 74.

7 Germán Santamaría, "Prohibir al sicario," *Revista Diners*, October 2000.

8 Mario Armando Valencia, *La dimensión crítica de la novela urbana contemporánea en Colombia* (Pereira, Colombia: Universidad Tecnológica de Pereira, 2009).

9 See Rory O'Bryen, *Literature, Testimony and Cinema in Contemporary Colombian Culture: Spectres of La Violencia* (Rochester, NY: Tamesis, 2008).

10 Anadeli Bencomo, "Geopolíticas de la novela hispanoamericana contemporánea: En la encrucijada entre narrativas extraterritoriales e internacionales," *Revista de Crítica Literaria Latinoamericana* 69 (2009): 34.

11 Harold Alvarado Tenorio, "La novela colombiana posterior a *Cien años de soledad*," *Cuadernos para el diálogo* 51 (2010, 6–25.

12 Marco Palacios, *Entre la legitimidad y la violencia: Colombia 1878–1994* (Bogotá: Grupo Editorial Norma, 1995), 310.

13 Palacios, 310.

14 Valencia, *La dimensión crítica.*

15 Valencia.

16 Héctor Abad, *Basura*, Colección Nueva Biblioteca (Madrid: Lengua de Trapo, 2000), 20.

17 This review is taken from the *Independent*'s online "Indy Choice" section. It was published on 13 November 2010 and can be found at https://www.independent.co .uk/arts-entertainment/books/reviews/oblivion-a-memoir-by-hector-abad-trans -anne-mclean-amp-rosalind-harvey-2131351.html.

18 Julius Purcell, "Oblivion: A Memoir by Hector Abad Faciolince—Review," *Guardian*, October 23, 2010, http://www.guardian.co.uk/books/2010/oct/24 /oblivion-memoir-hector-abad-faciolince-review.

19 This quote comes from *El olvido que seremos* and is part of an explanation that Abad gives about the lack of an implicit interlocutor in his work. According to him, he writes for his dead father, who "no leerá nunca." Héctor Abad, *El olvido que seremos* (Bogotá: Editorial Planeta, 2006), 22.

20 Alvarado Tenorio, *La cultura en la república del narco*, 58.

21 English, *Economy of Prestige*, 272.

22 María Helena Rueda, "Dislocaciones y otras violencias en el circuito transnacional de la literatura latinoamericana," *Revista de Crítica Literaria Latinoamericana* 69 (2009): 69–91.

Chapter 3 Narrating Disruption

1 This is a summary of the lettered city as understood by its foundational author, Angel Rama. For more on the lettered city, see Rama, *La ciudad letrada* (Hanover, NH: Ediciones del Norte, 1984).

2 José María Rodríguez García, *The City of Translation: Poetry and Ideology in Nineteenth-Century Colombia* (Basingstoke, UK: Palgrave Macmillan, 2010), 148.

3 See Jean Franco, *The Decline and Fall of the Lettered City: Latin America in the Cold War* (Cambridge, MA: Harvard University Press, 2002).

4 Marco Palacios, *Entre la legitimidad y la violencia: Colombia 1878–1994* (Bogotá: Grupo Editorial Norma, 1995), 197.

5 Palacios, 298.

6 Some scholars are hesitant to use the term *nueveabrileños* or to consider the rioting's source to be so squarely rooted in Gaitán's assassination. For more, see Alfredo Molano, *Los años del tropel* (Bogotá: CINEP-CEREC, 1985).

7 Rory O'Bryen, *Literature, Testimony and Cinema in Contemporary Colombian Culture: Spectres of La Violencia* (Rochester, NY: Tamesis, 2008), 25.

8 Gutavo Álvarez Gardeazábal, *Cóndores no entierran todos los días* (Barcelona: Ediciones Destino, 1972), 1.

9 Gardeazábal, 50.

10   See Daniel Pécaut, *Crónica de cuatro décadas de política colombiana* (Bogotá: Grupo Editorial Norma, 2006).

11   O'Bryen, *Literature, Testimony and Cinema*, 33.

12   O'Bryen, 10.

13   Anibal Quijano, "Coloniality of Power, Eurocentrism, and Latin America," *Nepantla: Views from South* 1, no. 3 (2000): 533–80.

14   Luis Fayad, *Los parientes de Ester* (Cieza, Spain: Alfaqueque Ediciones, 2008), 206.

15   In Charles Bergquist's chapter, "The Labor Movement (1930–1946) and the Origins of the Violence," in the volume *Violence in Colombia*, he discusses the paradoxes that accompany the influx of capital, the rise of coffee prices, and the lack of collective social benefit in Colombia during the 1960s and '70s. Bergquist, "Waging War and Negotiating Peace: The Contemporary Crisis in Historical Perspective," in *Violence in Colombia, 1990–2000: Waging War and Negotiating Peace*, edited by Charles Bergquist, Ricardo Peñaranda, and Gonzalo Sánchez G. (Wilmington, DE: SR Books, 2001), 195–212.

16   Fayad, *Los parientes de Ester*, 121.

17   Harold Alvarado Tenorio, "La novela colombiana posterior a *Cien años de soledad*," *Cuadernos para el diálogo* 51 (2010): 13.

18   Molano, *Los años del tropel*, 205.

19   For more on this see, Palacios, *Entre la legitimidad y la violencia*, 327; and the introduction to the English translation of Alonso Salazar's *No nacimos pa' semilla* (Bogotá: CINEP-CEREC, 1990).

20   Palacios, *Entre la legitimidad y la violencia*, 328.

21   Palacios, 321.

22   Juana Suárez and Carlos Jauregui, "Profilaxis, traducción y ética: Humanidad 'desechable' en *Rodrigo D. No futuro, La vendedora de rosas* y *La virgen de los sicarios*," *Revista Iberoamericana* 68, no. 199 (2002): 368.

23   For more on the philosophical problems addressed in the twentieth-century Latin American urban novel, see Amanda Holmes's *City Fictions: Language, Body, and Spanish American Urban Space* (Cranbury, NJ: Bucknell University Press, 2007).

24   Mario Mendoza, *Scorpio City* (Santafe de Bogotá: Seix Barral, 1998), 65.

25   Mendoza, 119.

26   Mendoza, 120.

27   Andrés Caicedo, *Que viva la música* (Bogotá: Plaza and Janes, 1985), 11.

28   According to Charles Bergquist in his introduction, "Colombian Violence in Historical Perspective," to the volume *Violence in Colombia*, "With advent of National Front traditional political violence ends. Its sequel of political banditry is repressed by 1966. After 1960, Cuban-inspired guerrilla groups (FARC, ELN, EPL), with some linked to previous Liberal resistance, proliferate. Governments continually resort to state-of-siege powers to contain internal dissent and social unrest. Under orthodox liberal policies adequate coffee prices, economy continues to grow and diversify, and multinational corporations enter Colombia in force" (xiii).

29   The magazine *Ojo al cine* was the "official" publication of the Cine Club de Cali and had only four issues between 1974 and 1976. The three directors of the Cine Club and a mutual cinephile friend formed the initial editorial team of the magazine: Andrés Caicedo, Luís Ospina, Ramiro Arbelaez, and Carlos Mayolo. Only Andrés Caicedo and Patricia Restrepo, who had joined the magazine since

the third issue, formed the editorial team of the last number. For a history of the Cine Club de Cali and Andrés Caicedo's lasting love with cinema, see the book-length compilation of his critical work *Ojo al cine* (Bogotá: Grupo Editorial Norma, 1999). Particularly informing are the introduction and the notes for each section by Sandro Romero Rey and Luís Ospina.

30 Antonio Caballero, *Sin remedio* (Bogotá: Alfaguara, 2004), 51.
31 Salazar, *No nacimos pa' semilla*, 9.
32 Salazar, 26, 32, 70.
33 In *The Decline and Fall of the Lettered City: Latin America in the Cold War* (Cambridge, MA: Harvard University Press, 2002), Jean Franco argues, "Unless we read irony into the account, the viewpoint is misogynist and racist. It is as if the novel in exaggerated fashion places before us the ultimate absurdity—the disassociation of the female reproduction machine and the male death machine, both of which function blindly, the one to reproduce and the other to exterminate" (225).
34 J. Franco, 225.
35 Fernando Vallejo, *La virgen de los sicarios* (Bogotá: Editorial Santillana, 1994), 7.
36 Vallejo, 10.
37 María Helena Rueda, "Dislocaciones y otras violencias en el circuito transncional de la literatura latinoamericana," *Revista de Crítica Literaria Latinoamericana* 69 (2009): 79.
38 For more on the intertextual resonances between Heraclitus and Vallejo, see O'Bryen, *Literature, Testimony and Cinema*. For information on Heraclitus's theorizations of time and universal reason, see Charles H. Kahn, *The Art and Thought of Heraclitus* (Cambridge: Cambridge University Press, 1979); and Roman Dilcher, *Studies in Heraclitus* (Hildesheim, Germany: Georg Olms, 1995).
39 Porfirio Barba Jacob, *Porfirio Barba Jacob: Poesia completa* (Bogotá: El Ancora Editores, 2000), 61.
40 Vallejo, *La virgen de los sicarios*, 19.
41 Vallejo, 15.
42 Vallejo, 42.
43 Vallejo, 56.
44 Vallejo, 61.
45 Vallejo, 90.
46 Vallejo, 90.
47 Vallejo, 98.
48 Vallejo, 68.
49 This is an extrapolation on Hermann Herlinghaus's reading from his article "La construcción del nexo de violencia y culpa en la novela *La virgen de los sicarios*," *Nomadas* 25 (2006): 184–204.
50 Herlinghaus, 189.
51 Vallejo, *La virgen de los sicarios*, 104.

Chapter 4   Recasting the Colombian National Story after the Inrush of the World

1 David Streitfeld, "Mario Vargas Llosa on Love, Spectacle and Becoming a Legend," *New York Times*, April 13, 2016, http://www.nytimes.com/2016/04/14/books/mario-vargas-llosa-on-love-spectacle-and-becoming-a-legend.html?_r=0.

2   See Silvana Paternostro's interview with Juan Gabriel Vásquez in *Bomb* magazine, January 1, 2010.

3   The Silicon Valley reference is from Patrick Gillespie, "How Colombia Went from Murder Capital to Tech Powerhouse," *CNN Business*, March 13, 2015, http://money.cnn.com/2015/03/13/investing/colombia-tech-silicon-valley/; and Vince Wong, "Andean Peaks and Silicon Valleys: Entrepreneurship in Colombia," SC Johnson College of Business, April 24, 2017, https://www.johnson.cornell.edu/article/emerging-markets-institute/research/emi-at-work/47013/andean-peaks-and-silicon-valleys-entrepreneurship-in-colombia/. The notion of "export reverie" is quoted from Ericka Beckman, *Capital Fictions: The Literature of Latin America's Export Age* (Minneapolis: University of Minnesota Press, 2013), x.

4   Beckman, *Capital Fictions*, xviii.

5   Juan Gabriel Vásquez, *El ruido de las cosas al caer* (Bogotá: Alfaguara, 2011), 9.

6   Vásquez, 27.

7   Vásquez, 63.

8   Vásquez, 91.

9   Vásquez, 131.

10 Vásquez, 131.

11 Vásquez, 133.

12 Vásquez, 138.

13 Vásquez, 137.

14 Vásquez, 138.

15 Vásquez, 193.

16 Vásquez, 201.

17 Vásquez, 202.

18 Vásquez, 203.

19 Vásquez, 255.

20 Vásquez, 331.

21 Vásquez, 332.

22 Vásquez, 403.

23 Vásquez, 407.

24 Vásquez, 420.

25 Vásquez, 430.

26 Jean Gabriel Vásquez, *Los informantes* (Bogotá: Alfaguara, 2004), 8.

27 Vásquez, 51.

28 See Mauro Libertella, "Los caminos de la historia," *Pagina 12*, February 4, 2007, http://www.pagina12.com.ar/diario/suplementos/libros/10-2422-2007-02-04.html.

29 Isabel Obiols, "Juan Gabriel Vásquez recrea en 'Los informantes' la Colombia de los años cuarenta," *El País*, October 13, 2004, http://elpais.com/diario/2004/10/14/cultura/1097704805_850215.html.

30 Vásquez, *Los informantes*, 278.

31 Vásquez, 490.

32 Vásquez, 499.

33 Vásquez, 530.

34 Vásquez, 530.

Bibliography

Abad, Héctor. *Basura*. Colección Nueva Biblioteca. Madrid: Lengua de Trapo, 2000.

——. *El olvido que seremos*. Bogotá: Editorial Planeta, 2006.

Adorno, Theodor. *Aesthetic Theory*. Minneapolis: University of Minnesota Press, 1997.

Adorno, Theodor, Walter Benjamin, Ernst Bloch, Bertolt Brecht, and Georg Lukács. *Aesthetics and Politics*. London: Verso, 2007.

Alvarado Tenorio, Harold. *La cultura en la república del narco*. Bogotá: Podenco, 2014.

——. "La novela colombiana posterior a *Cien años de soledad*." *Cuadernos para el diálogo* 51 (2010): 6–25.

——. "Les belles colombienne." *El País*, November 14, 2010. http://lacomunidad .elpais.com/la-lengua-viperina/2010/11/14/les-belles-colombienne.

Anderson, Benedict. *Imagined Communities*. London: Verso, 1983.

Appiah, Kwame Anthony. *Cosmopolitanism*. London: Penguin, 2006.

Aristizábal, Juanita. *Fernando Vallejo a contracorriente*. Rosario, Argentina: Beatriz Viterbo Editora, 2015.

Aristotle. *On Poetry and Style*. Indianapolis: Hackett, 1989.

Arnold, Mathew. *Culture and Anarchy*. Cambridge: Cambridge University Press, 1993.

Avelar, Idelber. *The Untimely Present: Postdictatorial Latin American Fiction and the Task of Mourning*. Durham, NC: Duke University Press, 1999.

Bach, Caleb. "Tomas Eloy Martinez: Imagining the Truth." *Americas* 50, no. 3 (1998): 14–21.

Baldick, Chris. *The Concise Oxford Dictionary of Literary Terms*. Oxford: Oxford University Press, 2008.

Barbero, Jesús Martín. "Transformations in the Map: Identities and Culture Studies." *Latin American Perspectives* 27 (2000): 27–48.

Barriendos, Joaquin. "Apetitos extremos: La colonialidad del ver y las imágenes-archivo sobre el canibalismo de Indias." *Postcolonial Displays* (2008), https:// transversal.at/transversal/0708/barriendos/es.

Baumgarten, Alexander. *Aesthetica*. Frankfurt: Hildesheim, 1961.

Bayly, Jaime. *La noche es virgen*. Barcelona: Anagrama, 1997.

Beckman, Ericka. *Capital Fictions: The Literature of Latin America's Export Age*. Minneapolis: University of Minnesota Press, 2013.

Bellatin, Mario. *Tres novelas: Salon de belleza, Jacobo el mutante, Bola negra*. Merida, Venezuela: El otro el mismo, 2005.

Bell-Villada, Gene. *Gabriel García Márquez's One Hundred Years of Solitude: A Casebook*. Oxford: Oxford University Press, 2002.

———. *García Márquez: The Man and His Work*. Chapel Hill: University of North Carolina Press, 2010.

Bencomo, Anadeli. "Geopolíticas de la novela hispanoamericana contemporánea: En la encrucijada entre narrativas extraterritoriales e internacionales." *Revista de Crítica Literaria Latinoamericana* 69 (2009): 33–50.

Bergquist, Charles. *Coffee and Conflict in Colombia, 1886–1910*. Durham, NC: Duke University Press, 1986.

———. Introduction to *Violence in Colombia, 1990–2000: Waging War and Negotiating Peace*, edited by Charles Bergquist, Ricardo Peñaranda, and Gonzalo Sánchez G. Wilmington, DE: SR Books, 2001.

———. *Labor in Latin America: Comparative Essays on Chile, Argentina, Venezuela, and Colombia*. Stanford, CA: Stanford University Press, 1986.

———. "Waging War and Negotiating Peace: The Contemporary Crisis in Historical Perspective." In *Violence in Colombia, 1990–2000: Waging War and Negotiating Peace*, edited by Charles Bergquist, Ricardo Peñaranda, and Gonzalo Sánchez G., 195–212. Wilmington, DE: SR Books, 2001.

Bhabha, Homi. *The Location of Culture*. New York: Routledge, 1994.

Bolivar, Simon. *El pensamiento de Simon Bolivar: Discrusos, proclamas y correspondencia*. Lima: Editorial san Marcos, 2006.

Borges, Jorge Luis. *Ficciones; El aleph; El informe de brodie*. Caracas, Venezuela: Biblioteca Ayacucho, 1986.

———. *Otras inquisiciones*. Buenos Aires: Emece, 1989.

Boullosa, Carmen. *La milagrosa*. Mexico City: Ediciones ERA, 1993.

Caballero, Antonio. *Sin remedio*. Bogotá: Alfaguara, 2004.

Caicedo, Andrés. *El atravesado*. Buenos Aires: Eloisa Cartonera, 2007.

———. *Los diplomas*. Separata Dramaturgica. Vol. La Revista Gestus, no. 11. Bogotá: Gestus, 2000.

———. *Ojo al cine* Bogotá: Grupo Editorial Norma, 1999.

———. *Que viva la música*. Bogotá: Plaza and Janes, 1985.

Casanova, Pascale. *The World Republic of Letters*. Cambridge, MA: Harvard University Press, 2004.

Cohn, Deborah. "A Tale of Two Translation Programs: Politics, the Market, and Rockefeller Funding for Latin American Literature in the United States during the 1960s and 1970s." *Latin American Research Review* 41, no. 2 (2006): 139–64.

Cornejo Polar, Antonio. *Writing in the Air: Heterogeneity and the Persistence of Oral Tradition in Andean Literatures*. Durham, NC: Duke University Press, 2013.

Cortázar, Julio. *Rayuela*. Nanterre, France: ALLCA XXe, 1991.

Crow, John. *The Epic of Latin America*. Berkeley: University of California Press, 1992.

Damrosch, David. *What Is World Literature?* Princeton, NJ: Princeton University Press, 2003.

Dilcher, Roman. *Studies in Heraclitus*. Hildesheim, Germany: Georg Olms, 1995.

Donoso, José. *The Boom in Spanish American Literature: A Personal History*. Translated by Gregory Kolovakos. New York: Columbia University Press, 1977.

———. *Historia personal del boom*. Buenos Aires: Sudamericana-Planeta, 1984.

Dove, Patrick. *The Catastrophe of Modernity: Tragedy and the Nation in Latin American Literature*. Lewisburg, PA: Bucknell University Press, 2004.

Dussel, Enrique. *Philosophy of Liberation*. Maryknoll, NY: Orbis Books, 1985.

———. *Twenty Theses on Politics*. Durham, NC: Duke University Press, 2008.

"Dutch Disease, The." *Economist*, November 26, 1977, 82–83.

Echevarría, Roberto González. *Myth and Archive: A Theory of Latin American Narrative*. Cambridge: Cambridge University Press, 1990.

Edwards, Jennifer Gabrielle. *The Flight of the Condor: Stories of Violence and War from Colombia*. Madison: University of Wisconsin Press, 2007.

English, James F. *The Economy of Prestige: Prizes, Awards, and Circulation of Cultural Value*. Cambridge, MA: Harvard University Press, 2005.

Eze, Emmanuel Chukwudi. *The Color of Reason: The Idea of "Race" in Kant's Anthropology*. Lewisburg, PA: Bucknell University Press, 1995.

Fanta Castro, Andrea. *Residuos de la Violenia: Producción cultural colombiana, 1990–2010*. Bogotá: Universidad del Rosario Press, 2015.

Fanta Castro, Andrea, Alejandro Herrero-Olaizola, and Chloe Rutter-Jensen. Introduction to *Territories of Conflict: Traversing Colombia through Cultural Studies*, edited by Andrea Fanta Castro, Alejandro Herrero-Olaizola, and Chloe Rutter-Jensen, 1–20. Rochester, NY: University of Rochester Press, 2017.

Fayad, Luis. *Los parientes de Ester*. Cieza, Spain: Alfaqueque Ediciones, 2008.

Felman, Shoshana. *Testimony: Crises of Witnessing in Literature, Psychoanalysis, and History*. New York: Routledge, 1992.

Fistioc, Mihaela C. *The Beautiful Shape of the Good: Platonic and Pythagorean Themes in Kant's "Critique of the Power of Judgment."* Edited by Roberto Nozick. New York: Routledge, 2002.

Franco, Jean. *The Decline and Fall of the Lettered City: Latin America in the Cold War*. Cambridge, MA: Harvard University Press, 2002.

Franco, Jorge. *Rosario Tijeras*. New York: Siete Cuentos Editorial, 1999.

Fresán, Rodrigo. *Jardines de Kensington*. Barcelona: Mondadori, 2003.

Freud, Sigmund. *"Beyond the Pleasure Principle" and Other Writings*. New York: Penguin, 2003.

———. *Civilization and Its Discontents*. New York: Norton, 1962.

———. *The Freud Reader*. Edited by Peter Gay. New York: Norton, 1995.

———. *Three Essays on the Theory of Sexuality*. New York: Basic Books, 1963.

———. *Totem and Taboo*. New York: Norton, 1952.

Fuguet, Alberto. *Las películas de mi vida: Una novela*. New York: Rayo, 2003.

García Canclini, Nestor. *Hybrid Cultures: Strategies for Entering and Leaving Modernity*. Minneapolis: University of Minnesota Press, 2005.

García Márquez, Gabriel. *Cien años de soledad*. Madrid: Real Academia Española, 2007.

Gardeazábal, Gutavo Álvarez. *Cóndores no entierran todos los días*. Barcelona: Ediciones Destino, 1972.

———. *Confesión de parte*. Bogotá: Instituto Tecnologico Metropolitano, 2007.

Gillespie, Patrick. "How Colombia Went from Murder Capital to Tech Powerhouse." *CNN Business*, March 13, 2015. http://money.cnn.com/2015/03/13/investing/colombia-tech-silicon-valley/.

Giraldo, Luz Mary. *En otro lugar: Migraciones y desplazamientos en la literatura colombiana contemporánea*. Bogotá: Pontificia Universidad Javeriana, 2008.

Goic, Cedomil. *Mitos degradados*. Atlanta: Rodopi, 1992.

Gómez, Blanca Inés. *Viajes, migraciones y desplazamientos: Ensayos de crítica cultural.* Bogotá: Pontificia Universidad Javeriana, 2007.

Gómez, Santiago Castro. "The Missing Chapter of Empire." *Cultural Studies* 21 (2007): 428–48.

Gómez, Sergio, and Alberto Fuguet, eds. *Mcondo.* Barcelona: Grijalbo Mondadori, 1996.

González, Aníbal. "Entrando en materia: Novela, poesía y cultura material en *El ruido de las cosas al caer.*" *Cuadernos de Literatura* 20, no. 40 (2016): 477–89.

González, Sady, photographer. "Tranvía quemándose—La agonía del transporte sobre rieles." Photograph. Bogotá, 1948. From Biblioteca Luis Ángel Arango del Banco de la República.

Guerrieri, Kevin. *Palabra, poder y nación: La novela moderna en Colombia de 1896 a 1927.* Ciudad Juárez, Mexico: Universidad Autónoma de Ciudad Juárez, 2004.

Gutierrez, Juan Duchesne Winter, and Felipe Gomez, eds. *La estela de Caicedo: Miradas críticas.* Pittsburgh: Instituto International de Literatura Iberoamericana, 2009.

Herlinghaus, Hermann. "La construcción del nexo de violencia y culpa en la novela *La virgen de los sicarios.*" *Nomadas* 25 (2006): 184–204.

———. *Renarración y descentramiento: Mapas alternativos de la imaginación en America Latina.* Madrid: Iberoamericana Editorial Vervuert, 2004.

———. *Violence without Guilt: Ethical Narratives from the Global South.* Basingstoke, UK: Palgrave Macmillan, 2009.

Herrero-Olaizola, Alejandro. "Gabriel Garcia Marquez global: Literatura latinoamericana e industria cultural." *Revista de Crítica Literaria Latinoamericana.* 69 (2010): 193–206.

Holmes, Amanda. *City Fictions: Language, Body, and Spanish American Urban Space.* Cranbury, NJ: Bucknell University Press, 2007.

Hopenhayn, Martin. *No Apocalypse, No Integration: Modernism and Postmodernism in Latin America.* Durham, NC: Duke University Press, 2001.

Hoyos, Héctor. *Beyond Bolaño: The Global Latin American Novel.* New York: Columbia University Press, 2016.

———. "La cultura material en las literaturas y culturas iberoamericanas de hoy." *Cuadernos de Literatura* 20, no. 40 (2016): 254–61.

Hoyos, Héctor Ayala, and Marília Librandi Rocha. "Theories of the Contemporary in South America." *Revista de Estudios Hispánicos* 48, no.1 (2014): 97–103.

Jacob, Porfirio Barba. *Porfirio Barba Jacob: Poesia completa.* Bogotá: El Ancora Editores, 2000.

Jacobs, Michael. "Oblivion: A Memoir, By Hector Abad." Review of *Oblivion,* by Héctor Abad. *The Independent,* November 12, 2010. https://www.independent.co .uk/arts-entertainment/books/reviews/oblivion-a-memoir-by-hector-abad-trans -anne-mclean-amp-rosalind-harvey-2131351.html.

Jameson, Fredric. "No Magic, No Metaphor: Fredric Jameson on 'One Hundred Years of Solitude.'" *London Review of Books* 39, no. 12 (2017). https://www.lrb.co.uk/the -paper/v39/n12/fredric-jameson/no-magic-no-metaphor.

———. *A Singular Modernity: Essay on the Ontology of the Present.* New York: Verso, 2002.

———. "Third-World Literature in the Era of Multinational Capitalism." *Social Text* 15 (1986): 65–88.

Joseph, Gilbert M., and Daniela Spenser, eds. *In from the Cold: Latin America's New Encounter with the Cold War.* Durham, NC: Duke University Press, 2008.

Kahn, Charles H. *The Art and Thought of Heraclitus*. Cambridge: Cambridge University Press, 1979.

Kant, Immanuel. *Critique of the Power of Judgment*. Cambridge: Cambridge University Press, 2000.

Krihnaswamy, Revathi, and John C. Hawley, eds. *The Postcolonial and the Global*. Minneapolis: University of Minnesota Press, 2008.

La desazón suprema: Retrato de Fernando Vallejo. Directed by Luís Ospina. 2003.

La virgen de los sicarios. Directed by Barbet Schroeder. 2002.

Levinson, Brett. *The Ends of Literature: The Latin American "Boom" in the Neoliberal Marketplace*. Stanford, CA: Stanford University Press, 2001.

Libertella, Mauro. "Los caminos de la historia." *Pagina 12*, February 4, 2007. http://www.pagina12.com.ar/diario/suplementos/libros/10-2422-2007-02-04.html.

Locane, Jorge. *Miradas locales en tiempos globales: Intervenciones literarias sobre la ciudad latinoamericana*. Madrid: Iberoamericana Editorial Vervuert, 2016.

Locke, John. *"Two Treatises of Government" and "A Letter Concerning Toleration."* New Haven, CT: Yale University Press, 2003.

López Baquero, Constanza. *Trauma, memoria y cuerpo: El testimonio femenino en Colombia (1985–2000)*. Madrid: Asociación Internacional de Literatura y Cultura Femenina Hispánica, 2012.

Lukács, Georg. *The Theory of the Novel*. Cambridge, MA: MIT Press, 1993.

Martin, Gerald. *Gabriel García Márquez: A Life*. New York: Vintage, 2008.

Martínez, Javier Bengoa. *Chile, the Great Transformation*. Washington, DC: Brookings Institution, 1996.

McClennen, Sophia A. *Ariel Dorfman: An Aesthetics of Hope*. Durham, NC: Duke University Press, 2010.

Mena, Lucila Inés. "La huelga de la compañía bananera como expresión de lo 'Real Maravilloso' americano en *Cien años de soledad*." *Bulletin Hispanique* 74, nos. 3–4 (1972): 379–405.

Mendoza, Annie. *Rewriting the Nation: Novels by Women on Violence in Colombia*. Tempe, AZ: Asociación Internacional de Literatura y Cultura Feminina Hispánica (AILCFH), 2015.

Mendoza, Mario. *Scorpio City*. Santafe de Bogotá: Seix Barral, 1998.

Mignolo, Walter. "Aiesthesis decolonial." *Calle 14* 4, no. 4 (2010): 10–25.

———. *The Darker Side of the Renaissance: Literacy, Territoriality, and Colonization*. Ann Arbor: University of Michigan Press, 2003.

———. *The Idea of Latin America*. Malden, MA: Blackwell, 2005.

———. *Local Histories / Global Designs: Coloniality, Subaltern Knowledge, and Border Thinking*. Princeton, NJ: Princeton University Press, 2000.

Mills, Charles. *The Racial Contract*. Ithaca, NY: Cornell University Press, 1997.

Molano, Alfredo. *Los años del tropel*. Bogotá: CINEP-CEREC, 1985.

Moretti, Franco. "Conjectures on World Literature." *New Left Review* 1 (January–February 2000): 54–68.

———. *Signs Taken for Wonders: Essays in the Sociology of Literary Forms*. London: Verso, 1988.

Negri, Antonio, and Michael Hardt. *Empire*. Cambridge, MA: Harvard University Press, 2000.

Nicholson, Brantley. "Entrevista con Fernando Vallejo: México DF, 10 de junio, 2011." *Chasqui: Revista de Literatura Latinoamericana*, November 2011, 220–227.

———. "Fernando Vallejo: Ciudadanía y la clausura de la literatura mundial." *Revista Calle* 5, no. 14 (June 2011): 69–78.

Nicholson, Brantley, and Juanita Aristizábal, eds. "El último gramático: Ensayos críticos sobre Fernando Vallejo." *Cuadernos de Literatura* 19, no. 37 (2015): 116–273.

Nicholson, Brantley, and Camilo Hernández Castellanos. "*Que viva la música*'s Sustained Prescience: Reading Andrés Caicedo's Anti-Bildungsroman Four Decades Later." *Cincinnati Romance Review* 43 (2017): 123–33.

Nietzsche, Friedrich. *The Birth of Tragedy*. Cambridge: Cambridge University Press, 2006.

Obiols, Isabel. "Juan Gabriel Vásquez recrea en 'Los informantes' la Colombia de los años cuarenta." *El País*, October 13, 2004. http://elpais.com/diario/2004/10/14 /cultura/1097704805_850215.html.

O'Bryen, Rory. *Literature, Testimony and Cinema in Contemporary Colombian Culture: Spectres of La Violencia*. Rochester, NY: Tamesis, 2008.

Oppenheim, Lois Hecht. *Politics in Chile: Democracy, Authoritarianism, and the Search for Development*. Boulder, CO: Westview, 1993.

Ortiz, Carlos Miguel. "El sicariato en Medellín: Entre la violencia politica y el crimen organizado." *Analisis Político* 14 (1991): 60–73.

———, ed. *Guerra en Colombia: Actores armados*. Bogotá: IEPRI, 2004.

Osorio, Flor Edilma Pérez. "Armed Conflict and Forced Displacement in Colombia: Data, Facts and Tendencies as of the Year 2000." In *Internationally Displaced People in Colombia, Victims in Permanent Transition*, edited by Sandro Jimenez Ocampo, 27–55. Bogotá: Ediciones Antropos, 2009.

Ospina, María. "Las naturalezas de la guerra: Topografías violentas de selva en la narrative contemporánea colombiana." *Revista de Crítica Literaria Latinoamericana* 40, no. 79 (2014): 243–64.

Pacheco, María Guadalupe Gutiérrez. *Representación estética de la hiperviolencia en la virgen de los sicarios de Fernando Vallejo y "paseo nocturno" de Rubem Fonseca*. Mexico City: Miguel Angel Porrua, 2008.

Palacios, Marco. *Entre la legitimidad y la violencia: Colombia 1878–1994*. Bogotá: Grupo Editorial Norma, 1995.

Palou, Pedro Angel, Eloy Urroz, Ignacio Padilla, Ricardo Chaez Cstaneda, and Jorge Volpi. "Manifiesto Crack." *Lateral: Revista de Cultura* 70 (2000): 53–70.

Paternostro, Silvana. "Interview with Juan Gabriel Vásquez." *Bomb* magazine, January 1, 2010.

Paz, Octavio. *Los hijos del limo: Del romanticismo a la vanguardia*. Barcelona: Seix Barral, 1974.

Pécaut, Daniel. *Crónica de cuatro décadas de política colombiana*. Bogotá: Grupo Editorial Norma, 2006.

———. *Orden y la violencia: Evolucion socio-politica de Colombia entre 1930 y 1953*. Bogotá: Grupo Editorial Norma, 2001.

Pineda Botero, Alvaro. *La esfera inconclusa: Novela colombiana en el ámbito global*. Medellín: Editorial Universidad de Antioquia, 2006.

Pippin, Robert. *Modernism and a Philosophical Problem: On the Dissatisfactions of European High Culture*. Malden, MA: Blackwell, 1999.

Polanyi, Karl. *The Great Transformation: The Political and Economic Origins of Our Time*. Boston: Beacon, 2001.

Porras, Maria del Carmen. "La familia Buendía en tiempos de globalización: 'Melodrama' de Jorge Franco." *Revista de Crítica Literaria Latinoamericana* 69 (2009): 207–26.

Prendergast, Christopher, ed. *Debating World Literature*. London: Verso, 2004.

Purcell, Julius. "Oblivion: A Memoir by Hector Abad Faciolince—Review." *Guardian*, October 23, 2010. http://www.guardian.co.uk/books/2010/oct/24/oblivion-memoir-hector-abad-faciolince-review.

Quijano, Anibal. "Coloniality of Power, Eurocentrism, and Latin America." *Nepantla: Views from South* 1, no. 3 (2000): 533–80.

Rama, Angel. *La ciudad letrada*. Hanover, NH: Ediciones del Norte, 1984.

Rancière, Jacques. *Hatred of Democracy*. London: Verso, 2007.

———. *The Politics of Aesthetics: The Distribution of the Sensible*. New York: Continuum, 2004.

Reber, Dierdra. *Coming to Our Senses: Affect and an Order of Things for Global Culture*. New York: Columbia University Press, 2016.

Restrepo, Carlos Mario Perea. "Pandillas y violencias urbanas: El suroriente de Bogotá." *Journal of Iberian and Latin American Studies* 7, no. 2 (2001): 39–62.

Restrepo, Laura. *Delirio*. Bogotá: Alfaguara, 2004.

Rivera, José Eustasio. *La vorágine*. Madrid: Cátedra, 2006.

Rodríguez García, José María. *The City of Translation: Poetry and Ideology in Nineteenth-Century Colombia*. Basingstoke, UK: Palgrave Macmillan, 2010.

———. "The Regime of Translation in Miguel Antonio Caro's Colombia." *Diacritics* 34, nos. 3–4 (2004): 143–75.

Roldan, Mary. *Blood and Fire: La Violencia in Antioquia, Colombia, 1946–1953*. Durham, NC: Duke University Press, 2002.

Romero, Simon. "Dueling Beauty Pageants Put Income Gap on View." *New York Times*, November 30, 2010. https://www.nytimes.com/2010/12/01/world/americas/01colombia.html.

Rueda, María Helena. "Dislocaciones y otras violencias en el circuito transnacional de la literatura latinoamericana." *Revista de Crítica Literaria Latinoamericana* 69 (2009): 69–91.

———. *La violencia y sus huellas: Una mirada desde la narrativa colombiana*. Madrid: Iberoamericana Editorial Vervuert, 2014.

Salazar, Alonso. *Born to Die in Medellín*. London: Latin American Bureau (Research and Action), 1990.

———. *No nacimos pa' semilla*. Bogotá: CINEP-CEREC, 1990.

Sánchez Prado, Ignacio. *América Latina en la "literatura mundial."* Pittsburgh: University of Pittsburgh Press, 2006.

———. *Strategic Occidentalism: On Mexican Fiction, the Neoliberal Book Market, and the Question of World Literature*. Evanston, IL: Northwestern University Press, 2018.

Santamaría, Germán. "Prohibir al sicario." *Revista Diners*, October 2000.

Santos, Lidia. "El cosmopolitismo de mercado: Del fin de las literaturas nacionales a la cultura de las celebridades (Brasil, Mexico y Chile)." *Revista de Crítica Literaria Latinoamericana* 69 (2009): 153–65.

Sarlo, Beatriz. *Escenas de la vida posmoderna: Intelectuales, arte y videocultura en la Argentina*. Buenos Aires: Ariel, 1994.

Sarmiento, Domingo Faustino. *Facundo*. Edited by Roberto Yahni. Madrid: Catedra, 2003.

Schiller, Friedrich. *On the Aesthetic Education of Man*. New Haven, CT: Yale University Press, 2004.

Shaw, Donald. *Antonio Skarmeta and the Post-Boom*. Hanover, NH: Ediciones del Norte, 1994.

———. *The Post-Boom and Spanish American Fiction*. Albany: SUNY Press, 1998.

Silva, José Asunción. *De sobremesa*. Madrid: Hiperion, 1996.

Siskind, Mariano. *Cosmopolitan Desires: Global Modernity and World Literature in Latin America*. Evanston, IL: Northwestern University Press, 2014.

Sommer, Doris. *Foundational Fictions: The National Romances of Latin America*. Berkeley: University of California Press, 1991.

Speranza, Graciela. *Atlas portátil de América Latina*. Barcelona: Anagrama, 2012.

Streitfeld, David. "Mario Vargas Llosa on Love, Spectacle and Becoming a Legend." *New York Times*, April 13, 2016. http://www.nytimes.com/2016/04/14/books /mario-vargas-llosa-on-love-spectacle-and-becoming-a-legend.html?_r=0.

Suárez, Juana. *Sitios de contienda: Producción cultural colombiana y el discurso de la violencia*. Madrid: Iberoamericana Editorial Vervuert, 2014.

Suárez, Juana, and Carlos Jauregui. "Profilaxis, traducción y ética: Humanidad 'desechable' en *Rodrigo D. No futuro, La vendedora de rosas* y *La virgen de los sicarios*." *Revista Iberoamericana* 68, no. 199 (2002): 367–92.

Thomas, Paul, and David Lloyd. *Culture and the State*. New York: Routledge, 1998.

Valencia, Mario Armando. *La dimensión crítica de la novela urbana contemporánea en Colombia*. Pereira, Colombia: Universidad Tecnológica de Pereira, 2009.

Vallejo, Fernando. *Años de indulgencia*. Madrid: Alfaguara, 2007.

———. *Barba Jacob el mensajero*. Madrid: Alfaguara, 2012.

———. *Chapolas negras*. Santafe de Bogotá: Editorial Santillana, 1995.

———. *El desbarrancadero*. Madrid: Alfaguara, 2008.

———. *El don de la vida*. Madrid: Alfaguara, 2010.

———. *El fuego secreto*. Bogotá: Planeta, 1986.

———. *Entre fantasmas*. Mexico City: Alfaguara, 1993.

———. *La virgen de los sicarios*. Bogotá: Editorial Santillana, 1994.

———. *Logoi: Una gramática del lenguaje literario*. San Diego: Fondo de Cultura Económica, 1983.

———. *Los caminos a Roma*. Bogotá: Planeta, 1988.

———. *Los días azúles*. Mexico City: Rayuela Internacional, 1995.

Vargas Llosa, Mario. Foreword to *Cien años de soledad*, by Gabriel García Márquez, i–xxx. Madrid: Real Academia Española, 2007.

———. "García Márquez por Vargas Llosa." *El País*, July 10, 2017. https://elpais.com /cultura/2017/07/07/babelia/1499445200_348553.html.

———. "Vargas Llosa rompe el silencio sobre García Márquez." *El País*, July 7, 2017. https://elpais.com/cultura/2017/07/06/actualidad/1499366796_414985.html.

Vásquez, Juan Gabriel. *El ruido de las cosas al caer*. Bogotá: Alfaguara, 2011.

———. *Los informantes*. Bogotá: Alfaguara, 2004.

Volpi, Jorge. *El insomnio de Bolivar*. Madrid: Debate Editorial, 2009.

———. *En busca de Klingsor*. New York: Rayo, 2008.

Wallerstein, Immanuel. *The Capitalist World Economy*. Cambridge: Cambridge University Press, 1979.

———. *European Universalism*. New York: New Press, 2006.

Wong, Vince. "Andean Peaks and Silicon Valleys: Entrepreneurship in Colombia." SC Johnson College of Business, April 24, 2017. https://www.johnson.cornell.edu /article/emerging-markets-institute/research/emi-at-work/47013/andean-peaks -and-silicon-valleys-entrepreneurship-in-colombia/.

Index

About the Author

BRANTLEY NICHOLSON is an associate professor of Spanish and Latin American studies at Georgia College in Milledgeville, Georgia. His research and teaching take up comparative-American studies and the theoretical questions of globalization, cosmopolitanism, and economics. His recent research has focused on postnational imaginaries in Chile and Colombia and the emergence of new global cities in the Andean region, such as Santiago, Bogotá, and Medellín.

About the Author